CW00501683

Creativity and Critique in Online Learning

"Accessibly written and timely, this book will be of interest to teachers in Higher Education charged with developing pedagogically sound online programmes to serve a wide, diverse and international student body. Interdisciplinary in scope, the book draws on interesting case studies from the Open University with relevance and application to other HE contexts. With refreshing honesty, the writers present a 'warts and all' analysis, acknowledging the difficulties and challenges as well as the affordances of online teaching and learning. This is very much a twenty-first-century text, offering great ideas and thoughtful critique of the key issues—essential reading for anyone currently teaching, or planning to teach, in a contemporary University."

—Dr Joan Woodhouse, *Associate Professor in Education,*
University of Leicester, UK

"This is a book written by practitioners for practitioners. It combines action research and theoretical analysis with practical tips for virtual practice. The lively case studies investigate how social networks of students and staff are learning through technology, and about technology enhanced learning. A diverse range of disciplinary contexts are set within the Open University's mission to promote openness in educational opportunity. The rapid adoption of digital learning in universities makes this enquiring and informative text both timely and useful."

—Dr Jane Roberts, *Learning and Teaching Innovation,*
Open University, UK

"This book is an excellent critical overview of the issues surrounding online teaching and learning in Higher Education. Using a series of complementary case studies focusing on the Open University, the book combines critical explorations of theory and research with accessible accounts of practice represented most clearly by the tips and discussion points to stimulate debate and which end each chapter. The chapters cover a broad range of issues pertinent to the use of digital technology in HE, from relatively established approaches such as online forums and online conferences to more recent developments such as creating MOOCs or incorporating social media tools into teaching and learning. The three themes identified in the concluding chapter, relating to digital technology's use in promoting student collaboration, building academic communities and redefining academic identities, should help to stimulate the kind of debate and further research which the book calls for in its conclusion. Most importantly perhaps, the case studies offer an opportunity for other academics and institutions to learn from practice in a longstanding pioneer in the field at a time when, like so many other institutions, it is facing significant threats as a result of the socio-economic pressures it so keenly explores."

—Michael Jopling, *University of Wolverhampton, UK*

Jacqueline Baxter • George Callaghan
Jean McAvoy
Editors

Creativity and Critique in Online Learning

Exploring and Examining Innovations
in Online Pedagogy

Editors
Jacqueline Baxter
Open University
Milton Keynes, UK

George Callaghan
Open University
Milton Keynes, UK

Jean McAvoy
Open University
Milton Keynes, UK

ISBN 978-3-319-78297-3   ISBN 978-3-319-78298-0   (eBook)
https://doi.org/10.1007/978-3-319-78298-0

Library of Congress Control Number: 2018946106

This Palgrave Macmillan imprint is published by the registered company Springer International Publishing AG part of Springer Nature.
The registered company address is: Gewerbestrasse 11, 6330 Cham, Switzerland

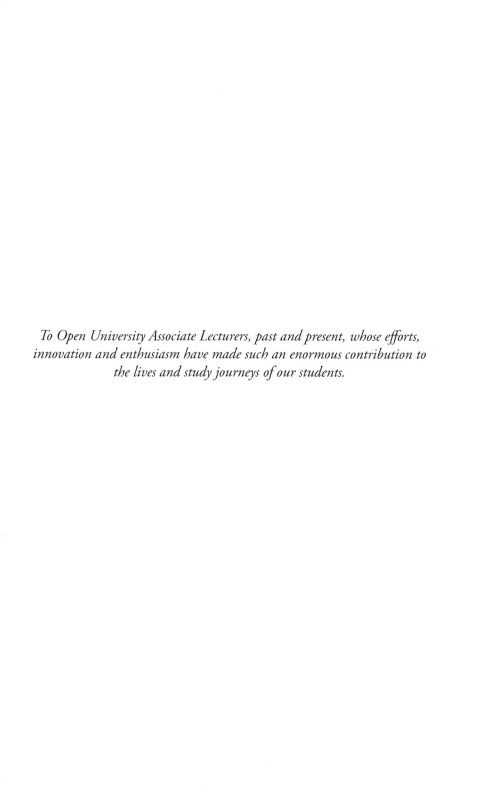

To Open University Associate Lecturers, past and present, whose efforts, innovation and enthusiasm have made such an enormous contribution to the lives and study journeys of our students.

Foreword

Clay Shirky suggests that it when a technology becomes so pervasive as to be invisible, then profound change occurs. In higher education, this might be the stage we are entering now with online learning. The change has been rapid, particularly give the glacial rate of change often observed in higher education. At the end of the 1990s the internet was seen as an interesting application, but not necessarily relevant to all subjects or modes of teaching. When creating the Open University's first elearning course in 1998, I recall a colleague confidently predicting "you'll be lucky to get fifty students who want to study like that." When we launched in 1999 we had 15,000 students. It seemed students did indeed want to study via the internet, and for distance education in particular it opened up a whole realm of possibilities.

For distance education, it was now possible to conduct group work without disruptive and expensive day schools, students could form communities online, and their sense of isolation greatly reduced. Course teams could respond to queries, change material without the need to send out printed addendum. Greater responsiveness and flexibility were now possible. For campus based students they could now watch lectures on demand, access notes after a lecture, and communicate with fellow students away from the physical location. In short, the technology made distance education more like face to face, and vice versa.

Since those early days the Virtual Learning Environment (VLE) or Learning Management System (LMS) has become a commonplace and essential piece of technology infrastructure in almost every university. Although the limitations of this technology and its application are often criticized, this overlooks how much we take its presence for granted. Online learning, and some form of blended approach is now the normal experience for nearly all students.

Despite this prevalence online a good deal of misconceptions and myths around online learning still persist. How, what and who we teach is affected by a shift online and yet the norms of face to face, or traditional distance education still dominate. A group activity that may take an afternoon in a face to face workshop may take three weeks when conducted online and require subtle negotiations and careful structuring. Similarly a printed unit that worked well in distance education may seem dry and wordy online, and miss opportunities for interaction. Often educators who have developed expertise in one setting get drawn into online teaching without any subsequent change in perspective.

Into this mix we can also add new developments, such as the use of social media, and Massive Open Online Courses (MOOCs). These are often accompanied by a good deal of hype and rhetoric. There can also be a tendency for a 'year zero' mentality to accompany many of these new developments. It was with something of a wry smile and weary resignation that many working in higher education greeted claims that MOOCs represented the first generation of online education, and then proceeded to encounter many of the issues that distance education had been working with for decades.

Much of the literature in online learning tends to focus on very practical '6 steps to successful teaching' type guides or more critical perspectives on the nature of the internet and the role of higher education. This book provides a much needed practical approach to online education while being grounded in pedagogic theory, drawing on the extensive experience of staff at the UK Open University across a range of disciplines. The coverage addresses many of the different areas associated with online learning, with an emphasis on its creative use for the benefit of students.

These themes – community, identity, scale, pedagogy, creativity – are at the core of the book, creating online learning that is as engaging as face to face education, while taking advantage of the benefits the technology affords. While this work is largely focused on a distance education setting, as I argued above, the distinction between online and face to face, or distance and campus-based is increasingly blurred. The work covered in this book provides a useful basis for all educators in successfully implementing various aspects of online education.

The Institute of Educational Technology   Martin Weller
Open University
Milton Keynes, UK

Contents

Notes on Contributors

Jane Barrett (now retired) was assessment lead for Faculty of Social Sciences and Lecturer in the Psychology Department (Open University, UK). She recently gained an online Masters Degree in Online and Distance Education from the OU, as well as holding a PhD in social psychology. During her OU career, Jane worked on the production team of several online modules. These modules included the first online module for the Psychology masters degree and a new large-population Level 2 module for the psychology programme. Jane has published pedagogical research and retains a scholarship interest in collaborative learning.

Jacqueline Baxter is Senior Lecturer/Associate Professor of Public Policy and Management at The Open University Business School. Her research interests lie in the areas of public governance and accountablity, particularly in the realm of education. Her books include: School Governance: Policy, Politics and Practices and most recently: School Inspectors: Policy Implementers, Policy Shapers in National Policy Contexts. Her background is in teaching and pedagogy and she has written extensively on this subject. She is a Senior Fellow of The Higher Education Academy and a Fellow of the Royal Society of Arts. She is also Editor in Chief of the Sage publication Management in Education and a Member of The Council of The British Educational Leadership, Management and Administration Society. She blogs at: www.jacquelinebaxter.org. Her LinkedIn profile can be found here: https://www.linkedin.com/in/dr-jacquelineaundr%C3%A9e-baxter-53206a12/. She tweets at @mieeditors and @drjacquebaxter.

George Callaghan is an Economist with the Open University. He has taught in the area of Personal Finance and Economics, co-editing the highly successful Personal Finance textbook which accompanies the module You and Your Money. He has conducted research funded by the Higher Education Academy into the use of ebooks in learning and is currently researching the pedagogy around using social media for University teaching. He is a Principal Fellow of the Higher Education Academy.

Paige Cuffe is an Associate Lecturer on undergraduate psychology modules and the Masters in Online and Distance Education and sits on the Board of Study for the Institute of Educational Technology at the Open University. As a consultant with a special interest in collaborative and technology enhanced learning, she has for eight years been involved in the planning and delivery of staff development for Associate Lecturers on adapting practice to online teaching and in supporting peer sharing of practice. A member of the Association of Learning Technologists and British Psychological Society, she has worked in online education for over a decade.

Karen Foley is a Lecturer in Learning and Teaching Innovation at the Open University and is responsible for developing and delivering the Student Hub Live, a platform of online interactive events that facilitate open access to an academic community. In previous roles, Karen was an academic consultant for the Faculty of Arts and Social Science, developing the concept of online interactive conferences (Student Connections) and synchronous and asynchronous formats to promote these (including online workshops, podcasts and audio dramas).

Ian Fribbance is the Executive Dean of the Faculty of Arts and Social Science. He has previously been Associate Dean of Teaching & Learning Enhancement in the Social Science Faculty. He has led several of the Faculty's curriculum innovations in personal finance and financial services. He won an Open University Teaching Award and a National Teaching Fellowship and is also a Fellow of the Higher Education Academy.

Hannah Gore joined The Open University in 2005, developing a range of projects centred in technology enhanced learning to leverage student and learner engagement. Hannah works with and syndicates content to OpenLearn, iTunes U, YouTube, Audioboom, Bibblio, Google Play, OERu, Facebook, and FutureLearn. At present these first and third party channels represent a combined rate of circa 10 million visitors per annum, with Hannah working towards the launch of further channels. As an advocate of lifelong learning, Hannah researched her doctorate in MOOC engagement with The Open University.

Helen Kaye is a Senior Lecturer in Psychology and currently Deputy Associate Dean (Teaching and Learning Innovation) in the Open University Faculty of Arts and Social Sciences. Her doctoral and post-doctoral research was in classical conditioning and cognitive learning theory. Helen was previously qualification director for Psychology at the OU and chaired the production and presentation of the final year module Investigating Psychology 3. She has authored textbook chapters and edited course books as well as publishing research papers. Helen maintains scholarship and research interests in learning and memory in various contexts.

Madeleine Knightley is a Chartered Psychologist and Staff Tutor with the Open University. Her research interests are in personal identity and development. She is undertaking ongoing training in positive psychological and cognitive behavioural approaches and techniques for improving health and well-being.

Rachel Manning is an applied social psychologist currently working with governmental and non-governmental organisations to provide independent research, training and consultancy. During 20 years spent in the higher education sector she drew on her interests in social identities and intra- and intergroup processes to inform her teaching practice and pedagogical research. Her broader research interests have primarily focused on the notions of 'prosocial' and 'anti-social' behaviours, informed by community, environmental and critical psychological perspectives.

Jean McAvoy is Senior Lecturer and Director of Teaching in the School of Psychology at the Open University. She has worked extensively across the psychology programme, including undergraduate, postgraduate and PhD supervision. Her specialist teaching is in research methodologies. As a critical social psychologist her own research focuses on processes of subjectification and the production of subjectivities, with a particular interest in the ways in which moral orders and transgression are constructed in ideological, discursive and affective practices.

Michelle Oldale is a person-centred psychotherapist, trainer and supervisor with experience in the Further and Higher Education sector. She is the co-author along with Michelle J Cooke of 'Making the Most of Counselling and Psychotherapy Placements'. Michelle's core values reflect the holistic nature of wellness and she is a licenced 'Well Now' facilitator. Currently a Part Time Post Gradate researcher with the Open University exploring Weight Stigma, Michelle has previously researched the therapeutic relationship in British Sign Language and Power in Relationship when the Therapist is Deaf, the Client is Hearing and a Sign Language Interpreter is present. www.michelleoldale.com

David J. Pell's 'first career' (28 years) was in local government as a professionally qualified public sector manager, environment health officer and housing manager serving as a director of health and housing for ten years and then as a director of wider community services. In 1993 he left to establish an environmental consultancy working mostly with the international Environment City Programme and to develop an academic 'second career' (25 years to date) as an Associate Lecturer with Sheffield Hallam University Business School and the Open University. He has researched, published and taught at all levels in both the natural and social sciences.

Graham Pike is Professor of Forensic Cognition at The Open University's School of Psychology and Director of Research for the Centre for Policing Research and Learning. He researches in forensic psychology, critical criminology and applied cognition, and focuses on issues of evidence and harm within the criminal justice system. He has a passion for public engagement and innovative online education, and has produced a number of Apps, MOOCs, blogs and websites, as well as a large number of supported distance learning courses in psychology and the social sciences.

Diane Preston is a Senior Lecturer in Human Resource Management in the Department of People and Organisations at the Open University Business School. She has many years of experience in teaching, research and management roles. She was Head of Department for five years and Associate Dean (Teaching and Learning) for nearly two. She has written and led many modules at all levels of study and has watched with interest how open and distance learning and pedagogy has developed. Her research interests cover many aspects of the management of people and management learning and development, including how individuals make sense of work and organisations and professionals moving into management.

Stefanie Sinclair is a Senior Lecturer in Religious Studies at The Open University, with a special research interest in religion and identity (gender and national identities in particular). She is a Senior Fellow of the Higher Education Academy and has led various projects critically exploring online and blended learning in HE, including a project on 'Assessing oral presentations at a distance' funded by the Higher Education Academy. She was awarded the 2017 Teaching and Learning Fellowship by the British Association for the Study of Religions in recognition of her contribution to excellence, innovation and transformation of the student learning experience in the study of religions.

Donna Smith With an academic background in politics and media, building on her experience of working in Westminster politics, her research has focused on UK politics, media, sexuality and representation. As an experienced higher education manager, designer, developer and tutor/lecturer, her focus also includes teaching and learning in the social sciences (politics in particular), with forums and participation a key interest.

List of Figures

List of Tables

List of Boxes

1

Introduction to Chapters: Creativity and Critique in Online Teaching and Learning: Innovations in Online Pedagogy

Jacqueline Baxter, George Callaghan, and Jean McAvoy

Introduction

Why creativity and why critique? These terms were not chosen by accident but rather to reflect that the realm of online teaching and learning is a contested area not only in the context of higher education, but more broadly. There are few areas of learning and teaching today that are not

J. Baxter (✉)
Department of Public Leadership and Social Enterprise, Open University, Milton Keynes, UK
e-mail: Jacqueline.baxter@open.ac.uk

G. Callaghan
Department of Economics, Open University, Milton Keynes, UK
e-mail: George.callaghan@open.ac.uk

J. McAvoy
School of Psychology, Open University, Milton Keynes, UK
e-mail: jean.mcavoy@open.ac.uk

1

venturing into the field, few institutions that are not asking themselves: can we do it better online?

But can online study really replicate the challenges and occasional joy of learning in a face to face environment? Can it foster relationships in the same way? Not only learner to learner but equally between teacher and learner. Perhaps one of the most pressing questions, and one we hear a great deal within our own particular context of The Open University, is, can it achieve the type of transformational learning that traditionally took place at residential schools and face to face tutorials? The type of learning that transforms the lives of individuals, radically altering their worldview, critical acuity and social mobility? Some would argue that these are the wrong questions- that we should instead be asking: what can online learning do that face to face learning can't; how can it help teach the 'hard to reach' and how can it provide learning for those that have failed in (or rejected) learning in a face to face context. In considering these questions we should also be asking ourselves what we can do to make online teaching appealing to those tasked with the challenge. How can we incorporate teachers' innate capacity for innovation and creativity into the online environment? How can we tap into their motivation to teach and provide a great learning experience for their students? How can we incorporate all of the elements that we know to work in face to face teaching environments and moreover how can we take them further in order to engage our learners?

One of the key issues around online teaching and learning is the fact that it is cost effective, rendering it a very attractive prospect for institutions labouring under today's tight economic constraints and highly marketized environment (see Chap. 2 for more discussion on this). This has prompted many of those in management positions (some of whom may have limited teaching experience), to extoll its virtues rather than to take an evidence based evaluative cold hard look at what it can do for teaching and learning.

This book uses case studies to engage with these questions and issues. We examine the benefits of various methods of teaching and learning online, whilst also analysing how effective these methods have proven to be in practice. In so doing the book aims to both inform and challenge those who are already teaching online or thinking of doing so in the near future. It looks to help those who are designing programmes of learning, in offering a comprehensive view of some of the tools that can be used to enhance the student experience, whilst also exposing areas of weakness that may well have the capacity to alienate learners and teachers if not incorporated carefully into the planned curriculum. Finally it explores the ways in which online teaching and learning can be creative for both teacher and learner, whilst acknowledging that no teaching method is perfect. The knowledge we are accumulating around digital learning is still, relatively speaking, in its infancy. This book presents a critical analysis of contemporary practice within a large University, examining practical teaching methods and discussing relevant pedagogical theory.

As a world leader in online and distance education and one of the world's largest universities, the OU's innovations in online teaching and learning make it a market leader. This book brings together some of the most creative practices in online education by some of the world's leading educators in online and distance teaching and learning. Taking an action research perspective on various aspects of online learning, the book brings theory and practice together to provide insights into various elements that go to make up distance teaching and learning. Real life case studies based at the OU illuminate innovative teaching and learning practices whilst also giving insight into the challenges and opportunities inherent within online teaching. The book also offers a critical perspective on these teaching practices: few pedagogies are perfect and the authors write from a critical perspective, drawing out what worked well and which aspects of the practice demand more thought and experimentation. To this end, each chapter concludes with a set of practical tips and discussion points to be used by university teachers. The book is also highly relevant for educational developers who may be getting to grips with some of the challenges inherent within online and distance learning.

The book is unique in focusing on the working practices of those that are delivering teaching within a range of disciplines. Rather than focusing on technical aspects of the teaching tools, as in the case of so many other books on the market, this book draws directly on the experiences and action research of those actively engaged in online teaching.

Chapter 2 begins with a discussion on the marketized context and climate in which higher education (HE) today is operating. It continues by exploring the very particular case of online education and its relationship with technology and the teacher. As a relatively new innovation for many HE teachers, it looks at past innovations and the mixed reception they received at that particular point in time, comparing this to some of the thoughts and feelings evoked by online learning and teaching. The final section of this chapter looks at the very particular case of the Open University and how case studies from this institution may be helpful to colleagues across the field of HE that are already teaching or have plans to teach online.

The case studies begin with Rachael Manning and Donna Smith in Chap. 3 who focus their work on building on the Open University's long-standing use of forums for teaching and learning. The chapter begins with a general consideration of how and why forums are used, through highlighting some of the more pertinent elements in the related literature, and most notably acknowledging one of the core perceived problems with forums: participation. They then move on to discuss the broader context within which forums sit, setting out some of the additional factors that impact on experiences of them and in the process, highlighting the 'structural' and 'functional' concerns that are related to the use of forums as spaces for learning. They conclude with suggestions for colleagues engaging with forums, based on their preceding analysis. In Chap. 4 Helen Kaye and Jane Barrett remain on the topic of forums, presenting empirical research investigating barriers to successful team work. They argue that poor group dynamics, particularly when working with strangers, are frequently cited by students as a major concern and highlight the importance of facilitating communication in situations where some group members fail to contribute fully. The chapter concludes by emphasising that, in any teaching model, strategic planning should include resources to nurture collaborative skills for students and their tutors. Turning to a different area and tool for learning, George Callaghan and Ian Fribbance in Chap. 5 examine the social media tool Facebook through the lens of teaching theory, reflecting in detail on the challenges such social media present to those working in Higher Education. They take examples such as the ethical aspects of working with Facebook and the threat such social media might present to deep learning. The chapter begins with a review of the literature surrounding social theory of learning, particularly on the debates around informal learning. There is then a discussion of social media in Higher Education in general and the use of Facebook in particular. Data from the Faculty Facebook page is used to illustrate how this technology stimulates and encourages informal learning. They continue by examining these developments within a critical perspective, in particular exploring the ethical and practical challenges of using commercially controlled software within an HE environment.

Exploring the area of assessment and multi-sensory learning in HE, Stefanie Sinclair uses Chap. 6 to consider why there is a need for a greater focus on creativity in higher education. From there she critically explores how digital technology can be used to facilitate creative, multisensory learning and assessment in higher education, particularly, though not exclusively, at a distance. The chapter introduces and critically appraises three forms of assessment used in Religious Studies and Philosophy modules at the Open University, including the assessment of digital audio recordings of oral presentations, presentation slides and a 'Take a picture' of religion activity involving digital photography.

In Chap. 7 David Pell reminds us that as well as affording outstanding opportunities for creative teaching and learning, there are other affordances which are less desirable: online cheating. He begins by arguing that there are few academic practitioners who are not worried about both detected and undetected cheating by apparently increasing numbers of their students, especially when aided by ever widening online opportunities. He asserts that this goes well beyond plagiarism from websites and uses this chapter to examine practices such as the 'digital paper mills' of the essay writing industry, collusion through the digital intimacy of social networks, 'mock surveys' for primary data, and assistance with assignment writing by parents or others having a vested interest in the student's success. In arguing that the opportunity to cheat is further aided by fewer real location closed book exams, by students being given access to plagiarism checking software and by a lack of time and/or will for practitioners to get on top of the problem, the chapter explains how some view the scale and nature of the problem and the forensic work needed in order to put any significant action beyond student capability.

In Chap. 8 Graham Pike and Hannah Gore look at two of the greatest challenges presented by MOOCs (massive open online course): how to engage and retain learners. Although often heralded as the next step in the evolution of online education, and despite the number of learners signing-up, MOOCs leave something to be desired with respect to the number of people who actually complete a course. This chapter explores some of the issues involved in retaining learners through an analysis of the design and development of one particular MOOC on the FutureLearn platform (*Forensic Psychology: Witness Investigation* by The Open University) and concludes with a discussion on the implications this might have for learning design and future development of MOOCs.

One of the key challenges for online teaching and learning is in the fostering of an academic Community. In Chap. 9, Karen Foley and Ian Fribbance take as a case study The Open University *Student Connections Conference* – an initiative from the Faculty of Social Sciences to facilitate development of an academic community. Using technologies such as podcasting and livestream, the Student Connections Conference and its accompanying PodMag have been created to establish a community of OU students and staff in a distance learning environment. Describing the conference as an innovative 2 day event, set in a studio in Milton Keynes with the audience all interacting online, the authors explain how, using bespoke interfaces developed by the Knowledge Media Institute at the Open University, participants can watch the livestream discussions from the studio and participate in these using the chat, interactive widgets, twitter and email. This chapter concludes with a discussion on the effectiveness of this format as a way of using new technologies to engage students and create a sense of academic community online.

Moving away from innovations in teaching and learning, the final chapters within the volume turn to how to support staff in such an environment. Beginning with Chap. 10 Paige Cuffe and Jean McAvoy explore the mechanisms put in place for supporting a group of over 200 tutors working together to deliver team teaching of pre-set online collaborative activities to a cohort of over 3000 students studying a first-year undergraduate psychology module. They describe the development of resources to aid this team teaching, from the perspective of the module team chair having overall responsibility for the module, and that of the consultant tutor who co-authored supporting resources and oversaw an online forum provided for the tutor team to raise questions, discuss implementation, and seek advice on issues arising. They summarise key themes arising in feedback from tutors and students, and note some of the changes implemented in response. The chapter concludes with recommendations for effective support of tutors conducting online team teaching. In Chap. 11 we turn from looking at online teams and how to support them to investigating how tutors feel when teaching online. In this study Michelle Oldale and Madeleine Knightley use a blend of educational and psychological literature to explore to what extent online teaching in all its forms allows tutors to be their real selves, and whether online environments allow tutors to express their identity and values in ways which contribute to successful teaching relationships. Taking a visual example of a tutor's reflections on a non-synchronous online forum it shows how thinking out loud about their values and identity colour the ways tutors respond in particular teaching contexts. The authors then conclude their chapter with a range of practical strategies to support the online expression of identity in the service of rewarding and engaging teaching relationships.

Finally, in Chap. 12 Diane Preston tackles the challenging issue of motivation in online teachers. She argues that moving to online teaching from a predominantly face to face teaching environment is a challenge for academics in higher education and one which can provoke anxiety in students and teachers alike. But, she also challenges managerialist discourses that suggest academics are resistant to change and unwilling to participate in technology enhanced learning (TEL) and are slow to adapt to new demands. Rather, speaking from her experience as a Head of Department, Diane offers a more positive view of academics' attitude to going online. She notes that one of the main reasons staff give for wanting to join the university is precisely to get involved directly in TEL at one of the most prominent on-line universities. Drawing on her research Diane argues that there is motivation out there in the academic community, which should be properly supported through recognition of the different skills required for online teaching and appropriate training, and which we can share and learn from as we move ever closer to online teaching in all its forms in higher education across the world.

The final chapter (chapter 13), reflects upon the main findings from the chapters. It once again discusses the important social and economic context of globalisation and neoliberalism which constrains and shapes higher education and its approach to digital learning. The creative potential of such technology in helping to build communities of learning is emphasised and changed academic identity discussed. The chapter also highlights the importance of developing a clear learning strategy at the outset and, crucially, the need for management to devote substantial resources to develop digital learning. We conclude by arguing that with investment, clear teaching objectives and good staff morale digital technology can help universities improve the learning and teaching they offers students and society.

References

Allen, E., & Seaman, J. (2017). *Digital learning compass: Distance education enrollement report* 2017 (Babson Survey Research Group. US Digital Learning Compass, Ed.).

Appadurai, A. (1996). *Modernity at large: Cultural dimensions of globalization* (Vol. 1). Minnesota: Minnesota Press.

Barak, A., & Gluck-Ofri, O. (2007). Degree and reciprocity of self-disclosure in online forums. *CyberPsychology and Behavior, 10*(3), 407–417.

Bates, T. (2014). *Teaching in a digital age.* https://opentextbc.ca/teachinginadigitalage/chapter/section-3-4-constructivism/

Baxter, J. (2010a). *Bien dans sa Peau: An investigation into the role of professional learning on the online teaching identities of HE Lecturers.* http://oro.open.ac.uk/26313/

Baxter, J. (2010b, December 7–11). Traversing the Borderlands: Online academic identities for a new HE world. In *Society for Research into Higher Education Newer Researchers Conference,* The Celtic Manor, Cardiff.

Baxter, J. (2011). *Who am I and what keeps me going? Profiling the distance learning student.* Positive Futures for higher education; connections, communities and criticality, The Celtic Manor, Wales.

Baxter, J. (2012). Who am I and what keeps me going? Profiling the distance student. *International Review of Research in Open and Distance Learning, 13*(4), 107–129.

Baxter, J. (2015). *The open university: A history* (Book review). London: Taylor and Francis, International Journal of Lifelong Learning.

Becher, T., & Trowler, P. (2001). *Academic tribes and territories: Intellectual enquiry and the culture of disciplines.* London: McGraw-Hill Education.

Beck, J., & Young, M. F. D. (2005). The assault on the professions and the restructuring of academic and professional identities: A Bernsteinian analysis. *British Journal of Sociology of Education, 26*(2), 183–197.

Boettcher, J. V., & Conrad, R. M. (2016). *The online teaching survival guide: Simple and practical pedagogical tips.* London: Wiley.

Boitshwarelo, B. (2011). Proposing an integrated research framework for connectivism: Utilising theoretical synergies. *The International Review of Research in Open and Distributed Learning, 12*(3), 161–179.

Carr, N. (2010). *The shallows:How the internet is changing the way we think, read and remember.* London: Atlantic Books.

Clarke, J. (2007). Citizen-consumers and public service reform: At the limits of neo-liberalism? *Policy Futures in Education, 5*(2), 239–248.

Davies, S. R., & Bartholomew, P. (2017). *How does technology -enhanced learning contribue to teaching excellence?* Digifest Birmingham Online at: https://www.jisc.ac.uk/digifest. Accessed 10 Oct 2017.

Deacon, B. (1997). *Global social policy: International organizations and the future of welfare.* London: Sage.

Dewey, J. (1916). *Democracy and education.* Pennsylvania State University. http://library.um.ac.id/images/stories/ebooks/Juni10/democracy%20and%20education%20-%20john%20dewey.pdf. Accessed 24 Aug 2016.

Duit, R., & Treagust, D. F. (1998). Learning in science: From behaviourism towards social constructivism and beyond. *International Handbook of Science Education, 1*(Part 1), 3–25.

Earney, L., Davies, S., McKean, P., & McGregor, A. (2017). *Jisc Digifest 2017-Plenary.* Jisc Digifest Birmingham, Birmingham City University, 14–15 March 2017.

Flavin, M. (2016). Technology-enhanced learning and higher education. *Oxford Review of Economic Policy, 32*(4), 632–645. https://doi.org/10.1093/oxrep/grw028.

Gale, K., Wheeler, S., & Kelly, P. (2007). Learning in cyberspace: An examination of changes in professional identity and practice style in an online problem-based learning environment. *Quarterly Review of Distance Education, 8*(4), 11.

Garrison, D. R., & Cleveland-Innes, M. (2005). Facilitating cognitive presence in online learning: Interaction is not enough. *The American Journal of Distance Education, 19*(3), 133–148.

Gourlay, L., & Stevenson, J. (2017). *Teaching excellence in higher education: Critical perspectives.* London: Routledge.

Harris, S. (2005). Rethinking academic identities in neo-liberal times. *Teaching in Higher Education, 10*(4), 421–433.

Henkel, M. (2005). Academic identity and autonomy in a changing policy environment. *Higher Education, 49*(1), 155–176.

Henry, M., Lingard, B., Rizvi, F., & Taylor, S. (Eds.). (2001). *The OECD, globalisation and education policy.* In G. Neave (Ed.), *Issues in higher education.* Bingley: Emerald Pubishing Limited.

Herbert, M. (2006). Staying the course: A study in online student satisfaction and retention. Online Journal of Distance Learning Administration, http://fsweb.bainbridge.edu/qep/files/teachingres/staying%20the%20course.pdf *9*(4), 1–12.

Huett, J. B., Kalinowski, K. E., Moller, L., & Huett, K. C. (2008). Improving the motivation and retention of online students through the use of ARCS-based e-mails. *The American Journal of Distance Education, 22*(3), 159–176.

Illeris, K. (Ed.). (2009). *Contemporary theories of learning : Learning theorists in their own words.* London: Routledge.

Janssen, D., & Kies, R. (2005). Online forums and deliberative democracy. *Acta Politica, 40*(3), 317–335.

Lee, J., & Leisa, M. (2017). Investigating students' perceptions of motivating factors of online class discussions. *The International Review of Research in Open and Distributed Learning*, [S.l.], *18*(5), ISSN 1492–3831. Available at: http://www.irrodl.org/index.php/irrodl/article/view/2883. Accessed 25 Aug 2017. doi: https://doi.org/10.19173/irrodl.v18i5.2883.

Lingard, B., Rizvi, F., & Taylor, S. (2003). Globalisation and changing education policy. In M. Henry, B. Lingard, F. Rizvi, & S. Taylor (Eds.), *The OECD, globalisation and education policy* (pp. 19–37). Bingley: Emerald.

Marsick, V. J., & Watkins, K. (1990). *Informal and incidental learning in the workplace.* London/New York: Routledge.

McQuiggan, C. A. (2007). The role of faculty development in online teaching's potential to question teaching beliefs and assumptions. *Online Journal of Distance Learning Administration, 10*(3), 1–13.

Muilenburg, L., & Berge, Z. L. (2001). Barriers to distance education: A factor-analytic study. *American Journal of Distance Education, 15*(2), 7–22.

O'Brien, B. S. (2002). Online student retention: Can it be done? In P. Barker & S. Rebelsky (Eds.), *Proceedings of world conference on educational Mutimedia, hypermedia and telecommunications*. Cheasapeake: AACE.

OECD. (1995). *Governance in transition: Public management reforms in OECD countries*. Paris: OECD.

Open University. (2016). *Annual report*. http://www.open.ac.uk/about/main/sites/www.open.ac.uk.about.main/files/files/ecms/web-content/about-annual-report-2015-2016.pdf. Accessed 7 Nov 2017.

Power, M. (1997). *The audit society: Rituals of verification*. Oxford: Oxford University Press.

Radice, H. (2013). How we got here: UK higher education under neoliberalism. *ACME: An International Journal for Critical Geographies, 12*(2), 407–418.

Rheingold, H. (2012). *Net smart: How to thrive online*. London: MIT Press.

Richardson, J. C., & Alsup, J. (2015). From the classroom to the keyboard: How seven teachers created their online teacher identities. *The International Review of Research in Open and Distributed Learning, 16*(1), 142–167.

Riding, R. J., & Sadler-Smith, E. (1997). Cognitive style and learning strategies: Some implications for training design. *International Journal of Training and Development, 1*(3), 199–208.

Rogers, C. (1995). *A way of being*. London: Houghton Mifflin Harcourt.

Rushby, N., & Surry, D. (2016, March). *Wiley handbook of learning technology*. London: Wiley-Blackwell.

Salmon, G. (1998). Developing learning through effective online moderation. *Active Learning, 9*(December), 3–8.

Salmon, G. (2002). *Moderating: The key to teaching and learning online*. London: Routledge.

Schreurs, B., Van den Beemt, A., Prinsen, F., Witthaus, G., Conole, G., & De Laat, M. (2014). An investigation into social learning activities by practitioners in open educational practices. *The International Review of Research in Open and Distributed Learning, 15*(4), 1–20.

Siemens, G. (2005). Connectivism: A learning theory for the digital age. *Journal of Instructional Technology and Distance Learning, 2*(1), 3–10.

Skinner, B. (1968). *The technology of teaching*. New York: Appleton-century-crofts.

Szucs, A., Tait, A., Vidal, M., & Bernath, U. (2009). *Distance and E-learning in transition: Learning innovation, technology and social challenges*. London: Wiley.

Thomas, A. (2007). *Youth online: Identity and literacy in the digital age*. London: Peter Lang Publishing.

Tobin, T. J., Mandernach, B. J., & Taylor, A. H. (2015). *Evaluating online teaching*. London: Wiley.

Turkle, S. (2011). *Life on the screen*. New York: Simon and Schuster.

Van der Veer, R. (2007). *Lev Vygotsky*. London: Bloomsbury.

Veletsianos, G. (2016). *Social media in academia: Networked scholars*. New York: Routledge.

Weinbren, D. (2014). *The Open University: A history*. Manchester: Manchester University Press.

Weller, M. (2011). *The Digital scholar: How technology is transforming academic practice*. Bloomsbury Open Access. https://www.bloomsburycollections.com/book/the-digital-scholar-how-technology-is-transforming-scholarly-practice/. Accessed 7 July 2016.

Wenger, E. C. (2008). *Communities of practice: Learning, meaning, and identity* (18th printing, first published 1998). Cambridge: Cambridge University.

Wolf, M. (2008). *Proust and the squid: The story and science of the reading brain*. London: Icon Books.

2

The Context of Online Teaching and Learning: Neoliberalism, Marketization and Online Teaching

Jacqueline Baxter, George Callaghan, and Jean McAvoy

Introduction

Online Teaching in the Marketised Environment

Higher education in the UK has been transformed due to political, social and economic changes that began in the 1970s. These transformations, based largely on shifts to the political economy of capitalism, not only

J. Baxter (✉)
Department of Public Leadership and Social Enterprise, Open University, Milton Keynes, UK
e-mail: Jacqueline.baxter@open.ac.uk

G. Callaghan
Department of Economics, Open University, Milton Keynes, UK
e-mail: George.callaghan@open.ac.uk

J. McAvoy
School of Psychology, Open University, Milton Keynes, UK
e-mail: jean.mcavoy@open.ac.uk

© The Author(s) 2018
J. Baxter et al. (eds.), *Creativity and Critique in Online Learning*,
https://doi.org/10.1007/978-3-319-78298-0_2

13

occurred in the UK, but took place across the world, facilitated via organisations such as the Organisation for Economic Cooperation and Development (OECD), The World Bank, the World Trade Organisation and the International Monetary Fund (Henry et al. 2001). These shifts have resulted in changes across education systems and led to the globalisation, privatisation and deregulation of public policy as a whole. In addition to this, "increasingly nomadic, highly mobile global capital has reduced the policy salience of governments at the nation state level" (Deacon 1997: 2), contributing to what Appadurai describes as the beginnings of the dissociation of politics from the territorial space of the nation (Appadurai 1996). It is against this background that governments in the developed countries of the global economy have pursued neo-liberal economic policies, rejecting the state interventionism that defined the period of the post war consensus. As a result, many nations have focused on ensuring the global competitiveness of their national economies, whilst looking to education to provide the skills and knowledge in order to be able to do this (Gourlay and Stevenson 2017),

Aligning with the global neo-liberal consensus, new public management forms have criticised old state bureaucracies as, "highly centralised, rule-bound, and inflexible organisations that emphasise process rather than results, [and] impede good performance" (OECD 1995: 7).This has resulted in the imposition of private sector ideals such as competition, a focus on performance and widespread use of governing by targets and numbers (Power 1997). These foci have essentially changed the purpose of the university, from the education of the elites in business, politics, culture and the professions, to the provision of marketable skills and research outputs to the 'knowledge economy' (Radice 2013: 408).

The changes to public service policy have profoundly affected the ways in which university education is conceptualised (Lingard et al. 2003). They have also created new ways of framing policy problems, creating normative discourses that urge universities towards a more global outlook with a priority on preparing students for work in a global economy. However, as Henry et al. outline, this must be done with far less resource as, "Leaner and meaner, the state now operates against a background of growing social instability, loss of social cohesion and deepening inequality" (Henry et al. 2001: 28). They have also changed perceptions of the student who, in policy terms, is interpellated as a fee paying consumer (Clarke 2007): an individual who is buying 'a product' and 'a service'. Education and student needs in this respect must be placed as central to the processes and policies surrounding education. This is reinforced by instruments such as The National Student Survey and the huge marketing campaigns instrumentalised by universities across the piece.

It is within this social, cultural, political and economic context that discourses surrounding online education have emerged: colouring and conditioning the ways in which both students and university staff perceive and embrace new technologies and new ways of teaching. Changes to the way in which HE is conceptualised have played out alongside the concomitant growth of online teaching and learning as Babson's recent report, based on the US distance learning market, indicates (Allen and Seaman 2017). The report illustrates that while enrolments on online distance learning courses continue to grow, the number of students physically attending post 16 education is shrinking, arguing that:

> Distance education continued its pattern of growth for yet another year. Fall 2015 saw more than 6 million students taking at least one distance course, having increased by 3.9% over the previous year. This growth rate was higher than seen in either of the two previous years. In higher education, 29.7% of all students are taking at least one distance course. The total distance enrollments are composed of 14.3% of students (2,902,756) taking exclusively distance courses and 15.4% (3,119,349) who are taking a combination of distance and non-distance courses. The vast majority (4,999,112, or 83.0%) of distance students are studying at the undergraduate level. Public institutions continue to educate the largest proportion of distance students (4,080,565, or 67.8%), while private non-profit institutions passed the private for-profit sector for the first time. (Page 7)

Yet according to a survey reported at the Joint Information Systems Committee (JISC) Digifest Conference (Earney et al. 2017), in spite of the billions of dollars being invested in edtech startups, only 21% of educators surveyed thought that we would come to rely on these companies for teaching and learning, whilst 69% believed that the expansion may result in a few tools we in the HE sector can adopt for teaching and learning. When asked "How important is organisational culture in the successful adoption of education technology", 100% of respondents replied either that it can totally make or break it (55%) or that it can significantly speed up or slow down its adoption (45%).

Technology and the Teacher

As Sarah Davies and colleagues point out: the "policy language surrounding technology enhanced learning [often] embodies a simple economic calculation: in exchange for the use of technology there will be enhanced forms of learning." (Davies and Bartholomew 2017). Highlighting that this is not necessarily the case, they emphasise that people are at the centre of the process and that neglect of the human element is to miss out on the very essence of what teaching and learning is all about. A number of researchers have also pointed out that the concept of nurture should be central to any institution adopting this type of learning and that this is created by "an environment that supports and rewards innovation; an environment that is critical, evidence-seeking and evidence creating, recognising the need to deploy human labour and development of institutional resilience through policy" (ibid: slide 54, see also, Tobin et al. 2015; Szucs et al. 2009; Rushby and Surry 2016).

In terms of nurture, many institutions appear to have some way to go, yet as Flavin, drawing on the idea of learning technology as disruptive technology, points out, "If we look at what students and lecturers do, rather than what we would like them to do, we will have a firmer evidence base from which to progress and an enhanced knowledge of actual practices with ICTs to support learning and teaching, which can comprise an influence on the kind of modules and programmes we design and on the way we structure and support learning in higher education. There is something to be learned from disruptive behaviour." (Flavin 2016: 22).

The turn towards online learning throughout education can and does elicit contrasting responses, from the giddy excitement of early adopters right through to the head shaking cynicism of the old timers (Weller 2011; Veletsianos 2016).

Looking Back: Reactions to Innovation

Online teaching, when viewed in terms of the long history of teaching and pedagogy, is still in its infancy. We are still developing language to talk about it; examining new ways to promote its development, and still in many ways resistant to the thought that it may eventually replace face to face teaching. In order to place this in context it is first useful to examine the ways in which earlier pedagogical innovations were received when they first started to emerge. One example of this is the practice of writing, and Rheingold, in his book on digital literacy, cites an interesting fifth century BC extract from the work of Plato on writing:

> The fact is that this invention will produce forgetfulness in the souls of those who have learnt it. They will not need to exercise their memories, being able to rely on what is written, calling things to mind no longer from within themselves by their own unaided powers, but under the stimulus of external marks that are alien to themselves. So, it's not a recipe for memory, but for reminding, that you have discovered. And as for wisdom, you are equipping your pupils with only a semblance of it, not with truth. (Rheingold 2012: 50)

Clearly the response to being able to record and reflect upon human activity in written format was not universally welcomed. If we jump forward to the invention of the printing press there were also those who saw threats and limitation, for example the eighteenth century French philosopher Diderot who expressed concern that the increasing availability of books would constrain learning as there would be too much choice (an early version of information overload) (Rheingold 2012: 99). More recently there are those who are critical of the web's capacity to increase learning (Carr 2010), those who argue that we should be constantly aware of its threats and limitations (Wolf 2008) and those who seek to develop digital literacy skills which allow us to leverage the capacity of the web, to use it to augment our mental capacities (Rheingold 2012; Weller 2011; Veletsianos 2016).

What is clear is, as Veletsianos writes in his 2016 book on digital scholarship, that "The history of scholarship is largely intertwined with the history of technological innovation" (2016: 13). He goes on to at describe how we are seeing an ideological shift occurring among scholars from established frameworks of academic scholarship and discourse, towards structures that are more participatory and empowering, as, "Participation in social media allows the scholar to connect with others (e.g., other scholars, practitioners, the general public) in ongoing discussion and reflection (2016: 23). Just as earlier cultures worked with and through challenges with increasing information by developing encyclopedias, libraries, card indexes and reference systems, so our contemporary culture necessarily must develop tactics which allow scholars and students to create critically reflective learning communities through using digital networks and information.

Teaching and Learning Online

There are now many volumes that focus on online teaching and learning, these range from Gilly Salmon's seminal work on online forums (Salmon 1998; Salmon 2002), to more recent work which examines online identities (Thomas 2007; Gale et al. 2007), faculty development online (McQuiggan 2007; Boettcher and Conrad 2016) and other aspects of online learning such as motivation (Anderson 2004; Baxter 2012; Huett et al. 2008; Lee and Martin 2017). The field is moving fast and is informed not only by advances in technology, pedagogy and neuroscience, but by the ways in which online engagement is integrated into the lives of individuals in the form of news, online banking, social interaction and how we choose everything from household goods to holidays. Previous research has shown that the ways in which teachers learn about online teaching are not purely confined to formal learning but are assimilated through a blend of life experiences and interactions with their students and other teachers. It also demonstrates that issues such as student motivation, retention and completion have to be considered in new ways in order to explore the progression and retention of online learners (see for example, Baxter 2012).

This is not to suggest that traditional approaches to pedagogy must be put aside; on the contrary, new forms of teaching are based on a number of insights from behaviourist, cognitivist, humanist and social constructivist understandings of learning. In many ways, designing online courses has prompted higher education lecturers to think more deeply than ever about how their students learn and interact with their material. Unlike a traditional classroom, design of online learning material is challenging due to the fact that when we write, we cannot actually see the student interacting with the material. We are not privy to verbal cues such as that 'just don't get it look' or that 'lightbulb moment' that makes face to face teaching so rewarding.

Many modules at the Open University – the site of the case studies in this book – are designed by drawing primarily on social theories of learning. For those unfamiliar with the ideas behind this, they describe learning as a participatory process, where learners are part of communities, where they learn through practical experience and where they can shape their identity as learners. One of the key writers of influence in this field is Etienne Wenger, whose idea of communities of practice have done much to advance thinking in the field (see for example: Wenger 2008).

The key elements of this theory, illustrated in Fig. 2.1, show how learning is both a social activity whilst also affecting individual identities and ways of being in the world. This way of learning will often incorporate other views of learning such as behaviourism and cognitivism (Riding and Sadler-Smith 1997), taking such elements as the necessity for rapid feedback and firm learning outcomes (behaviourism), or acknowledging that far from being *tabula rasa*, students bring much in terms of their own experiences to learning, whilst each learning in different ways from one another (cognitivism) (Illeris 2009; Duit and Treagust 1998). Alongside this the humanist perspective has raised awareness of the affective dimensions of learning and the importance of relevance of the learning experience to the life of the individual (Rogers 1995).

The rich history of pedagogy and psychological theories of learning have yielded some very productive elements for online teaching. Such as, for example, the work of behavioural theorists such as Skinner (1968), whose teaching machine provided early pointers to later computer aided learning, and has parallels with the multiple-choice tests students run through in MOOCs. Similarly, elements of cognitive learning theory, with its emphasis on the internal functioning of the brain, can be seen in artificial intelligence and adaptive learning (Bates 2015). In addition to this, online

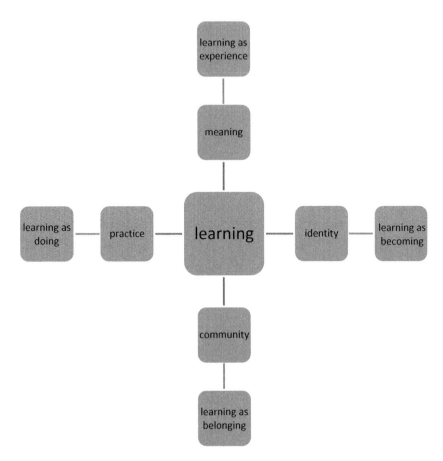

Fig. 2.1 Components of social learning theory adapted from Wenger (2008)

teaching has benefitted from being able to draw from the vast pedagogic literature emanating from the field of compulsory education as well as that in the field of traditional Higher Education methodologies (Schreurs et al. 2014). Bates (2015) eloquently summarizes the constructivist approach by describing that: "...constructivists emphasise the importance of consciousness, free will and social influences on learning... Constructivists believe that knowledge is essentially subjective in nature, constructed from our perceptions and mutually agreed upon conventions."

Wenger builds on the work of early social theorists of learning, including the American philosopher John Dewey (1916) and the Russian psychologist and educationalist Lev Vygotsky (writing in the 1920s and 1930s) (Van Der Veer 2007). The core of these theoretical arguments is that learning is to a very large extent influenced by social setting. The lived experience of an individual within their wider culture, family, and peer groups, local communities and so on helps to shape their identities and inform their competencies and capabilities as learners. In turn, this then provides them with skills enabling them to be active participants in their various communities. Social theories of learning are often contrasted with the formal learning which takes place in traditional classrooms. As John Dewey, an early and influential exponent of this theory, wrote:

> Hence one of the weightiest problems with which the philosophy of education has to cope is the method of keeping a proper balance between the informal and the formal, the incidental and the intentional, modes of education. When the acquiring of information and of technical intellectual skill do not influence the formation of a social disposition, ordinary vital experience fails to gain in meaning, while schooling, in so far, creates only "sharps" in learning—that is, egoistic specialists. (Dewey 1916: 13)

Dewey argues that humans should recognise and value the learning which takes place within communities. These include family, social and work networks. He sees learners as performing best when they were active participants in their own education. This implies that teachers make connections between subject content and real lived experience.

It is clear to see how this early work informs Wenger's emphasis on a social theory of learning. He is perhaps best known for developing the idea of communities of practice, writing: "… it is a perspective that locates learning, not in the head or outside it, but in the relationship between the person and the world, which for human beings is a social person in a social world" (2008: 1). This theoretical position recognises the role of informal learning that is the knowledge building and knowledge sharing which takes place outside formal theatres of learning such as the classroom. Marsick and Watkins (1990) provide the following summary of some key differences between formal and informal learning:

Formal learning is typically institutionally-sponsored, classroom-based, and highly structured. Informal learning, a category that includes incidental learning, may occur in institutions, but it is not typically classroom-based or highly structured, and control of learning rests primarily in the hands of the learner… Informal learning can be deliberately encouraged by an organization or it can take place despite an environment not highly conducive to learning. Incidental learning, on the other hand, almost always takes place although people are not always conscious of it. (1990: 12)

One aspect of the learning communities Wenger describes is that they are complex, involving constant interplay between formal and informal learning. Another important characteristic of such communities is that they are dynamic. This implies that learners can actively participate and shape their learning community. They do not passively accept given knowledge, whether through formal or informal channels, but rather critically interact with teachers and other students. Wenger describes this as developing a learning imagination through which they consciously engage with their learning environment, constantly create and re-create an image of themselves and their world.

We would argue that such a perspective, which emphasises the role of the informal, the social, is appropriate to many of the aspects of online learning covered in this book. In particular, our understanding of how social media can be used for informal learning and how technology can help to create communities of learning, can be informed by this theoretical framework. One can imagine that early theorists such as Vygotsky, with a focus on the role of culture in shaping mental life, would be interested in how the new digital culture is influencing education. Dewey too, would be interested in how the web might create more active learners, with students making connections between learning and their lived experience.

This focus on creating communities of learning through digital means also links to the theory of connectivism which has been developing since the mid 2000s (Schreurs et al. 2014; Boitshwarelo 2011). This represents an attempt to conceptualize learning in a digital age. One of its earliest proponents is Siemens, who argues that much learning and knowledge now exists outside of the individual, within the web:

Connectivism is driven by the understanding that decisions are based on rapidly altering foundations. New information is continually being acquired. The ability to draw distinctions between important and unimportant information is vital. The ability to recognize when new information alters the landscape based on decisions made yesterday is also critical. (Siemens 2005: 23)

While this theory is in the early stages of development, the idea that knowledge exists primarily inside digital systems and networks, is a useful addition to the pedagogical debate.

In order to fully understand how theories of learning adapt and evolve within the online context it is vital to consider the role of the teacher within these processes. The Open University has a rather unique way of approaching teaching with 5000 Associate Lecturer staff who directly support, teach and mark students' work and provide other forms of student support. In addition, Central and Regional Academic staff manage teaching, produce modules and carry out research into pedagogy and within specific fields of academic study. In the next part of this chapter we discuss the role of academics more broadly in the online teaching and learning environment.

Academics in Online Teaching

The role of academics in online teaching has drawn much from the field of identity formation. Debates around how and why you teach online have posed challenges to established notions of academic tribes and territories (Becher and Trowler 2001), and have gone so far as to challenge the very nature of disciplines. One of the key elements within this is the hegemonic claim that technology often appears to have staked within the whole rationale and practice of teaching. Early writing on the impact of technology on the academic focuses on the ideas brought to bear by writers such as Sherry Turkle and her seminal volume "Life on the screen: Identity in the age of the internet" (Turkle 2011), which describes how teaching with technology initially suppresses the teacher as bricoleur who draws from a number of rich sources to inform teaching and relegates them to the 'plodding' linear stages of their initial development as teachers. This idea has since been taken up by a number of researchers into academic identities (Muilenburg and Berge 2001; Baxter 2010a, b), who question the very notion of academic identity and autonomy in a digital age (see also Henkel 2005; Richardson and Alsup 2015).

Many early researchers into how delivering online changes the whole notion of what it means to be a teacher, certainly believed that the early adopters of such teaching were conditioned by technological hegemonies which changed their style of delivery and seriously impeded their ability to teach their subject (Henkel 2005). The sense of anomie experienced by many academics was compounded by the feeling that teaching online was largely driven by neo-liberal ideals and cost saving exercises on the part of universities – a feeling that is perhaps unsurprising given the climate in which higher education is operating (see also Harris 2005; Beck and Young 2005). However as technologies have progressed and become more integrated into the working lives of academics, researchers have moved on from this position, to looking at how academics manipulate their digital worlds and identities within those online environments (see for example Barak and Gluck-Ofri 2007; Garrison and Cleveland-Innes 2005; Janssen and Kies 2005).

The challenges of online teaching do not only rest with academics but with students too and the ways in which they in turn create sustainable and salient identities that promote retention and progression (Baxter 2011; O'Brien 2002; Herbert 2006). Management of academics that teach online is not without its challenges, particularly in terms of their retention and ongoing job satisfaction (see for example Chap. 12 this volume). It is particularly unhelpful when individuals or policies focus on the technologies at the expense of the human element of teaching – as if individuals were somehow an optional extra in the teaching and learning experience! These beliefs have been around for some time and judging by the recent Digifest conference (2017) they are still often foremost in the minds of those who design teaching and learning policy within HE.

The Open University: The Case

The Open University is now such an integral part of the national and international HE landscape that it is difficult to imagine the extent of the political opposition it faced as the first *University of the Air*. A university that fulfilled its unique promise in eradicating the entry requirements that characterized conventional universities and permitting universal access for all and one that aimed to banish the pedagogically pedestrian in its quest to seek out new ways to engage students. A university that challenged the transmission mode of teaching by introducing new collaborative ways of working and pedagogies that placed as much emphasis on the processes engendered by the learning, as the learning itself. With its once unique approach to teaching and learning the OU was one of the first institutions which employed technology to emphasise, "the discursive, adaptive, interactive and reflective" (see Baxter 2015 on Weinbren 2014).

Since the OU's launch in 1969 more than 2 million people have studied and achieved their learning goals with the organisation (Open University 2016). The OU today is also the largest provider of HE for people with disabilities, with more than 22,000 people with disabilities studying there in the period 2015/16. Its flexible approach and unique profile means that 76% of registered OU students work full or part time during their studies, 23% of OU UK undergraduates live in the 25% most deprived areas and 31% of new undergraduates are under 25.

As the only UK University dedicated to distance learning the institution has a long history of delivering high quality online learning. As well as paid for modules and qualifications it also offers a wide range of Massive Open Online Courses (MOOCs) through its company FutureLearn, and since 2006 45 million people have accessed this free learning (OU 2016). Its modules are historically recognised for their critical take on a subject and the teaching is well known for its creativity, participatory and innovative qualities. As such it is well placed to offer insights into both the practices and pedagogies of online teaching and learning as the rest of this book reflects.

References

Allen, E., & Seaman, J. (2017). *Digital learning compass: Distance education enrollement report* 2017 (Babson Survey Research Group. US Digital Learning Compass, Ed.).

Anderson, T. (2004). *Teaching in an online learning context* (2nd Rev. ed.). Athabasca: Athabasca University Press.

Appadurai, A. (1996). *Modernity at large: Cultural dimensions of globalization* (Vol. 1). Minnesota: Minnesota Press.

Barak, A., & Gluck-Ofri, O. (2007). Degree and reciprocity of self-disclosure in online forums. *CyberPsychology and Behavior, 10*(3), 407–417.

Bates, T. (2015). *Teaching in a digital age.* https://opentextbc.ca/teachingina-digitalage/chapter/section-3-4-constructivism/

Baxter, J. (2010a). *Bien dans sa Peau : An investigation into the role of professional learning on the online teaching identities of HE Lecturers.* http://oro.open.ac.uk/26313/

Baxter, J. (2010b, December 7–11). Traversing the Borderlands: Online academic identities for a new HE world. In *Society for Research into Higher Education Newer Researchers Conference*, The Celtic Manor, Cardiff.

Baxter, J. (2011). *Who am I and what keeps me going? Profiling the distance learning student.* Positive Futures for higher education; connections, communities and criticality, The Celtic Manor, Wales.

Baxter, J. (2012). Who am I and what keeps me going? Profiling the distance student. *International Review of Research in Open and Distance Learning, 13*(4), 107–129.

Baxter, J. (2015). *The open university: A history* (Book review). London: Taylor and Francis, International Journal of Lifelong Learning.

Becher, T., & Trowler, P. (2001). *Academic tribes and territories: Intellectual enquiry and the culture of disciplines.* London: McGraw-Hill Education.

Beck, J., & Young, M. F. D. (2005). The assault on the professions and the restructuring of academic and professional identities: A Bernsteinian analysis. *British Journal of Sociology of Education, 26*(2), 183–197.

Boettcher, J. V., & Conrad, R. M. (2016). *The online teaching survival guide: Simple and practical pedagogical tips.* London: Wiley.

Boitshwarelo, B. (2011). Proposing an integrated research framework for connectivism: Utilising theoretical synergies. *The International Review of Research in Open and Distributed Learning, 12*(3), 161–179.

Carr, N. (2010). *The shallows: How the internet is changing the way we think, read and remember.* London: Atlantic Books.

Clarke, J. (2007). Citizen-consumers and public service reform: At the limits of neo-liberalism? *Policy Futures in Education, 5*(2), 239–248.

Davies, S. R., & Bartholomew, P. (2017). *How does technology -enhanced learning contribue to teaching excellence ?* Digifest Birmingham Online at: https://www.jisc.ac.uk/digifest. Accessed 10 Oct 2017.

Deacon, B. (1997). *Global social policy: International organizations and the future of welfare.* London: Sage.

Dewey, J. (1916). *Democracy and education.* Pennsylvania State University. http://library.um.ac.id/images/stories/ebooks/Juni10/democracy%-20and%20education%20-%20john%20dewey.pdf. Accessed 24 Aug 2016.

Duit, R., & Treagust, D. F. (1998). Learning in science: From behaviourism towards social constructivism and beyond. *International Handbook of Science Education, 1*(Part 1), 3–25.

Earney, L., Davies, S., McKean, P., & McGregor, A. (2017). *Jisc Digifest 2017-Plenary.* Jisc Digifest Birmingham, Birmingham City University, 14–15 March 2017.

Flavin, M. (2016). Technology-enhanced learning and higher education. *Oxford Review of Economic Policy, 32*(4), 632–645. https://doi.org/10.1093/oxrep/grw028.

Gale, K., Wheeler, S., & Kelly, P. (2007). Learning in cyberspace: An examination of changes in professional identity and practice style in an online problem-based learning environment. *Quarterly Review of Distance Education, 8*(4), 11.

Garrison, D. R., & Cleveland-Innes, M. (2005). Facilitating cognitive presence in online learning: Interaction is not enough. *The American Journal of Distance Education, 19*(3), 133–148.

Gourlay, L., & Stevenson, J. (2017). *Teaching excellence in higher education: Critical perspectives.* London: Routledge.

Harris, S. (2005). Rethinking academic identities in neo-liberal times. *Teaching in Higher Education, 10*(4), 421–433.

Henkel, M. (2005). Academic identity and autonomy in a changing policy environment. *Higher Education, 49*(1), 155–176.

Henry, M., Lingard, B., Rizvi, F., & Taylor, S. (Eds.). (2001). *The OECD, globalisation and education policy.* In G. Neave (Ed.), *Issues in higher education.* Bingley: Emerald Pubishing Limited.

Herbert, M. (2006). Staying the course: A study in online student satisfaction and retention. *Online Journal of Distance Learning Administration, 9*(4). https://eric.ed.gov/?id=EJ1108805

Huett, J. B., Kalinowski, K. E., Moller, L., & Huett, K. C. (2008). Improving the motivation and retention of online students through the use of ARCS-based e-mails. *The American Journal of Distance Education, 22*(3), 159–176.

Illeris, K. (Ed.). (2009). *Contemporary theories of learning : Learning theorists in their own words*. London: Routledge.

Janssen, D., & Kies, R. (2005). Online forums and deliberative democracy. *Acta Politica, 40*(3), 317–335.

Lee, J., & Martin, L. (2017). Investigating students' perceptions of motivating factors of online class discussions. *The International Review of Research in Open and Distributed Learning*, [S.l.], *18*(5), ISSN 1492–3831. Available at: http://www.irrodl.org/index.php/irrodl/article/view/2883. Accessed 25 Aug 2017. doi: https://doi.org/10.19173/irrodl.v18i5.2883.

Lingard, B., Rizvi, F., & Taylor, S. (2003). Globalisation and changing education policy. In M. Henry, B. Lingard, F. Rizvi, & S. Taylor (Eds.), *The OECD, globalisation and education policy* (pp. 19–37). Bingley: Emerald.

Marsick, V. J., & Watkins, K. (1990). *Informal and incidental learning in the workplace*. London/New York: Routledge.

McQuiggan, C. A. (2007). The role of faculty development in online teaching's potential to question teaching beliefs and assumptions. *Online Journal of Distance Learning Administration, 10*(3), 1–13.

Muilenburg, L., & Berge, Z. L. (2001). Barriers to distance education: A factor-analytic study. *American Journal of Distance Education, 15*(2), 7–22.

O'Brien, B. S. (2002). Online student retention: Can it be done? In P. Barker & S. Rebelsky (Eds.), *Proceedings of world conference on educational Mutimedia, hypermedia and telecommunications*. Cheasapeake: AACE.

OECD. (1995). *Governance in transition: Public management reforms in OECD countries*. Paris: OECD.

Open University. (2016). *Annual report*. http://www.open.ac.uk/about/main/sites/www.open.ac.uk.about.main/files/files/ecms/web-content/about-annual-report-2015-2016.pdf. Accessed 7 Nov 2017.

Power, M. (1997). *The audit society: Rituals of verification*. Oxford: Oxford University Press.

Radice, H. (2013). How we got here: UK higher education under neoliberalism. *ACME: An International Journal for Critical Geographies, 12*(2), 407–418.

Rheingold, H. (2012). *Net smart: How to thrive online*. London: MIT Press.

Richardson, J. C., & Alsup, J. (2015). From the classroom to the keyboard: How seven teachers created their online teacher identities. *The International Review of Research in Open and Distributed Learning, 16*(1), 142–167.

Riding, R. J., & Sadler-Smith, E. (1997). Cognitive style and learning strategies: Some implications for training design. *International Journal of Training and Development, 1*(3), 199–208.

Rogers, C. (1995). *A way of being*. London: Houghton Mifflin Harcourt.

Rushby, N., & Surry, D. (2016, March). *Wiley handbook of learning technology*. London: Wiley-Blackwell.

Salmon, G. (1998). Developing learning through effective online moderation. *Active Learning, 9*(December), 3–8.

Salmon, G. (2002). *Moderating: The key to teaching and learning online*. London: Routledge.

Schreurs, B., Van den Beemt, A., Prinsen, F., Witthaus, G., Conole, G., & De Laat, M. (2014). An investigation into social learning activities by practitioners in open educational practices. *The International Review of Research in Open and Distributed Learning, 15*(4), 1–20.

Siemens, G. (2005). Connectivism: A learning theory for the digital age. *Journal of Instructional Technology and Distance Learning, 2*(1), 3–10.

Skinner, B. (1968). *The technology of teaching*. New York: Appleton-century-crofts.

Szucs, A., Tait, A., Vidal, M., & Bernath, U. (2009). *Distance and E-learning in transition: Learning innovation, technology and social challenges*. London: Wiley.

Thomas, A. (2007). *Youth online: Identity and literacy in the digital age*. London: Peter Lang Publishing.

Tobin, T. J., Mandernach, B. J., & Taylor, A. H. (2015). *Evaluating online teaching*. London: Wiley.

Turkle, S. (2011). *Life on the screen*. New York: Simon and Schuster.

Van der Veer, R. (2007). *Lev Vygotsky*. London: Bloomsbury.

Veletsianos, G. (2016). *Social media in academia: Networked scholars*. New York: Routledge.

Weinbren, D. (2014). *The Open University: A history*. Manchester: Manchester University Press.

Weller, M. (2011). *The Digital scholar: How technology is transforming academic practice*. Bloomsbury Open Access. https://www.bloomsburycollections.com/book/the-digital-scholar-how-technology-is-transforming-scholarly-practice/. Accessed 7 July 2016.

Wenger, E. C. (2008). *Communities of practice: Learning, meaning, and identity* (18th printing, first published 1998). Cambridge: Cambridge University.

Wolf, M. (2008). *Proust and the squid: The story and science of the reading brain*. London: Icon Books.

3

Creating Spaces for Learning: Online Forums

Rachel Manning and Donna Smith

Introduction

The changing landscape of Higher Education (HE) provision has meant that a range of educators are necessarily engaging with some of the various challenges of web-based teaching media. The perceived flexibility of 'blended'[1] approaches to the provision of learning environments in particular has contributed to the increasing use of online provision (Irvine et al. 2013). Within blended learning contexts, asynchronous online discussion forums can be seen as particularly attractive, as they are not reliant on students and tutors being in 'the same place at the same time', thus allowing for a more flexible engagement with learning (Kim et al. 2016). As Kim et al. explain, asynchronous online discussion forums can be a means through which to support critical discussion, social interaction and reflection. As

R. Manning • D. Smith (✉)
School of Politics, Philosophy, Economics, Development and Geography,
Open University, Milton Keynes, UK
e-mail: Donna.Smith@open.ac.uk

© The Author(s) 2018
J. Baxter et al. (eds.), *Creativity and Critique in Online Learning*,
https://doi.org/10.1007/978-3-319-78298-0_3

such, these forums can be seen as an example of where universities are trying to reimagine teaching spaces. However, discussion of the use of online forums for education often centres on the interaction (or, most often, lack of it) within them. Yet, while they can end up as relatively unused and neglected, we argue in this chapter (and Helen Kaye and Jane Barrett in the next) that online forums still have potential for teaching.

In this chapter, while attending to issues of forum participation, we will also discuss forums in their broader context, and how such contextual issues inform potential approaches to their use. We will focus on the issues of forum structure and function, rather than the finer detail of interactional facilitation. Thus, while our focus is, in a sense, one level removed from the more 'micro' issues of within-forum interactional management, the issues that concern us in this chapter nonetheless impact on such processes, as we will see. Therefore, in our analysis, we will examine how some of the various ways in which forums are conceived and operationalised can impact on their effectiveness. While the detail of our analysis focuses on the use of forums at The Open University (OU), our discussion is informed by our use of forums across various HEIs, as well as relevant broader literature.

Our discussion is informed by our particular perspectives on forums: as tutors and lecturers who use forums, but also as managers of design elements of forums (including their membership), as managers of colleagues tutoring in forums and as developers of modules and programmes of learning more generally. Thus, while we both are long standing educators, we bring to this our practical experience of managing these learning spaces and managing the tutors that use them. Moreover, while the focus of the case studies we present in this chapter are drawn from an OU context (and from a particular faculty), our discussion of them in this chapter is informed by our wider HE experiences. This allows us to highlight broad principles which should hold true across different technologies and institutions.

We begin with a general consideration of forums, through highlighting some of the more pertinent elements in the related literature, and most notably acknowledging one of the core perceived 'problems' with forums: participation. We will then move on to draw our attention to the broader 'extra-forum' context within which forums sit, in order to set out some of the additional factors that nonetheless impact on experiences within them. Our key point is to highlight what we have termed *structural* and *functional* concerns that are related to the use of forums as spaces for learning. We then move on, taking a heuristic approach, to set out a series of case studies of forum design and use in order to illustrate how a concern with structure and function can facilitate a productive engagement with forum use. Finally, we make some key suggestions for colleagues engaging with forums, based on our analysis. In doing so we adopt a broadly pragmatist position: in examining online forums devised for various different pedagogical purposes, by different instructors, in different disciplinary contexts, our aim is to identify common issues and themes. This is done by offering a reflective analysis of some of the factors that can influence the effectiveness of online forums as a pedagogical tool.

Forums: Panacea or Lost Cause?

Forums are among some of the oldest online technologies, and are also (e.g. in the form of Facebook) some of the most ubiquitous, existing on a variety of different platforms (Wallace 2016). Online forums are seen as a particularly useful space for use in HE (Groves and O'Donoghue 2009; Choi et al. 2005). The use of online forums as a space for discussion, for example, is seen as having (at least potential) benefit to learners, particularly those for whom online channels are the only ones available to them. Such opportunities to engage with others (fellow students and/or tutors) can provide important learning spaces for developing understanding, for example of complex material, where time to think 'offline' renders the asynchronous space a valuable tool. Likewise, they represent a potential space for interaction and collaboration where 'traditional' (face to face) opportunities for these core activities may be lacking (e.g. in solely or primarily distance institutions) – one of seemingly various perceived 'Achilles heels' of distance education (e.g. Hulsmann 2009).

This longevity, and the prior familiarity that many internet users have with forums, can pose both opportunities and challenges for their use in HE contexts. Assumed familiarity can mean that they are implemented with little thought as to how well they will 'work'. Moreover, differing expectations can lead to particular forms of implementation being experienced as frustrating. One aim of this chapter, then, is to encourage the consideration of the various ways in which forums can be designed and used, and to attend to the different expectations that users may have of them.

While internet forums are broadly conceived as online message boards, where, as a minimum, forum members can post messages/text and respond to the posts of others, members may also be able to start their own discussion topics, upload documents, link to other web-based resources, report inappropriate content, etc. Likewise, forums can serve a variety of functions, including straightforward information provision, the sharing of resources, and an additional means through which to facilitate the sense of learning community (Liu et al. 2007). Moreover, their utility as a relatively 'permanent' container of developing content (in the sense that text is stored in the space until those in a position to do so decide otherwise), mean that such spaces can be returned to and content reviewed by students at any time within the limits set out by the designer (Balaju and Chakrabarti 2010). Writing about the potential of technology, Weller (2011, p. 67) notes, 'there is nothing inherent in the technologies themselves that force users to behave in a specific manner'. Thus, the technology of forums can similarly be used in a variety of ways, for a variety of purposes – for example to set out information stores for easy access by educators and students (to which, of course, both can add their own content), or as 1:1 forums to facilitate tutor-student project supervision (which may include discussion, but is equally a type of 'storage' space for information that can be updated). Similarly, various different configurations of information sharing can be done via forums, as a means through which to facilitate engagement with the 'abundance' of learning materials (and 'knowledge') that Weller (2011) highlights. The specific range of functionality available to forum users will be subject to a range of decisions, as we discuss below.

As we have already noted, it is concerns over levels of engagement and the effectiveness of forms of asynchronous online discussion that have led to questions of their ultimate utility. For example, various authors have pointed to the problems and barriers students find in engaging with online discussion (Kim et al. 2016; Smith and Smith 2014). While, for example,

Weller's example of a 'communities of practice' pedagogy illustrates the potentially developmental nature of participation (or contribution) to online communities, questions remain regarding the ability of forums to function as effective learning spaces. Smith and Smith's (2014) research discusses the notion of 'active' and 'passive' participation in forums: 'active' participation is when a student posts, and 'passive' when a student views a thread but does not post themselves. They note that this does not mean that the passive student is not engaged, as they may learn by observation of others (Dennen 2008). Linked to this, it has been suggested that more 'passive' forms of engagement are not necessarily indicative of less success on a module (e.g. in terms of outcome grades). As Smith and Smith 2015 (p. 1), note in relation to a study of two (now, discontinued) Year 1 OU social science modules, while students who did not engage actively or passively were likely to fail, those who passively engaged to an 'average' or 'high' level were 'not only more likely to pass, but achieve almost as high a score as those students who both actively and passively engage in a module'. Thus, while we might naturally assume that 'participation' is always crucial to effective learning, participation in forums – while often assumed to be of central importance to their effectiveness – is not as straightforward an educational 'good' as it might first appear and therefore warrants further investigation. We will return to this issue later in this chapter.

Thus, doubts over the utility of online forums can raise questions regarding their inclusion as an effective learning medium. For example, there are indications that online discussion forums can be seen as less useful in the context of blended module delivery (Zhou and Chua 2016). On the other hand, their potential in supporting learning means that they still have the capacity to contribute to effective online provision. As Kember et al. (2010) note: "Using features which promote constructive dialogue and interactive learning activities encourages a deep approach to learning, the development of communication skills and enhanced understanding of content." (p. 1183).

The need for 'participation', then, (and particularly 'active participation') depends on the function of the forum. We question whether struggles to effect 'participation' are always necessary, and question its centrality as a concern. Instead, we would suggest, the need for participation (and its form – e.g. whether 'active' or 'passive') is related to what the forum is for (both in terms of its contents and its role within the broader course or module). Aligning the purpose, or *function,* of the forum and assessment can be a useful driver of participation, where this is seen as a core route through which a desired forum function can be achieved. In which case, it may be useful to consider the different possible purposes that a single forum can achieve, if assessment is being used to drive participation within it. Conversely, if 'active' participation is not a goal of the module, then the focus can shift. The key point here, then, is that a focus on 'participation' (particularly when crudely defined or quantified) needs to be justified in terms of its importance for realising the specific aims of a specific forum in the context of the broader module. We will develop this point further below.

Forums in Context

Forums are of course just one element of a wider range of provision often made available as part of a 'blended' learning environment (De George-Walker and Keeffe 2010). Thus, while we here focus in detail on forums in particular, they obviously sit within a broader context of learning that may or may not be under the control of a forum user and/or designer. Relatedly, while some educators will be involved in pedagogical decisions that precede (but have implications for) the 'action' that occurs within a 'live' forum, this is not necessarily the case. Moreover, institutional factors will of course have implications for student experience and learning – and, as such, are a constituent of the more general 'structural' factors that impact on learning design and student experience (which also include the systems and technological limitations of any given institutional context).

In addition, while learning is clearly socially embedded (see for example Weller 2011), it is, we would argue, equally particularised. Students are of course embedded in broader learning systems, whether we consider them to be connectivist learners (i.e. relatively autonomous learners who navigate a networked environment of knowledge, see Siemens 2005; Kop 2011), or not. Students' own prior experiences of different forum formats, and of previous educational forums (e.g. on other modules or other

HEI's) will of course impact on their experiences and expectations of the forum used in any particular learning context (Baxter and Haycock 2014). Much like the observation of Wiley and Mc Andrew et al. (2009, cited in Weller 2011, p. 108) in relation to open educational resources, some learners will not be seeking social interaction, and will therefore avoid context for discussion – and therefore forums – altogether. While we consider learning to be social, and forums inherently so, building community is not necessarily facilitated by forums. In the context of the abundance of learning content and resources (Weller 2011), and the shifting dominance of traditional modes of education, the attraction of within-module forums to students may be limited.

Finally, it is also instructive to briefly note some of the particular issues relating to 'part time' learning. Of course, the reality for many students – even those nominally designated as 'full time' – will be a parallel obligation to paid employment and/or domestic commitments (Burston 2016). However, for those deliberately choosing 'part time' study, time constraints may feature significantly in learning activity. As such, a proliferation of learning media can in itself become a drain on time, as students must navigate an array of available spaces. Thus, aside from some of the more complex arguments relating to forums and pedagogy, it is worth bearing in mind central basic tenets of human-computer interaction (HCI). More generally, the basic message here is that any requirement for forum participation should be carefully thought through in terms of wider learning and teaching strategies (at the module level and beyond).

Working with Forums: Structure, Function and Control

For the purpose of our discussion in this chapter, we will distinguish between different core elements of online forums which are useful to consider in developing forums, and in analysing the contribution of forums to student learning. For the purpose of this chapter, we characterise the dimensions along which these elements differ as 'structural' and 'functional'. This allows us to highlight the importance of the relationship between how forums are designed and how they are experienced and used. Our discussion and analysis of forums in these terms is intended as a heuristic resource for planning their use as part of overall learning design. Moreover, while we are not suggesting that forums are a neutral medium for teaching, we nonetheless propose that there are few essential characteristics of forums, given their variety of both structure and function. Thus, we aim to offer our analysis and reflections as informing ways of approaching forums creatively as educators, in ways that can work with and around the various contextual factors that may impact on experiences of them.

In order to facilitate our discussion and analysis of the potential creative use of forums, we refer to *structure* in terms of issues relating to the more mechanical aspects of forums. These are issue such as who has access to a particular online forum space, at what times (i.e. how long/at what points in the life of the module will a particular forum be in use), how many forums on a module, together with elements of what they look like: how many threads, permissions relating to who can do what in the forum. There are of course additional, basic structural issues relating to the specific technology used, for example the user interface. Such basic structural features again have the potential to influence the use of such forums that are beyond the control of the tutor/manager.

We will use the notion of *function*, on the other hand, to refer to the purpose of the particular learning space (i.e. the forum), and as such is driven by learning strategy (and which may be facilitated by structure). Thus, structure and function are not neatly separable. Nonetheless, we suggest that, considering these two aspects of forums is a useful exercise in planning forum delivery. Individual forums may serve a number of different functions. Alternatively, some functions may only be served by a particular forum. Thus, the different 'functions' that each forum might serve can potentially be incorporated into the same or different forums. Likewise, the same forum might serve different pedagogies (see Weller 2011). As Weller (2011) notes, the crucial question for educators is how to use available tools to tap into their potential without destroying what makes them valuable. As noted above, it is the perceived flexibility of forums in particular (most notably due to their commonly asynchronous nature) that is seen as rendering them particularly valuable (e.g. Hrastinski 2008).

Not all decisions relating to structure and function will be under the control of the person designing the learning– either because they are the decisions of others, or because of technological limitations. In planning to use forums, therefore, a useful first step would be to familiarise oneself with what decisions are practically possible. On a 'first run' of using forums, basic technological functions may be primary concerns, and it is often through one's own experience of how things 'work' in use, followed by reflection and evaluation of this initial experience, that will primarily inform one's own future practice, as well as preferred theoretical perspective. One may, of course, not be in a position to choose any element of the learning environment at all – particularly in terms of form/structure, but also in terms of purpose/function (although the latter is often more amenable to manipulation, at least in terms of the approach to facilitating interaction, or supporting the purpose/function of the forum). Thus, in practice, many of the important decisions around forum design (the technology used, access of it, etc.), may belong to others.

The freedom one has (or not) for using forum spaces may well, of course, be a source of frustration or conflict in terms of the achievement of one's learning and teaching strategies. Moreover, when control over structural and functional decisions is located in different places, there can also be conflict between elements and/or the proliferation of spaces (e.g. forums). Ultimately, when adding forums to the same online learning space (i.e. module site), care should be taken with respect to both the communication of their purpose, and the articulation between any additional forum and others available to students.

As noted, what we are calling structure and function are inherently bound – and point to additional issues such as the perceived or desired relationships between tutors and students. Thus, particular structures may also be bound up in assumptions about this relationship (e.g. tutor group specific forums, where there is an expectation of an ongoing, developing relationship, compared with a structure in which the particular tutor/moderator is largely irrelevant, and the focus is on information exchange, such as question and answer-type forums).

Core learning design principles (e.g. constructive alignment) together with basic human-computer-interaction (HCI) principles point to the need for clarity in the presentation of online learning spaces. As Anderson et al. (2001, p. 6) note, "the teacher's task is to create a narrative path through the mediated instruction and activity set such that students are aware of the explicit and implicit learning goals and activities in which they participate. Macro-level comments about course process and content are thus an important motivation and orientation component of this category of teaching presence." Likewise, Bedersen et al. (2015) further illustrate the utility of HCI principles in that, "Many fundamental issues in HCI are, at their core, questions about learning. And many key opportunities for improving learning are, at their core, sites for improving HCI."

One of the key points here, as we have noted, is that the temptation to proliferate learning spaces can be a risky strategy, particularly when used to mitigate against the perceived limitations of others' structure/function decisions. At the very least, 'conflict' between learning spaces should be considered and avoided (we will illustrate this point further in our case studies below). Ultimately, we would argue that whoever makes each decision around structure and function should ensure that the rationale for each is made clear to other users: communication of the rationale for forums is a core element of their effectiveness. Conversely, as educators who are working with the decisions of others, one should seek to ensure that those making the decisions are required to set out their rationale. Of course, stated aims for a forum may not be realised. However, it is only through being explicit about them that we can (1) ensure that students are effectively informed and (2) reflect on and evaluate our (and others) practice – and revise where appropriate.

Illustrative Case Studies

A considerable amount of research on online forums focuses in one way or another on the communicative or language element of forums. While, of course, such features of forum experience are crucial, our focus here is on the larger structures that surround online forum activity, and those which are largely determined prior to any student engagement (and, therefore, can be impervious to 'live' alteration during the course of a particular module). Our focus is a pragmatic one, drawing on a detailed engagement with the use of forums by both students and tutors, rather than focusing on ideal scenarios. In so doing, we are aware that actual use can run contrary to original intentions. Thus, there is a need for continual review and reflection in relation to the use of learning technologies.

Our discussion and analysis here is based on tutoring and management of a broad range of modules from the social sciences within the OU. We will therefore look critically at what works and does not work, from the perspective of those managing online forums, as well as managing tutors who teach through forums. In the discussion that follows, while drawing on this broad practice, we also refer to some specific modules that serve as illustrative cases. We will refer to the modules as follows (Table 3.1):

Table 3.1 Modules/forums discussed in the chapter

Forums and examples discussed[a]		
Chapter reference	Type of forum	Studied by
Module A	Individual tutor group forum	Undergraduate Year 1 students; usually the first module of study; discontinued module
Module B	Multi tutored clustered forum Assessed forum	Undergraduate Year 1 students; usually the first module of study; replaced Module A
Module C	Single forum covering whole module (aka a module-wide forum)	Undergraduate Year 3 students
Module D	Single forum covering whole module (aka a module-wide forum)	Undergraduate Year 2 students
Module E	Collaborative forum Assessed forum	Undergraduate Year 2 students
Module F	Collaborative forum	Undergraduate Year 1 students; usually the second module of study

[a]All of the modules discussed in this table are in-presentation in 2017, with the exception of Module A which ceased presentation a few years prior

Common Forum Structures

In this section, we set out some examples from OU modules of structural and functional forum features and decisions relating to them. These form the basis for examining our own learning around their effectiveness as learning spaces. We do not attempt to include every single sub-type of forum, but the most common ones we have used while working at the OU. These sub-types, while discussed in an OU context, may be familiar to those working at other HEIs, albeit the naming conventions may be different.

Individual Tutor Group Forums

Tutor group forums are a space for a tutor to moderate a forum for a group of students assigned to them. Only the students in that particular group can access the forum space, which on OU modules is usually around 15–20 students. On OU modules this type of forum is often used as a 'noticeboard' style space, useful for the tutor to post advice and guidance and tutorial notes and presentations, and for students to ask questions about the module they are studying, study skills issues, and assessment (a simple example of 'function'). The forum will be open for the duration of the module, and will be often be the tutor's first port of call when checking for student queries, alongside their email. Students may also use it as a social space, to discuss wider study issues with other students, as well as for general chat – although tutors often report (and our forum moderation suggests) that this is not popular with many students. We know that many students use other social media platforms, such as Facebook, for this activity. In their study of forums and student identities Baxter and Haycock (2014) note that students viewed social interactions in forums as being of less value than those about academic content; this could be at play here.

Tutor group forums can therefore be a useful space for establishing the tutor-student relationship, and for making sure that students who have not attended a tutorial (whether face to face or online) can access appropriate guidance and support. However, that is not to say that tutor group forums are always successful. For a start, there may be other forums which compete for students' time, in particular clustered forums (a forum which multiple tutor groups can access, see below) or module-wide forums (a forum which every tutor and student on the module can access, see below), meaning the tutor group forum can become secondary. Due to the limited number of students who can access a tutor group forum, it can also be difficult for the forum to gain momentum in relation to the number of posts students make, meaning the forum could feel intimidating to those who do want to post but have not yet done so. This can in turn be dispiriting for the tutor moderating the forum, and mean they in turn make fewer posts, contributing to the problem. Tutor group forums can also feel superfluous if the function is not properly explained to students and the purpose of the forum is not written into the module materials with students guided to use them at appropriate points.

Module A is an example of a tutor group forum which, in our experience, did not work as well as we originally hoped. As managers on this module we had the opportunity to set up tutor group forums for each tutor alongside a clustered forum (and a centrally set-up and run module-wide forum). We did so feeling it was important to establish a space for tutors to work with students in a tutor group setting, thus enhancing the group dynamic. However, it became clear that these spaces were not frequently used by many students or tutors; feedback from tutors suggested this was due to the presence of the cluster and module-wide forums which seemed 'busier' and were therefore more appealing and less intimidating for students. For subsequent presentations of the module, we made the decision to discontinue tutor group forums with tutors asked to concentrate on the cluster forum instead.

This is not to say that tutor group forums are never successful (i.e. the desired level of participation is achieved, or students use them in the way envisioned). What is important is that they are integrated into the module, that tutors and students understand their function, and that the presence of other sorts of forums which compete for students' time is thought about carefully before being set up (they too need an explicit function). Our experiences as managers suggest that tutor group forums can be successful if the tutor running it is enthusiastic, encourages students to post, and advertises the forum in tutorials and by email. They may also be useful for modules when students do more independent study, are more confident, and rely on the group dynamic less. This allows tutors to post extension activities for students who want to stretch themselves, without students feeling overwhelmed, and for students and tutors to engage in discussion about wider issues linked to the module. Of course, this still relies on tutors being engaged and students understanding the place of the forum in their studies.

Clustered Forums

Clustered forums are forums which multiple tutor groups can access, but are a level lower than full, module-wide forums. For OU Social Sciences modules this is usually between four and ten groups of students (so, between 60 and 200 students), although can be bigger or smaller, based around geography if there is face to face teaching (so the same students have the chance to meet each other both in person and online) or a simple division of overall student numbers into workable groups of activity. All tutors and students in the cluster can access this forum, with tutors working together to moderate it, often taking turns. It is a useful place to post tutorial notes and presentations (particularly if those tutorials were for the entire cluster rather than on a tutor group basis) and for questions and answers about the module and its assessments. The forum is open for the entirety of the module, and often becomes a student's first port of call, particularly if there are no tutor group forums.

The advantages of a clustered forum are many. First of all, there are more students available to post, making the forum seem busier and hopefully more welcome. Students can also experience the input of multiple tutors, helping to establish the notion of an academic community; this can be particularly important if the module is an interdisciplinary one, as each tutor may have a different academic background and students therefore get the opportunity to interact with tutors with different expertise and skills. Students also get the opportunity to read tutorial notes and presentations developed by other tutors as well as their own, and to discuss them with students from other groups.

Potential negatives include the possible erosion of the tutor group-student dynamic. However, to mitigate this, tutors can set up a tutor group thread within the clustered forum, if they want to target their own students (it is useful in such contexts to ensure there is some discussion between tutors on what activities and topics are best located in such threads, as opposed to the general clustered area). There should also be regular contributors to the main forum threads and ideally tutors would be supporting their students via email messages and telephone calls. For those managing the tutoring team this of course entails regular reviewing of the forums as well as appropriate staff development activities to ensure tutors are aware of their role.

On *Module B* tutor group forums were a possibility, but the authors decided to only use a clustered forum from the very beginning, with tutors taking turns to moderate. Tutors were provided with very clear guidance from the start about the purpose of the forum. Permanent threads were also posted at the top of the cluster forum detailing to students what the function of the cluster forum was, which tutors were moderating it, the computing code of conduct, and wider points about the other types of tuition available on this module (making the post a useful 'one stop shop' for learning and teaching information). Some tutors fed back that they would rather have a tutor group forum (as it is seen as creating a stronger tutor-student link), even though they had a tutor group specific thread within the clustered forum; it was therefore important to speak to these tutors individually to explain why we decided against using both cluster and tutor groups forums. It was also important to moderate the forum to check that all tutors were contributing as required, as some tutors were unused to this approach and it had yet to become a standard way of working. Finally, it enabled us to gather best practice for dissemination for future presentations of the module.

Module-Wide Forums

Module-wide forums are open to every student studying a module on a particular presentation; in the OU context, this could mean thousands of students on large-scale Year 1 social science modules. They are usually moderated by a member of the module team (in the OU context, the group of academics and other team members who write the module and design the teaching and learning strategy), although sometimes by a tutor (if so, they then feed back to the module team any problems or queries). This kind of forum often runs for the entire presentation of a module, usually focusing on clarifying bits of the module or assessment questions, as well as answering general queries.

If run well, they can be popular spaces for discussion about the module. Indeed, research by Haycock (2008) suggests that many students prefer larger national module forums to smaller tutor group ones (over 50% of 2000 students surveyed). It also enables members of the module team who may not teach students in actual tutorials, but instead write the modules (teaching students 'through the material') which tutors then use in their teaching, to keep abreast of student issues and also to be part of the academic community alongside tutors and students. Module-wide forums can therefore be very dynamic spaces. Informal feedback suggests, though, that this can intimidate students. Not only are they accessible by every student studying the module that presentation, the academics whose names appear in the module materials may moderate them.

Some students may feel uncomfortable with this exposure. Concerns about social presence and embodiment (Bayne 2005) are issues at play here, echoed by Haycock's (2008) research which suggested that a substantial proportion of students expressed concern about how they portrayed themselves online. Module-forums can also have a very big pull, more so even than clustered forums; some tutors feel frustrated by the fact they are trying to build up a community of learning in a clustered forum – community being a core element in the construction of student identities (Johnson 2001 cited Baxter and Haycock 2014) – only to be 'trumped' by the module-forum. Clear boundaries for the module team, tutors, and students are therefore essential. In other words, the structure must be well thought through and communicated to stakeholders.

Second and third year module-wide forums often appear busy (lots of student posts). In our experience, by this stage many students are more comfortable with using forums, working with academics, and their studies more generally. ***Module C**,* for example, has a very busy and informative module-wide forum, moderated by the module team chair. It includes information based threads about assessment and online learning opportunities, as well as being a space for students to post queries about module content, study skills and wider discussion points about the subject more generally. This helps to tie the module team, via the chair, into student concerns, which will in turn be useful for subsequent presentations of the module and any changes that need to be made to enhance the student experience.

There are other types of module-wide forum aside from ones which are open to the whole of the presentation. For example, *Module D* has 'block forums', time-limited forums which open for specific sections or blocks of the module, thus focused on the module content relevant to particular weeks of study. Such forums can be particularly useful for focusing students on the linked assessment, and also seem contained and purposeful to users. This type of forum highlights the need for all forums to have a clear rationale for those moderating and using them: their function must be clear.

Another type of module-wide forum used by many social sciences modules at the OU is a welcome forum. Welcome forums usually open for a few weeks before the official start of the module and close when the module-wide forum opens. The purpose of the forum is to welcome students to the module, in-between their receipt of module materials, but before the module officially starts (and sometimes before a tutor has been assigned to each group of students). Giving students an 'early' space to discuss the module allows their queries about the module and their studies as a whole to be answered, and can therefore be useful for students new to study/on their first module. However, it can be confusing for students when the welcome forum is closed down and they are then directed to other forums to use for the rest of the module, such as the module-wide forum. It is often better, therefore, to combine the functions of the welcome forum into the module-wide forum to avoid this problem. Certainly, in our experience it is good practice not to move students from forum to forum if possible, as the momentum that is built up, alongside the feeling of academic community which students have established, may be undermined. In the same manner, it is good practice to leave forums open for a clearly defined amount of time after the module has finished, so students can continue any useful conversations without feeling abruptly cut off.

Common Forum Functions

If tutor group, clustered and module-wide are ways of *structuring* forums, their actual *function* is a bisecting issue of importance. So, it's not just about how forums are set up, it is important to consider how they are intended to be used by students and tutors, as well as to consider how they are actually used. We inevitably touched upon some forum functions when discussing structure (for example, using a forum as a notice-board, or using a forum to answer new student queries). In this section, we have chosen to focus on two functions in particular: collaborative forums and assessed forums. This is not an indication that we consider these functions to be more important that other functions, merely a reflection of two quite distinct (but at the same time interlinked) forum functions, both of which raise pertinent issues in relation to the bisection of forum function/structure.

Collaborative Forums

All of the forums described so far can also have a collaborative function. That is, students can be asked to collaborate in them, often linked to assessment, but also for group work or to critically assess the contribution of others. In recent years in social sciences this type of forum function has been used more at the OU, partly because of the current UK government focus on the importance of employment skills gained in higher study.

As one example, *Module E* asks students to find material, comment on the material found by others and discuss it collaboratively, before using this material to write an assessment. Students are not judged as a group, but instead on their individual contribution. The key aim of this assessment is to judge students' ability to work together as a team, with the work worth 15% of the related piece of assessment. Students are provided with clear guidance about what good teamwork entails and a clear description of the learning outcomes their tutors will be using to assess their work, in particular: contribution to a collaborative team, contribution to analysis and discussion of the resources, and the extent and quality of contribution. This forum task is can therefore be described as collaborative working in action, where learners make a 'joint effort to construct knowledge and solve problems together' (Vuopala et al. 2016, p. 2). Here collaboration is grounded in the social constructivist approach of learning construction via interaction (Dillenbourg et al. 2009; Vuopala et al. 2016). It can be useful for students to be encouraged to assign roles to each member of their group; this not only gives each student a sense of purpose, it also encourages them to work with and for each other with a shared sense of responsibility.

Scholarship of this collaborative forum (see Smith 2016) has shown that the vast majority of students participate. Indeed, data from the 2013–2014 presentation of this module shows that only 19 out of 514 (3.70% of students) who had access to the forum received a zero for the forum element of the assessment, suggesting they did not do it. However, it is also clear that most students only do the minimum amount needed to pass; the participation data sourced from the module website shows that students are most likely to post a small number of replies to the collaborative forum, with the mode value 4, with most students starting zero threads (28%) or only a few (22% started one thread, 15% two threads, 13% three threads). It is difficult not to ask whether collaborative forums can usefully assess student collaboration, particularly if students are assessed individually. Indeed, students are often assessed individually rather than as a team because of the expectation that many students will not participate at all or will minimally participate, which almost defeats the purpose of the activity in the first place. However, this does not mean that collaborative forums can *never* work – it depends what the module team wants students to achieve. The learning outcomes of the above-described collaborative forum were contribution to a collaborative team, contribution to analysis and discussion of the resources, and the extent and quality of contribution. The data suggests the first two outcomes were (partially) met, but the third less so for many students.

This module has three other collaborative forums before the final assessed one discussed above, the aim of which was to help students practice working with other students in forums before they were actually assessed on it. Interestingly, the first forum is fairly popular in terms of active participation/postings, but this drops for the third in particular (the first forum had 1526 student visits, the second 1435, the third 1186, and the fourth forum, described above, 2593). This points to the fact that having the correct *number* of forums is just as important as the right type of forum. Indeed, it is clear from participation levels on **Module F**, which has a large number of non-assessed collaborative forums which open up at different points in the module, one after the other, that participation in the forums generally drops off across the presentation of the module. The number of collaborative forums on Module F was in fact reduced between two presentations of the module. This is important because there is no point assigning tutor time to these activities if they are not used for the purpose that was intended. Indeed, collaborative forums can entail lots of work on behalf of the tutor and this effort needs to be worthwhile: function needs to meet structure.

Assessed Forums

The assessment of student participation in forums is also a function of some debate. Students can be assessed for completing a forum task on an individual basis; for example, on **Module B** students have to make a post in a forum for their first assignment (worth 5% of the linked assessment) but do not have to respond to other posts. Students can also be assessed for working with others to complete a task in a forum and/or can also be asked to integrate the work completed in the forum into a more formal written assessment (as on **Module E,** discussed above). Whatever students have been asked to do, their participation is a required part of the module in that if they do not do it, they will not gain the allocated marks.

'Compulsory' participation versus 'voluntary' participation in forums has been the subject of scholarship for many years. Indeed, Palmer et al. noted in 2008 that while there is some evidence to suggest that voluntary participation leads to enhanced learning outcomes (Weisskirch and Milburn 2003), the amount of contribution individuals make is likely to be low unless there is an incentive for posting (Graham and Scarborough 2001). More recently Andresen (2009, p. 252) notes that many students need incentive to participate whether in an online or face to face setting: 'Given the importance of the discussion in the learning process at both the theoretical and empirical level, an appropriate measure of participation should be a component of each learner's grade for the course. Though there are always learners who wish to participate in discussions, face-to-face or online, many learners need an incentive to participate in class discussions.'

As Hew and Cheung (2012) realise, one way to induce participation is through the assignment of a mark. There is a question of how many marks should be assigned; it needs to be enough to encourage participation, but not so many that it is inappropriate for the level of student engagement required. Palmer et al. (2008) suggests 10% of the module as a whole, something supported by Smith's (2016) study of *Module E*, where the forum element is worth 15% of the linked piece of assessment (which is in turn worth 10% of the overall module mark).

In terms of assessed forums, it is important to explain the purpose to students, integrate it into the module (in terms of both content and a clear pathway to the forum) and ensure the most appropriate type of forum is used for the task at hand (i.e. tutor group forums may be useful for tasks which require less discussion). It may also be useful to divide students up into smaller groups depending on the task, although not so small that there are too few students to create meaningful discussion. Interestingly, though, research suggests that active participation in forums can be low even if there is a mark assigned. Indeed, as noted above, on *Module E* most students start few threads in the forum and post a low number of replies – they do the bare minimum to pass (Smith 2016). This of course leads one to question whether or not the assessment of forum activity is always a useful way to assess student learning.

What is clear from looking at both assessed and collaborative forums is that many students use forums as INDIVIDUAL/PASSIVE/INFORMATION (for example, as a notice board), rather than SOCIAL/ACTIVE/EXPEREINCE (Conole et al. 's 2004 terms). This suggests that module writers and designers need to accept this and adapt their forum use to suit, or try and encourage more participation by other means, such as awarding a significant amount of marks for participation. Whatever decision is made, the structure of the forum and its function(s) are key; well-designed module content is essential with forums integrated into teaching and learning strategy and aims in a clear, coherent and purposeful manner. The key questions are: which student learning outcomes might be met by which type of forum? What is an appropriate teaching and learning strategy to achieve them? Do students need an incentive to participate and if so what's appropriate in the context of the learning outcomes and the module as a whole? Unless these (function-focussed) questions are answered in the design stages of the module, it is possible that the teaching and learning strategy will be inadequate.

Conclusions

Our online practices will always tend to be influenced by the spaces available to exercise our pedagogical expertise – as well as, of course, our students' engagement with us in these spaces. Our aim here is to encourage working creatively and imaginatively within such constraints, using the decisions and spaces that we have available to us. Weller (2011) suggests it is not technology itself that necessarily makes students behave a certain way. Indeed, we believe what's important is not necessarily the technology behind forums, but rather their structure and function. Weller (2011, p. 67) goes on to note that 'successful use of … technologies often requires the adoption of certain approaches or cultural norms'. So, educators need to be aware of these norms (pre-existing ones or those that develop) and work with them (Baxter and Haycock 2014).

One starting point for those designing and teaching modules, is to better understand what it is they want to get out of forums. Forums are by no means a panacea, particularly in distance provision. Nonetheless, they have a range of potentially useful functions and benefits to students. It is clear that forums can work well, if structure and function is aligned, as suggested in our discussion about the module-wide forums used by Modules C and D. It is also clear they may not work as well as intended or meet the intended aims, if structure and function is not aligned, as suggested (in part) by Module E. We make some suggestions below about the kinds of issues that must be considered by those designing forums as well as by those teaching them; by doing so, it is more likely that structure and function will bisect successfully. Sharpe and Benfield (2005) write, 'it is not enough to hope for a match between students' understanding of how they learn, their conceptions of teaching process, and the teachers' intentions. It is clear that we need to be more explicit in our explanations to students of the purposes of online work and our expectations for the activities they will undertake. This might need to be quite explicit.' So, alongside considerations of structure and function, student expectations are important is as their understanding of learning aims and outcomes (Anderson et al. 2001).

There are, though, wider questions about the general utility of forums. As this chapter suggests we have spent a significant amount of time assessing what works and does not in relation to specific module contexts. And yet, despite these efforts we have still not identified the exact best design for function and structure. We are not suggesting that this means forums should necessarily be written out of a teaching and learning strategy or replaced with commercial social media (although that *could* be a solution for a module, if it is proving difficult to align structure and function). What is essential is that each module, in its own particular context (learning outcomes, assessment strategy, student workload, tutor workload) considers what is/is not being achieved and to modify their strategy accordingly.

Tips and Discussion Points

- Structure and function bisect and must complement each other. So, make sure each forum has a clearly defined function (utilising a consistent naming strategy, cross-module), well-integrated into the module in terms of both design/pathway and learning aims and outcomes
- The function of each forum should be clearly explained in the module materials and by tutors as appropriate; it can also be useful to have an 'information' thread in each forum, detailing the purpose of the forum, who is moderating it, and guidance on appropriate conduct
- Tutors also need to understand the function of the forums they are moderating and what their role is; information briefings are essential
- Consider the number of forums which students can access across the presentation; if there are too many, student participation may drop off. Again, structure and function is key
- Consider the different types of forum students can access and what is appropriate; it may be essential that students access both tutor group, clustered, and module-wide forums because of the assessment aims, or it may be an unnecessary over-proliferation and lead to some of the forums being under-utilised

- Think carefully about when to open forums; it can be useful to open a forum before the module has officially started, helping students to settle into the module
- Try to avoid shutting down one forum and moving students on to another, as it can ruin any momentum that has built up
- Do not shut forums down abruptly at the end of the final piece of assessment; make it clear to students when the forums will finally shut, giving them space to finish conversations
- Allow students to utilise forums for social conversation if appropriate (it may not be on some forums, such as assessed ones), although bear in mind students may use social media for this rather than a formal tutor-moderated forum
- Keep in mind that evidence suggests many students need an incentive to use forums. One way to incentivise students is to make a forum appear worth their while, with clear connection to learning outcomes. Another way is to assign grades for participation and/or for completion of an activity – although the amount of marks available has to be significant, rather than small
- Moderation is important, whether by tutors or by those who wrote the material; the latter can help to link authors to students, encourage a dynamic academic community, and be helpful when changes to the module are being considered
- Do not assume that only 'active' students are learning; 'passive' students may learn vicariously through others. While the latter should be encouraged to join in (and it is important that they do if the forum is collaborative and/or assessed), and module materials should direct them to do so, it should be understood that students approach forums differently.

Note

1. We refer to 'blended' learning environments in terms of its more popular usage, i.e. the combination of traditional face-to-face learning activities with online (Oliver and Trigwell 2005), but equally acknowledge ongoing debate around the utility of the term 'blended learning' (e.g. Irvine et al. 2013).

References

Anderson, T., Rourke, L., Garrison, R., & Archer, W. (2001). Assessing teaching presence in a computer conferencing context. *Journal of Asynchronous Learning Networks, 5*(2), 1–17.

Andresen, M. A. (2009). Asynchronous discussion forums: Success factors, outcomes, assessments, and limitations. *Educational Technology and Society, 12*(1), 249–257.

Balaji, M. S., & Chakrabarti, D. (2010). Student interactions in online discussion forum: Empirical research from "media richness theory" perspective. *Journal of Interactive Online Learning, 9*(1), 1–22.

Baxter, J., & Haycock, J. (2014). Roles and student identities in online large course forums: Implications for practice. *International Review of Research in Open and Distance Learning, 15*(1), 20–40.

Bayne, S. (2005). Deceit, desire and control: The identities of learners and teachers in cyberspace. In R. Land & S. Bayne (Eds.), *Education in cyberspace* (pp. 21–41). Abingdon: RoutledgeFalmer.

Bederson, B. B., Russell, D. M., & Klemmer, S. (2015). Introduction to online learning at scale. *ACM Transactions on Computer-Human Interaction (TOCHI), 22*(2), 5.

Burston, M. A. (2016). I work and don't have time for that theory stuff: Time poverty and higher education. *Journal of Further and Higher Education* (online first). https://doi.org/10.1080/0309877X.2015.1135885

Choi, I., Land, S. M., & Turgeon, A. J. (2005). Scaffolding peer-questioning strategies to facilitate metacognition during online small group discussion. *Instructional Science, 33*, 483–511.

Conole, G., Dyke, M., Oliver, M., & Seale, J. (2004). Mapping pedagogy and tools for effective learning design. *Computers and Education, 43*(1–2), 17–33.

De George-Walker, L., & Keeffe, M. (2010). Self-determined blended learning: A case study of blended learning design. *Higher Education Research and Development, 29*(1), 1–13. https://doi.org/10.1080/07294360903277380.

Dennen, V. (2008). Pedagogical lurking: Student engagement in non-posting discussion behaviour. *Computers in Human Behaviour, 24*(4), 1624–1633.

Dillenbourg, P., Järvelä, S., & Fischer, F. (2009). The evolution of research on computer supported collaborative learning: From design to orchestration. In N. Balacheff, S. Ludvigsen, T. de Jong, A. de Lazonder, & S. Barnes (Eds.), *Technology-enhanced learning: Principles and products* (pp. 3–19). New York: Springer.

Graham, M., & Scarborough, H. (2001). Enhancing the learning environment for distance education students. *Distance Education, 22*(2), 232–244.

Groves, M., & O'Donoghue, J. (2009). Reflections of students in their use of asynchronous online seminars. *Educational Technology and Society, 12*(3), 143–149.

Haycock, J. (2008). *Making first class impressions.* Paper presented at the 3rd open CETL conference: Building bridges, The Open University, Milton Keynes.

Hew, K. F., & Cheung, W. S. (2012). *Student participation in online discussions: Challenges, solutions and future research.* New York: Springer Science+Business Media.

Hrastinski, S. (2008). Asynchronous and synchronous e-learning: A study of asynchronous and synchronous e-learning methods discovered that each supports different purposes. *EDUCAUSE Quarterly, 31*(4), 51–55.

Hülsmann, T. (2009). Access and efficiency in the development of distance education and E-learning. In U. Bernath, A. Szücs, A. Tait, & M. Vidal (Eds.), *Distance and E-learning in transition* (pp. 119–140). Hoboken: Wiley.

Irvine, V., Code, J., & Richards, L. (2013). Realigning higher education for the 21st century learner through multi-access learning. *Journal of Online Learning and Teaching, 9*(2), 172.

Kember, D., McNaught, C., Chong, F., & Cheng, K. (2010). Understanding the ways in which design features of educational websites impact upon student learning outcomes in blended learning environments. *Computers and Education, 55*(3), 1183–1192.

Kim, D., Park, Y., Yoon, M., & Jo, I. H. (2016). Toward evidence-based learning analytics: Using proxy variables to improve asynchronous online discussion environments. *The Internet and Higher Education, 30*, 30–43.

Kop, R. (2011). The challenges to connectivist learning on open online networks: Learning experiences during a massive open online course. *The International Review of Research in Open and Distributed Learning, 12*(3), 19–38.

Liu, X., Magjuka, R. J., Bonk, C. J., & Lee, S. H. (2007). Does sense of community matter. *Quarterly Review of Distance Education, 8*(1), 9–24.

Oliver, M., & Trigwell, K. (2005). Can 'blended learning' be redeemed? *E-learning, 2*(1), 17–26.

Palmer, S., Holt, D., & Bray, S. (2008). Does the discussion help? The impact of a formally assessed online discussion of final student results. *British Journal of Educational Technology, 39*(5), 847–858.

Sharpe, R., & Benfield, G. (2005). The student experience of E-learning in higher education: A review of the literature. *Brookes eJournal of Learning and Teaching, 1*(3), 1–22.

Siemens, G. (2005). Connectivism: A learning theory for the digital age. *International Journal of Instructional Technology and Distance Learning, 2*(1). http://www.itdl.org/Journal/Jan_05/article01.htm.

Smith, D. (2016). *Looking behind the headlines: Participation in assessed collaborative forums and implications for assessment.* International conference of education, research and innovation, Seville, 2016.

Smith, D., & Smith, K. (2014). The case for 'Passive' learning – The 'silent' community of online learners. *European Journal of Open, Distance and E-Learning, 17*(2), 85–98.

Smith, D., & Smith, K. (2015). *Understanding passive learning in online distance education.* International Conference of Education, Research and Innovation, Seville, 2015.

Vuopala, E. M., Hyvönen, P., & Järvelä, S. (2016). Interaction forms in successful collaborative learning in virtual learning environments. *Active Learning in Higher Education.* Epub ahead of print 30 November 2015. https://doi.org/10.1177/1469787415616730.

Wallace, P. (2016). *The psychology of the internet.* Cambridge: Cambridge University Press.

Weisskirch, R. S., & Milburn, S. S. (2003). Virtual discussion: Understanding college students' electronic bulletin board use. *The Internet and Higher Education, 6*(3), 215–225.

Weller, M. (2011). *The digital scholar: How technology is transforming academic practice,* Bloomsbury Open Access. https://www.bloomsburycollections.com/book/the-digital-scholar-how-technology-is-transforming-scholarly-practice/

Zhou, M., & Chua, B. L. (2016). Using blended learning design to enhance learning experience in teacher education. *International Journal on E-Learning, 15*(1), 121–140. Chesapeake, VA: Association for the Advancement of Computing in Education (AACE).

4

Making Online Teams Work

Helen Kaye and Jane Barrett

Collaboration and Employability

Team working in the twenty-first century is an essential employability skill, enabling students to compete for jobs (Reddy et al. 2013) and therefore one that graduates should acquire as part of their education. However, admission to a degree is traditionally considered by university students and staff to reflect skills and knowledge of an academic nature. The distinction between academic subject knowledge and employability creates tension between what students and employers deem to be important products of a first degree.

The psychology degree provides an interesting testing ground for considering these tensions because of the subject matter of psychology itself. A core aspect of psychology concerns the complexity of social groups and group processes, especially when applied to learning. As part of their scholarship, psychology students gain an insight into these structures and

H. Kaye (✉) • J. Barrett
School of Psychology, Faculty of Arts and Social Sciences,
Open University, Milton Keynes, UK
e-mail: Helen.Kaye@open.ac.uk

© The Author(s) 2018
J. Baxter et al. (eds.), *Creativity and Critique in Online Learning*,
https://doi.org/10.1007/978-3-319-78298-0_4

processes. Applying such insight should facilitate self-reflective and insightful engagement with team work and collaboration. Furthermore, the complexity of social processes mean that we cannot naively assume that simply putting several students into the same online space will create a team. Rather we must learn how to provide effective environments to facilitate group formation and teamwork.

Psychology and Collaboration

Collaboration and team work are recognised by the QAA (2016) as important skills for employability. Psychology graduates ought to "recognise what is required for effective teamwork and articulate their own strengths and weaknesses in this regard." (p. 10) Similarly the British Psychology Society (BPS 2015) expects Psychology graduates to "be sensitive to, and take account of, contextual and interpersonal factors in groups and teams" (p. 17). Psychology programmes can address this expectation by integrating team working into the curriculum. For example, the project work that is an integral part of a psychology degree provides opportunities for group work in the design and execution of experimental procedures, as well as discussion of ethical issues in research proposals. Dissemination of findings too provides opportunities for engaging with peer review. (Reddy et al. 2013).

This chapter focusses on online learning, particularly student experiences of online team work. Collaboration presents challenges, and the long history of psychological studies into group processes attests to this, identifying problems with reaching consensus, polarization, social loafing, etc. – see Brown (2000). Online collaboration brings with it additional and exacerbated challenges – as well as benefits. This chapter considers online collaboration and team work from the viewpoints of students and their tutors as well as exploring the tutor role in helping students apply their academic psychological learning to their own learning processes.

A series of empirical studies is presented exploring how psychology students experience online collaboration, including a demonstration of how they engage in team work via a simulated forum. These studies were conducted at the Open University (OU), where very large numbers (thousands) study, usually part-time, for their Psychology degree. The teaching materials and activities are produced by a small team of full-time academic staff and individual students are supported by tutors who are qualified psychologists mostly working for the OU on a part time basis.

Learning to Collaborate

Advances in technology have led to increased use of electronic media in education and forums may be seen as online equivalents of face-to-face teaching (Andresen 2009). In the OU, the practical psychology work that occurred in residential, "summer schools" frequently now takes place in an online environment relying on forums. However, there are substantial differences in pedagogy and affordances between the media. Interactivity differs in an online asynchronous forum, because of the delay between posting a message and receiving a response. Communication differs too, in face-to-face, synchronous interactions, non-verbal communication can supplement impoverished speech (Roschelle 1992), but that is unavailable to participants in an online forum. Forum discussions may thus be fragmented, incoherent, disrupted or inconclusive (Calvani et al. 2010).

Conversely other researchers have explored learning in forums and argued that features of the online environment can facilitate active learning including the creation of knowledge through collaboration (Hiltz and Meinke 1989). The goal here is to build a learning community and social network: 'a social group with an identity and a shared purpose and social ties' (Hiltz et al. 2007, p. 59). The focus is on collaboration and team work; with activities designed to share and build knowledge about a subject area. Hilltz and colleagues argue that as forums allow engagement "anytime, anywhere" students can take control of their learning, allowing themselves time to develop and present their responses and ideas. An online environment also allows for anonymity and the potential for role-playing thus increasing students' freedom to engage in learning activities in a variety of contexts, (Andrews and Haythornthwaite 2007; Hiltz et al. 2007).

Intuitively it seems that learning in a group, whether virtual or actual, should be beneficial in enabling students to learn more about subject content by pooling their ideas. The next section considers some of the challenges that students encounter when working together online to produce a joint output.

Perceived Benefits and Challenges to Working Together

Students must engage with asynchronous learning environments in order to benefit from the opportunities offered by them. Understanding students' experiences of working in a group is key for teachers to address the preferences, perceived needs and motivation of learners. Box 4.1 presents a case study which compares student experience in these different media.

Several factors may have contributed to the poor group dynamics revealed by our survey:

First, inexperience with technology, evidenced by the low level of forum usage prior to the module start may have made students reticent to participate wholeheartedly. Swan (2002) refers to the "critical importance of active … discussion to students' perception of satisfaction and learning in online courses" (p. 35). In a study of collaborative learning, Fung (2004) reported low participation rates amongst students inexperienced with on-line learning.

Secondly, students may have found working with strangers challenging. Our (unpublished) observations of project work in another module suggest that the lack of choice for students in being assigned to groups of 4 or 5 where they generally don't know each other may contribute to their negative attitudes. This other module was the final year (OU Level 3) cognitive psychology module which required students to attend residential school. Students whose circumstances prevented their attendance were offered an online alternative, and could choose to pair with another student or to work singly. Those who opted to work in a pair could choose their partner. Over 97% of students who chose to pair-up reported that the arrangement was successful. It is unclear whether group size, the opportunity to choose one's partner, or the academic experience of the students contributed to the difference in satisfaction ratings. Another factor, "Social loafing" may have contributed to dissatisfaction with group work. It is well documented that in a group situation individuals may work less hard than when they are alone (Karau and Williams 1993). There is also evidence that this may be accentuated when group members are not physically co-located (Chidambaram and Tung 2005). The perception that other group members are not contributing sufficiently, or

Box 4.1   Summer School or Forums?

Psychology students at The OU who were studying for a BPS accredited degree up until 2016 could choose to complete their second year (OU Level 2) project module at residential school or by participating in an on-line equivalent. The content and outputs of these modules were identical, both required students to work in small groups to design and carry out an empirical study. The presentation however was different: the on-line equivalent relied exclusively on asynchronous learning networks, mainly forums, whereas by its nature residential school involved synchronous face–to-face communication. Additionally, there were differences in terms of time of year the two types of module were offered as well as in their duration and study intensity. At the end of both modules students submitted an assessment, this was an individual piece of work analysing and reporting the group project. Students achieved similar grades in these two modules when previous academic achievement was taken into account. However, our survey revealed that student satisfaction differed between the modules.

This case study, conducted in 2012, involved administering an online questionnaire to psychology undergraduates who had attended residential school or its online equivalent. A representative sample of 267 students completed the survey (136 residential school; 121 online learners).

The survey identified different factors governing student choice, many unrelated to preferences for the medium itself: for residential school, social aspects were important, students wanted to meet other students and immerse themselves in completing their project during an intensive period of studying psychology. Those choosing the online module were more concerned that the work fitted into their lives. Important factors included the perceived cost of residential school, and unavoidable home or work commitments. After completing their module, students were asked to identify the best and worst aspect of the experience. For students who chose the online module, flexibility and working from home were the best aspects; whereas for residential school participants social interaction was paramount. Although both groups also cited working in groups as a positive experience, a worrying finding was the frequent citation of group dynamics as the worst aspect of the on-line version. Their comments referred to poor communication among group members and accusations of laziness.

"freeloading" was a major source of dissatisfaction in our case study indicated by comments such as "(it was) difficult working with lazy people".

The link between lack of effective communication and perceived slacking accords with Piezon and Donaldson's (2005) review of online social loafing. They stress the importance of communication among group members in tackling loafing and recommend that roles within groups are clearly defined. Kear (2010) notes the importance of social chat in facilitating peer support within online groups and thus reducing loafing. Goodwin et al. (2001) found that assessing group work reduced social loafing, but some students still chose not to participate in online discussion, even though they forfeited 10% of the marks awarded for group work. Clearly disinterest in participation affects the group as well as individual achievement and must be tackled.

Sociability and Non-Participation

Many investigations into online group behaviour report that group members who do not actively contribute may nevertheless read messages posted by their colleagues. Oliver and Shaw (2003) characterise students as strategic learners – adept at deciding what helps them in their studies, and optimising (or at least minimising) their study time. Those students who read but don't post, so called "lurkers", perhaps consider that there is insufficient benefit in posting to justify the effort. If participation is rewarded, for example if it is assessed then students may "play the game" and make appropriate postings, though as Goodwin et al. (2001) demonstrated this not always so. Preece et al. (2004) surveyed a broad spectrum of 375 interest groups (representing 77,582 individuals), drawn from MSN's-online communities service to investigate why people post or lurk. Lurkers, by their very nature, are a difficult population to sample, and their response rate, although representing 18.4% of valid survey returns, was very low (2.3%). The sample's demographics were comparable with a general sample of internet users, suggesting that their participants were a representative sample of that population. In other words the lurkers had no obvious distinguishing characteristics. When asked about their lack of participation most felt that they 'didn't need to post', because they got what they needed from browsing the contributions of others, this matches Oliver and Shaw's findings. Almost 30% needed to find out more about the community before posting a message. The response 'didn't like the group' also occurred frequently, as did 'shy about posting'. Thus, a substantial number of lurkers indicated that affective sociability factors were important in their decisions about participation. Preece and colleagues suggested that improving software usability and sociability factors might encourage lurkers to participate. These factors resonate with those we identified in our study of student dissatisfaction with online project work.

Bishop (2007) suggested that lurkers could become integrated into a social network by changing their beliefs so that they want to act on, as well as read, postings. This could be accomplished by introducing dissonance by for instance, posting a message to challenge beliefs about not needing to post a message. This begs the question of who should be introducing dissonance and challenging beliefs. An obvious candidate for doing so is the tutor.

The Tutor's Role in Facilitating Collaboration

Many of the theoretical underpinnings of research into collaborative learning have evolved from constructivist and social constructivist developmental perspectives. Roschelle defined collaborative learning as: "a coordinated, synchronous activity that is the result of a continued attempt to construct and maintain a shared conception of a problem" (Roschelle and Teasley 1995; cited in (Dillenbourg 1999, p. 12)). For Roschelle (1992) learning is a convergence process that parallels how scientists develop concepts: an "attractive possibility that students develop their concepts in the course of learning to participate in … practices of enquiry" (p. 272). Roschelle argued further that conversational interaction between peers creates a situation whereby they can negotiate and co-construct shared meaning about concepts and experiences achieving deeper understanding by the process of convergent conceptual change. As the children in his study collaborated on a mutual task, developing shared knowledge and common history, their talk became ambiguous and elliptical; and their discourse was 'fundamentally situated' in the sequencing of utterances and in the learning situation itself (p. 269). This approach positions the investigation of collaborative learning within the socio-cultural approach, where it is viewed as a social activity mediated by tools and artefacts. Hence, what is required is an environment where a tutor facilitates meaning making and knowledge construction within student groups rather than transmitting knowledge to students, the 'guide on the side', rather than the didactic 'sage on the stage' (King 1993); learners are "explorers" who work together to solve problems. This view emphasises the importance of understanding the learning process itself as well as its outcomes.

An action research study which explored online teaching of critical thinking skills illustrates how a tutor may influence the group dynamics within an online forum. This study was conducted by Jane Barrett (unpublished, 2007–2008) under the auspices of the OU CETL (Centre for Excellence in Teaching and Learning).

Box 4.2   Does a Forum Need a Leader?

Psychology students were invited to take part in a two-week voluntary enrichment activity. In it the principles of constructivist learning were put into practice. 32 students signed up for the forum; 23 read the first task message and downloaded it; 18 students posted more than one message. Students could work independently with the materials provided but, to increase understanding of critical thinking skills; they were encouraged to interact in an online, asynchronous forum. Most students found this approach helpful and appreciated the generally supportive environment, though some experienced problems in understanding its underlying constructivist pedagogy. The tutor (JB) could track students' activity on the forum; allowing discussions and task downloads to be monitored. An issue arose concerning what constitutes an authoritative source and as Barrett noted in her reflexive notes at the time: 'Most threads are one-off messages, but a few are taking off' and later 'It's strange how discussions seem to peter out. Do students lose interest? Are they just trying to impress?' (JB, 15/1/2008). During a post-forum evaluative interview, one interviewee commented 'I don't want to read blogs because actually I don't care what people who don't know anything about it think about it'. The lack of spontaneous discussion may have reflected similar attitudes. The tutor was visible throughout, encouraging critical thinking about issues arising from the activity. The effect of tutor presence undoubtedly influences group dynamics: It may facilitate deeper thinking by encouraging many-to-many interactions; however students may interact only with the tutor thus reducing discussions and devaluing collective peer knowledge.

JB's reflections indicated dilemmas about gauging the frequency and level of intervention by the tutor in the forum to encourage collaboration amongst peers rather than information gathering by independent activity. Initially, JB made few postings, giving students time to post their ideas, later JB provided hints for debates and issues for consideration.

Issues about authority and student engagement become especially relevant where students must work together collaboratively to produce a joint output, and when marks are awarded for those outputs. Tutors in the forums are well placed to observe group dynamics and to make decisions about when and whether to intervene. The next section considers group dynamics from the tutor's perspective.

Collaborative Learning and the Tutor

The research literature highlights a tension between recognising the reluctance of students to participate (and collaborate) and the extent to which tutors should be involved. In a survey of medical students, tutor enthusiasm was the only tutor related factor rated by students as being particularly important in encouraging contributions (Oliver and Shaw 2003). Tutor presence may be beneficial in developing a sense of community, but judging the optimal participation level is important in order to avoid inhibiting collaboration between students (An et al. 2009).

Collaborative learning involves the social construction of knowlege within a community and implies an active role for students in supporting one another in a symmetrical relationship where no-one is a recognised authority. This process can be distinguished from the knowledge transmission model illustrated in Fig. 4.1a. According to Roschelle (1992), their interactions with one another and the inevitable intellectual conflicts lead to convergence and, ultimately, develop deeper understanding of concepts. Dysthe (2002) investigated the interactions and learning potential of an asynchronous forum analysing the postings of a group of 10 postgraduate philosophy students. The tutor withdrew from the discussion after setting students an 'authentic' assignment which was open-ended with no right or wrong answer. Tutor presence was thereafter represented by teaching resources and students were instructed to post their ideas on the forum. Dysthe analysed turn-taking on the premise that postings can be directed towards one or many (monologic or dialogic) and can be part of an intersubjective construction of meaning. The patterns of student interaction were analysed as a 'communicogram' (see Student A in Fig. 4.1b), providing evidence of this collaborative process.

Qualitative content analysis of the postings revealed that students were engaged in meaning-making involving reciprocity and engagement with the thoughts and ideas of others, which contrasts with the relative simplicity of the transmission model (Fig. 4.1a). Dysthe (p. 345) claimed that the collaborative process is a product of different factors: providing an authentic assignment, symmetrical (rather than asymmetrical)

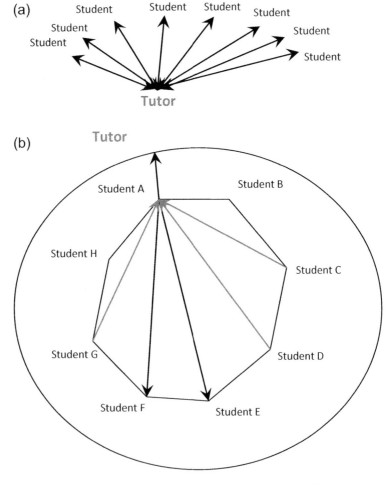

Fig. 4.1 Two models of learning, (a) a transmission model and (b) a "communico-gram" based on Dysthe (2002) representing collaborative learning

interactions between peers, and the tutor role which fosters the symmetrical relationship between peers.

Defining an "effective interaction" is important (Calvani et al. 2010).
A high participation rate may indicate a lively collaborative group, but
could be focused on banal, superficial and individual contributions.
Dysthe studied the collaborative activity of the students, in terms of their
interaction dynamics and the content of their postings. Had she focused
on participation rate, which was low, there might be less optimism about
the learning potential of collaboration. Generalization to an undergraduate population is problematic because this small-scale study was focused
on post-graduate students, who may well have gained skills in collaborative working already. Whether peer-to-peer collaboration would be successful with undergraduates is an empirical question yet to be addressed.

Murphy (2004) devised a coding frame to analyse collaborative interactions on online forums, based on a conceptual model which charted
progressive stages from interaction to collaboration. In this model "interaction" involves sharing individual information and develops through
stages of reflecting on one's own, then others', perspectives and finally to
developing shared goals and constructing an artefact together, this can be
termed true "collaboration". Murphy analysed messages posted to an
online forum used by trainee teachers during an undergraduate methods
course and found that most of the postings were at the 'interaction' stage.
She suggested that working together and being tasked with producing a
shared artefact might promote shared goals, discourage students from
concentrating on individual contributions and encourage progression
from 'interaction' to 'collaboration'.

Tutors' Perceptions 'Best and Worst Groups'

A further exploration of OU Psychology students' dissatisfaction with
group working examined the group dynamics of these student teams
through the lens of their tutors (Kaye et al. 2013; see Box 4.3).

Two main issues emerge from this study. First, effective teams require
more than simply grouping students and giving them a task– some students cope with this, but others do not. Understanding the reasons for

> **Box 4.3   Team Working: The Tutors' View**
>
> A questionnaire was sent to all tutors employed on the online project module presented in 2013 (52 tutors, 25 responded), immediately after the module ended. Tutors were asked to ponder how well the 5 or 6 groups they had taught on the module had worked and to identify their "best group and worst group". With those two groups in mind they answered a number of questions including: "What made your chosen group 'the best' ['the worst']"?
>
> Whilst their 'best' groups had diverse characterisations, tutors provided a more coherent picture of their 'worst' groups, with non-contributors being a major cause of tension. Tutors perceived differences between the 'best' and 'worst' groups in terms of how they managed their projects, their group dynamics and their successful completion of the project. Whereas 'best' groups were more likely to be democratic in the way they allocated tasks, the 'worst' groups were more likely to have leaders. This leadership was characterised as being an uneasy alliance with one person making a decision and doing most of the work, while other members of the group (for whatever reason), lagged behind or made little contribution to the forum. There were differences in the group dynamics, with those in the 'best' groups exhibiting mutual regard for one another; whereas those in the 'worst' groups were likely to be dependent on their tutors, needing regular forum intervention for facilitation, decision-making, and resolution of disputes. Finally, the 'best' groups were perceived as being more likely to succeed than the 'worst' groups in producing the group output, though of course the outcome may have affected the tutors' classifications of the groups.

these differences between teams remains a challenge. Secondly, this study supported earlier findings (e.g. Goodwin et al. 2001) that some students do not engage with a collaborative task, even when there are tangible benefits in doing so. The next section explores an attempt to facilitate engagement.

An Online Team Building Exercise

Mercer (1995) used the term interthinking to describe the way that the cognitive and social aspects of talking together can enhance creativity in face-to-face groups of young children. Littleton and Mercer (2013) argue that interthinking can occur in online groups of students too where the "talk" is via a computer keyboard. However groups and teams face challenges particularly in asynchronous settings where the exchange of information, clarifications and conflict resolution can be laborious and time-consuming. Additional challenges include discussions taking unexpected turns that can mean students waste time and energy pursuing an idea only to find that it has become irrelevant when they next access the forum. Littleton and Mercer argue that the groups who establish ground rules for the conduct of members working together are less likely to be adversely affected by these challenges. They suggest that ground rules help generate a discursive environment that facilitates the development of interthinking and hence collaboration.

In an attempt to facilitate the development of collaborative skills, we carried out a small-scale study in which psychology undergraduates worked in 3 small teams on tasks in an asynchronous online learning environment. A set of teaching materials was provided on a bespoke website which enabled students to familiarise themselves with the materials prior to the forum opening. The students were allocated to forums where the tutor provided minimal input.

The key task was for each team to produce a jointly negotiated set of ground rules related to working together in small teams, based on their experiences in three tasks: designing a business card, advertising their team; solving some puzzles; designing a multi-cultural dinner party... They were asked to confine their discussions to the online forums so that all students could participate at their own convenience and also so that all conversations were documented.

Students were given more tasks than they could complete independently, to encourage them to work together and a variety of tasks to provide an opportunity to allocate roles within the team according to individual capabilities.

To illustrate an example of interthinking and collaboration in one of these online groups, Box 4.4 presents the postings of 3 students (designated Blue, Orange and Green) who were working together on a set of "ditloid" puzzles.

In this interaction Student Blue contributed to only two of the tasks, mainly by indicating agreement with suggestions made by the other two (Orange and Green). However, she did start the thread on this puzzle

> **Box 4.4   Solving a Word Puzzle**
>
> Blue – 19:48
> Hi, Not very good at this one, but so far:
> 1. 8 = T on an O - 8 toes on an orangutan?
> 2. 8 = P in the SS -?
> Orange – 21:02
> [...] Not sure about the orangutan's toes but I'll take your word for it.
> Green – 21:13
> I've had that somewhere else before on like a puzzle thing and was 8
> tentacles on an octopus – but that doesn't mean that is right for this one lol
> Orange – 21:28
> Ooh yes that would work. What do you think [...]?
> Blue – next day, 18:30
> Great work! Let's go with 8 tentacles on an octopus, it's much better than
> 8 toes on an orangutan!

posting the answers to the 5 sets of clues. Orange responds, completing the puzzles that Blue couldn't get and expressing some disbelief about the 8 T on an O. Green posts her suggestion, saying she's seen this before, but adding 'but that doesn't mean that is right for this one'. This appears to be a very non-threatening way of putting forward her idea. Orange posts agreement, but asks blue 'what do you think?' Thus, including blue in the decision making. Blue replies in agreement – but not until the next day.

The interaction seems to be an example of interthinking where the team solved the puzzle, and members showed mutual regard for each other; both characteristics of best groups identified by Kaye et al. (2013). The team later discussed the ground rules for working together. Orange posted initially on ground rules and Green agreed contributing a further rule, and adding that because of family issues, she could not contribute as much as she wanted to in this task. Blue read the posts but did not take part in this discussion or any other subsequent to the ditloid puzzle task.

Although, this appears to be a good example of effective team working, it also highlights the kind of subtle dilemma that a tutor encounters: why didn't Blue continue to contribute to the discussions? Was she feeling humiliated by what she might have seen as a gaffe, even though her other answers were right? Or did she feel that the others knew more than she did? Or perhaps, as many students claim, external factors such as work pressures were responsible for the lack of contribution. This group showed little evidence of working as a team, except in this instance, subsequently failing to complete all the tasks. Another group in this study demonstrated that in the absence of an authoritative tutor, a student can fill the gap becoming 'a driving force' directing the activities of the others. It was also noticeable that students worked separately on the tasks, cooperatively rather than collaboratively.

Six participants provided feedback about the task. A selection of their comments is presented in Box 4.5.

Their feedback indicated that these students recognized the importance of setting ground rules for the community, to optimize discussion and collaborative learning. The comments convey a sense that, in these tasks, online synchronicity, which is not easily achieved in an online forum, was seen as necessary for the group to function efficiently and equitably.

Box 4.5   Students' Responses to the Question "What Did You Learn from the (Collaborative) Activity?"

"I learnt that for the online project to be successful all the members please the group need to work together and share with others anything that they think may contribute to the discussion. I also learnt that sharing the tasks based on the individuals' strengths would make working on the tasks more efficient."

"When the task is time-limited it is tempting to have a go yourself before discussing who will be responsible for each task – especially when everyone is not online all of the time (and members of your group drop out). This may, however alienate some people. Also that it can be hard to get your meaning across in text, you have to be very careful about the language and tone that you use."

"I learnt that setting ground rules first is a good idea as you can set a time for everyone to log on. Also it is a good idea to pick a leader who will collate all ideas together instead of 4 people trying to do it. Also I learnt that not everyone will pull their weight and some people end up doing more work than others."

"Not all people work in the same way."

"That it can be difficult if a task has a short time limit as knowing when people would be online and who would participate etc."

"I learned that it can be quite difficult working in a group online if not all members are able to participate regularly and put in the same effort and leaving the bulk of the work to one or two members of the group."

This simulated forum illustrated that a group of volunteer students could complete tasks with minimal tutor input, cooperating on a task by adding to one another's postings. Student feedback indicated that they understood the differences between synchronous and asynchronous communication and had learned some techniques for effective teamwork including understanding how to allocate roles based on capabilities and capacities of others; and the importance of establishing ground rules for interactions. Collaboration, where they produce something better than they would alone with 'deeper' learning is desirable, but difficult to achieve in online forums. Vuopala et al. (2016) analysed instances of successful collaborative learning in groups where both synchronous and asynchronous online environments were available. They found the asynchronous tools were used mostly for "task related interactions" – students posted knowledge rich theoretical material and devised plans for tackling the tasks that were set. In contrast more postings overall were made in the synchronous condition and these were "group related interactions" concerning social and informal matters such as sharing personal information. The authors concluded that successful collaboration requires both types of exchanges and they are supported by different learning environments.

This chapter began by noting that there is an expectation that psychology graduates will have a practical appreciation of collaborative work, so we must provide an environment that ensures that everyone can achieve this. Observing group work in an online forum demonstrates that we need to motivate students and equip tutors with the skills to facilitate collaborative learning.

The Tutor's Role

The team building exercise employed a tutor to oversee the forum rather than to teach. Her role was limited to answering questions and encouraging students to complete the tasks – 'monitoring and regulating interactions' which can be a way ' to increase the probability that some types of interaction occur' Dillenburg (1999, p. 6).The website resources substituted for the teacher's role allowing us to gauge students' behaviour when only instructions and resources were available.

The tutor's comments illustrate the sensitive judgements and skills necessary to accommodate the requirements of the group and the constraints of the task. She said of Group B "it appeared that no one was prepared to take responsibility for the group's performance. I felt they lacked the necessary team working skills to achieve anything beyond their individual competences". "If I were supporting the groups through a module I would certainly have intervened fairly quickly with group B to prevent them from getting behind [...]". The tutor survey demonstrated that tutors can reflect on and question the underlying factors in student behaviour. The comments also suggest that leadership was required, questioning Dysthe's model of collaborative learning (Fig. 4.1b).

Collaboration and using information technology to achieve it have been identified by Binkley et al. (2012) as "twenty-first-century skills" necessary for success in contemporary society. Similarly Hakkinen and colleagues (2017) argue that understanding how to collaborate and how to facilitate collaboration are new skills to most students, and must be learned. In the context of teacher training, they propose that student teachers should engage with different teaching methods and tools; using a social constructionist model where knowledge resides amongst a community of learners, rather than a one-to-many transmission model of knowledge by teachers to students. They suggest focussing on 'inquiry based pedagogical designs' (p. 26) to facilitate collaborative skill development. In the context of undergraduate education a similar argument can be made that university teaching staff should be trained in how to facilitate collaboration.

The Open University provides tutors with staff development in online teaching and learning. Although this was originally delivered in an ad hoc fashion, tutors are now encouraged to study an online course, (developed by McDonald 2006) allowing them to develop and practice online teaching skills. Many tutors are new to online collaborative exercises, such things were unavailable when they were students, and the course provides hands-on experience of online group work. On completing the self-guided course, tutors are awarded a certificate (Fig. 4.2).

Such evidence of online competence is indicative of a baseline level of skill in online teaching; however the question remains whether such a basic course can tackle the intricacies of supporting students engaged in collaborative activities to develop twenty-first century skills.

Fig. 4.2 Jane Barrett's certification of online teaching skills

Conclusions

As well as being essential employability skills, collaboration and effective teamwork contribute to deeper learning; and nowadays occur frequently in informal and formal online networks. However, many students are reluctant or unable to work together online, even when there are immediate negative consequences for failure to engage. Working together, in an online environment presents challenges as well as benefits. Online learning allows students to sustain an existing lifestyle, but negotiating group dynamics may prove an insurmountable challenge for learning with peers unless students have an understanding of how to work effectively in a team. Thus, learning about team working becomes a vital skill for students to learn.

Tutors are well placed to help and support students in developing and flexing their team-working muscles, tutors can work at the group or individual level and are skilled at detecting subtle nuances of student behaviour. Dysthe's model, where students construct knowledge by working with their peers, may be difficult to achieve in the initial years of an undergraduate degree. It is also challenging for tutors to step back while students work things out for themselves, particularly when the process is lengthy and deadlines are looming.

Helping students to achieve effective group and team work involves empowering tutors to use their facilitation skills with confidence; The OU provides institutionally approved basic staff development about how to teach online and how to facilitate team working. However, informal opportunities for peer support and collaboration within a tutor network are also important if skills are to develop further. Providing spaces where tutors can exchange and debate teaching and learning issues related to online collaboration and teamwork, are valuable ways of supporting self-reflection and continuing professional development.

Tips and Discussion Points

* Decide what you want to achieve from students working together. A joint output which is assessed at the group level, is different from individually assessed work resulting from group work.

- Acknowledge the importance of sociability factors in group work. Give students opportunities to get to know one another and to feel secure in the online environment before introducing an assessed task.
- Recognise that group working skills need to be developed. The goal for novice learners may be to contribute to a task, whereas that for experts may be to co-create an artefact.
- Consider the optimal level of tutor involvement, in the context of the learning strategy, the goal of the task and student expertise.
- Invest appropriately. Successful group work is resource intensive. Students need time and opportunity to become proficient in working together online. Tutors need time to develop appropriate teaching materials and opportunities to hone their online and facilitative skills.

References

An, H., Shin, S., & Lim, K. (2009). The effects of different instructor facilitation approaches on students interactions during asynchronous online discussions. *Computers and Education, 53*(3), 749–760.

Andresen, M. A. (2009). Asynchronous discussion forums: Success factors, outcomes, assessments, and limitations. *Educational Technology and Society, 12*(1), 249–258.

Andrews, R., & Haythornthwaite, C. (2007). Introduction to e-learning research. In R. Andrews & C. Haythornthwaite (Eds.), *The sage handbook of E-learning research* (pp. 1–52). Los Angeles/London: Sage.

Binkley, M., Erstad, O., Herman, J., Raizen, S., Ripley, M., Miller-Ricci, M., & Rumble, M. (2012). Defining twenty-first century skills. In P. Griffin, B. McGaw, & E. Care (Eds.), *Assessment and teaching of 21st century skills* (pp. 17–66). New York: Springer.

Bishop, J. (2007). Increasing participation in online communities: A framework for human-computer interaction. *Computers in Human Behavior, 23*(4), 1881–1893.

British Psychological Society. (2015). *Standards for the accreditation of undergraduate, conversion and integrated Masters programmes in psychology*. http://www.bps.org.uk/system/files/Public%20files/PaCT/Undergraduate%20Accreditation%202016_WEB.pdf. Accessed 18 Jan 2017.

Brown, R. (2000). *Group processes: Dynamics within and between groups* (2nd ed.). Oxford: Blackwell.

Calvani, A., Fini, A., Molino, M., & Ranieri, M. (2010). Visualizing and monitoring effective interactions in online collaborative groups. *British Journal of Educational Technology, 41*(2), 213–226.

Chidambaram, L., & Tung, L. (2005). Is out of sight, out of mind? An empirical study of social loafing in technology-supported groups. *Information Systems Research, 16*(2), 149–168.

Dillenbourg, P. (1999). What do you mean by collaborative learning. In P. Dillenbourg (Ed.), *Collaborative learning: Cognitive and computational approaches* (pp. 1–19). Amsterdam: Pergamon.

Dysthe, O. (2002). The learning potential of a web-mediated discussion in a university course. *Studies in Higher Education, 27*(3), 339–352.

Fung, Y. H. (2004). Collaborative online learning: Interaction patterns and limiting factors. *Open Learning, 19*(2), 135–149.

Goodwin, C., Graham, M., & Scarborough, H. (2001). Developing an asynchronous learning network. *Educational Technology and Society, 4*(4), 39–47.

Häkkinen, P., Järvelä, S., Mäkitalo-Siegl, K., Ahonen, A., Näykki, P., & Valtonen, T. (2017). Preparing teacher-students for twenty-first-century learning practices. (PREP 21): A framework for enhancing collaborative problem-solving and strategic learning skills. *Teachers and Teaching, 23*(1), 25–41. https://doi.org/10.1080/13540602.2016.1203772.

Hiltz, S. R., & Meinke, R. (1989). Teaching sociology in a virtual classroom. *Teaching Sociology, 17*(4), 431–446.

Hiltz, S. R., Turoff, M., & Harasim, L. (2007). Development and philosophy of the field of asynchronous learning networks. In R. Andrews & C. Haythornthwaite (Eds.), *The sage handbook of E-learning research*. Los Angeles/London: Sage.

Karau, S. J., & Williams, K. D. (1993). Social loafing: A meta-analytic review and theoretical integration. *Journal of Personality and Social Psychology, 65*(4), 681–706.

Kaye, H., Barrett, J. P., & Knightley, W. M. (2013). Student preference for residential or online project work in psychology. *Psychology Learning and Teaching, 12*(2), 196–202.

Kear, K. (2010). Collaboration via online discussion forums: Issues and approaches. In H. Donelan, K. Kear, & M. Ramage (Eds.), *Online communication and collaboration*. Abingdon/Oxon: Routledge.

King, A. (1993). From sage on the stage to guide on the side. *College Teaching, 41*(1), 30–35. www.jstor.org/stable/27558571.

Littleton, K., & Mercer, N. (2013). *Interthinking: Putting talk to work*. London: Routledge.

MacDonald, J. (2006). *Blended learning and online tutoring: A good practice guide*. Aldershot: Gower.

Mercer, N. (1995). *The guided construction of knowledge: Talk amongst teachers and learners*. Clevedon: Multilingual Matters.

Murphy, E. (2004). Recognising and promoting collaboration in an online asynchronous discussion. *British Journal of Educational Technology, 35*(4), 421–431.

Oliver, M., & Shaw, G. P. (2003). Asynchronous discussion in support of medical education. *Journal of Asynchronous Learning Networks, 7*(1), 56–67.

Piezon, S. L., & Donaldson, R. L. (2005). Online groups and social loafing: Understanding student-group interactions. *Online Journal of Distance Learning Administration, 8*(4). http://www.westga.edu/~distance/ojdla/winter84/piezon84.htm. Accessed 1 Feb 2017.

Preece, J., Nonnecke, B., & Andrews, D. (2004). The top five reasons for lurking: Improving community experiences for everyone. *Computers in Human Behavior, 20*(2), 201–223.

QAA. (2016). *Subject benchmark statement: Psychology*. http://www.qaa.ac.uk/en/Publications/Documents/SBS-Psychology-16.pdf. Accessed 1 Feb 2017.

Reddy, P., Lantz, C., & Hulme, J. (2013). *Employability in psychology: A guide for departments*. York: Higher Education Academy. tinyurl.com/kthejrs. Accessed 18 Jan 2017.

Roschelle, J. (1992). Learning by collaborating: Convergent conceptual change. *The Journal of the Learning Sciences, 2*(3), 235.

Swan, K. (2002). Building learning communities in online courses: The importance of interaction. *Education, Communication and Information, 2*, 23–49.

Vuopala, E., Hyvönen, P., & Järvelä, S. (2016). Interaction forms in successful collaborative learning in virtual learning environments. *Active Learning in Higher Education, 17*(1), 25–38.

5

Facebook and Informal Learning

George Callaghan and Ian Fribbance

Introduction

The digital, networked and open nature of technological development is leading to a transformation of many different aspects of academic practice. Indeed, in his book The Digital Scholar (2011) Martin Weller argues that: "… the potential impact… on scholarship is revolutionary, as it could lead to changes to research definition, methodology, the publishing industry, teaching, the role of institutions and collaboration." (2011: 9). This chapter focuses on using the social media technology of Facebook to explore the strengths and weaknesses of such channels as part of informal learning. It adopts a case study approach drawn from the Open University's

G. Callaghan (✉)
Department of Economics, Open University, Milton Keynes, UK
e-mail: George.callaghan@open.ac.uk

I. Fribbance
Faculty of Arts and Social Science, Open University, Milton Keynes, UK

© The Author(s) 2018
J. Baxter et al. (eds.), *Creativity and Critique in Online Learning,*
https://doi.org/10.1007/978-3-319-78298-0_5

Faculty of Arts and Social Science's (FASS) Facebook page to analyse social media within the theoretical framework of informal learning.

This is an important area for Higher Education, because as social media become more commonly used by students as channels of communication and conduits of information, Universities need to think through and experiment with different ways of using such technology as part of their teaching and learning strategies.

We have written in an earlier publication (Callaghan and Fribbance 2016) on how Facebook can be used to create a community of learning in a distance learning environment. In this chapter, we focus on examining the social media tool Facebook through the lens of teaching theory. We also reflect in detail on the challenges such social media present those working in Higher Education, for example the ethical aspects of working with Facebook and the threat such social media might present to deep learning.

In terms of the structure of the chapter itself, it begins with a review of the literature surrounding social theory of learning, particularly on the debates around informal learning (Wenger 2008, 2010). This is followed by a discussion of social media in Higher Education in general and the use of Facebook in particular. Data from the Faculty Facebook page is then used to illustrate and comment upon how this technology can stimulate and encourage informal learning. There is then a longer section which discusses these developments within a critical perspective, in particular examining the ethical and practical challenges of using commercially controlled software within an HE environment. This section also explores possible ways Universities might meet and (possibly) overcome these challenges, including developing new competencies and skills for both teachers and students. The concluding section then presents a summary and points to useful areas of future research.

Social Theory of Learning

The American philosopher and writer John Dewey was one of the early exponents to emphasize the essentially social nature of learning. In his book Democracy and Learning, first published in 1916, he writes:

> In the final account, then, not only does social life demand teaching and learning for its own permanence, but the very process of living together educates. It enlarges and enlightens experience; it stimulates and enriches imagination; it creates responsibility for accuracy and vividness of statement and thought. (Dewey 1916: 10)

While he argues that there is a place for formalized education, he also highlights that through lived experience and practice much important learning takes place in communities. This emphasis on the importance of social learning is built upon by later writers on educational theory. For example, Marsick and Watkins (1990, 2001), develop the idea of informal learning which is rooted in a social setting and less structured than class based education (with formal learning objectives and outcomes).

Much of the literature around informal learning focuses on workplace learning (Marsick and Watkins 1990, 2001; Marsick et al. 2006). The framework of learning these academics use is based on recognising the crucial role of social and economic context. As Marsick and Watkins argue these create, re-create and reinforce particular value and power systems:

> When people learn in families, groups, workplaces, or other social settings, their interpretation of a situation and consequent actions are highly influenced by social and cultural norms of others. Yet, people often do not deeply question their own or others' views. (Marsick and Watkins 2001: 31)

This quote neatly describes the depth and strength of informal learning; a constant unconscious process reinforced through all forms of social activity. But the last sentence from the extract above also highlights a possible drawback, it cannot be assumed that social learning will automatically be critical and reflective. Clearly this could (and has in the past) led to problematic value systems being the norm (for example: racism, sexism, fascism). As we discuss later in this chapter, it is possible for social media such as Facebook to reinforce such problems by recycling bias, bigotry and fake news. The challenge for HE providers is to add a critically reflective element to the tremendous communication potential inherent within social media.

Perhaps one of the most influential educationalist theorists working in the field of social learning is Etienne Wenger. He builds on the work of anthropologists such as Jean Lave (1988), which argues that the context of learning influences its success. One example is that in comparing how citizens make mathematical calculations when buying groceries and how they work through similar calculations conducted in a classroom, they do better in the first case. In other words, the social situation within which knowledge is applied influences the outcome (Wenger and Lave 1991).

While Wenger acknowledges that educators should adopt a perspective which "… places learning in the context of our lived experience of participation in the world." (2008: 3) he recognises that individual agency is still important. He argues for the development of a new vocabulary around learning and that individuals should foster an "educational imagination" (2008: 272). So, for example, Universities should encourage students to orientate their identity so they are constantly looking out to an ever-changing world, while simultaneously looking inwards to reflect upon their own reactions and responses to this world.

Marsick et al. (2006) describe how such insights provide a valuable addition to social learning theory:

> These three factors – imagination, engagement, and alignment – enhance our understanding of social reflective learning. They add the following to our model: (1) an understanding of how valuing difference enriches social learning, (2) a deepened appreciation of the social context for learning, and (3) respect for the challenges involved in aligning viewpoints as meaning is negotiated within the social context. (2006: 797)

In terms of how this theory might be applied within educational design Wenger writes that: "A learning community must push its boundaries and interact with other communities of practice." (2008: 274). While acknowledging that Facebook, at least at the level of a large academic faculty, is unlikely to create the depth of interaction required by an academic community of practice (Jakovljevic et al. 2013), it does offer a platform for discussion and information sharing which contribute to the process of creating learning communities.

For example, there is potential for universities to use such informal learning channels to make connections between students and Faculty staff and between students themselves. They can also provide links to core course content, advertise Faculty events, and show videos of academic discussions and seminars. Finally, there is the potential to engage in more academic interaction through lecturers debating issues using social media platforms such as Facebook. The FASS (Faculty of Arts and Social Sciences) Facebook page we discuss in this chapter allows us to analyse these different possibilities.

Social Media and Facebook in Education

Before going on to examine the Faculty of Arts and Social Science Facebook page, we will first provide a brief review of the literature around using such technology in education. The trend related to social media is clear: individuals in general are spending more time on social media and more time on mobile devices. For example, one report highlights that of the two hours and 51 minutes' people based in the UK spend every day on line in 2015, 17% was on social media sites, up from 12.2% in 2014 (Guardian 2015). These social changes have inevitable implications for Universities. Wenger's comments that in designing an educational community, practitioners should "… become self-conscious about appropriating the styles and discourses of the constellations in which it expects to have effects" (2008: 274), are prescient. He argues that if students are inhabiting virtual spaces then educators should be using that space in designing, developing and delivering their formal and informal learning.

The academic literature on this topic clearly identifies social media as an area higher education institutions should consider (Callaghan and Fribbance 2016). For example, Guy (2012) writes in an overview of the literature: "As educators look for ways to engage and motivate students, social media technologies are becoming a viable supplement to the traditional learning environment…" One interesting aspect of much of the literature surrounding the use of social media such as Facebook in HE settings is that the distinction between formal and informal learning is rarely made explicit. Rather studies talk about academic teaching space on the one hand and social or personal space on the other. For example, Guy's summary study reports that while students and staff consistently spend time on Facebook only "…a low percentage of users are engaging in such for academic practice" (Guy 2012: 2).

Similarly, Liu (2010), concludes that social reasons take priority over academic learning for using Facebook, and Tess (2013), in another review of the (again predominately US) literature on the use of social media in higher education, finds little evidence of success in stitching social media into formal learning. Also Manca and Ranieri's (2013) overview of academic studies, which examines the use of Facebook for teaching, finds that although students want their University to use new technology, they resist it as a formal tool within their education.

However, there is evidence in the literature which suggests that social media can help create and support learning communities through informal learning. This includes Hung and Yuen's (2010) study that social media can improve communication between teachers and learners, Kent and Leaver's (2014) edited book on practical examples of using Facebook in Universities and our own study on how social media such as Facebook can foster a learning community (Callaghan and Fribbance 2016). These studies point to social media as being an excellent example of an informal learning space, where a community of practice can be developed. At its best such space offers the opportunity for students to make connections with University staff, recognises their agency, develop reflective practices and enhance their (informal and formal) learning.

To realize such potential requires recognition of the validity and importance of informal learning amongst both students and, crucially, teachers. There is only limited evidence to date that academics are enthusiastically engaging with social media in their teaching. While there is evidence which illustrates that a large number of academics use social media for professional purposes, for example Veletsianos (2016: 39) reports that social media platforms such as Twitter are very useful in building academic networks, there are fewer examples of it being a mainstream element of teaching. He writes: "While early adopters often extol the benefits of new technologies, attempts at using technology to enhance scholarly practice have so far been met with skepticism and reluctance"

(2016: 17). Similarly, Chen and Bryer's (2012) find that while educators used social media for personal and professional (research and networking) they are less willing to use it in teaching.

In terms of why this might be, Veletsianos found that Faculty staff have concerns about the time commitment and threat to privacy, particularly in trying to navigate between the personal and professional through social media tools such as Facebook. The point about privacy emerges frequently in his study: in a number of interviews academics report that they are highly sensitive to the open nature of social media (Facebook in particular) and adopt protective strategies, which include restricting the topics they post on and limiting access to the profiles. He also argues that because participation in social media is not linked to promotion and (in the US and Canada) tenure, there may be a reluctance to engage. (Veletsianos 2016).

An additional, more deep-seated reason, might be that there is relatively conservative consensus around epistemology in academia which reifies the collection, analysis and presentation of formal knowledge within ever more specialized fields. Here research takes primacy, teaching involves lectures where the expert delivers knowledge and promotion goes to experts in narrow technical areas. Within this context the idea that learning is normal, that informal learning is important and that social media reflects and fuels the potential for such learning, is a threat. This might help explain the reluctance of the academy to adapt traditional teaching methods. As Veletsianos writes, ideas of social learning: "Are noteworthy for the mere reason that they break away from norms of 20th century university scholarship about fundamental epistemological questions regarding what knowledge is, how it is gained, how it is verified, how it is shared, and how it should be valued." (2016: 21).

The ubiquity of digital technology and the potential to connect and encourage learning through social media mean, however, that Higher Education Institutions, should at the very least be experimenting with how social media can help in the design and delivery of teaching material. The next section explores some potential options through examining data from one Faculty's Facebook page.

Faculty Facebook Page: Data

The last section looked at the literature on social media and Facebook in Higher Education. We now move on to explore in more detail the Open University's Faculty of Arts and Social Science Facebook (FASS) page. The origin of this was a desire to explore innovative methods to create a feeling of belonging to a Faculty within a diverse and geographically highly dispersed student group. As Taylor (2013) has argued "… one challenge is (for the OU) to get into spaces and places where users and potential students are already browsing" (2013: 8). This is what the Faculty Facebook page is doing and, as we argue elsewhere (Callaghan and Fribbance 2016) the Facebook page goes some way to fostering an academic community.

The page has a number of key features. These include links to other Faculty and University digital assets, such as the free online material provided through the OpenLearn platform. In an attempt to break down the barriers between teacher and student the Facebook page also has videos of academic staff discussing the development of learning material and photos of academics out of the workplace. More dynamic interaction includes regular weekly activities. Examples include posts which encourage students to share study skills tips, posts which invite students to share their motivations for study and occasionally more light hearted posts which invite students to share examples of unusual places or locations when they have studied.

A particular challenge in using Facebook within an educational context (shared with commercial users) is to launch posts onto the screens of those who follow your pages. Facebook's algorithms control the number of people who receive posts without paying, (known as organic reach), and in 2014 the company changed the formula which dramatically cut such free postings to below 10% of those who link to a page. The intention is to get the business user to boost reach by paying Facebook. Over time the Faculty project has done this and in 2016 was spending around £300 per month on boosting pages. So, for example £25 might help a post reach 5–10,000. The ethical issues of Universities supporting such commercial tactics are discussed in a later section. A combination of boost and organic reach has meant that the reach of the Faculty Facebook page, measured by the number of likes, has grown over the years (see Chart 5.1).

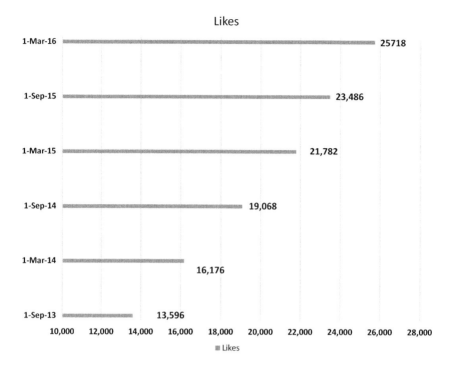

Chart 5.1 Faculty Facebook page number of likes (2013–2016)

What this chart indicates is that over time the number of people who like the Facebook page has grown dramatically. While this clearly does not indicate depth of interaction it does illustrate breadth: a growing number of users are viewing the site and interacting in some way with the content.

Other data shows that the largest audience are women aged 35–44-18% of people who viewed the page. It's also interesting to note the heavy reliance on smartphones, with most students (65%) using a mobile device to engage with the content.

Much of engagement involves likes, comments, shares and watching videos. A minority of students participate more intensively through the 'Friday Thinkers' postings. These involve a Faculty academic early on Friday posting a question about an aspect of arts or social science that is in the news or relates to a research interest then moderating the discussion which takes place throughout the day. The most popular academic areas for question are Politics, Economics and Sociology:

- Can social scientists explain why some young European Muslims are attracted to Islamist political ideology and violence?
- What did we learn about the state of UK democracy from the 2015 election?
- Why is immigration now such an important social issue in the UK?

To give a flavour of the discussions and interactions the extract below contains details from a string of postings related to the EU Referendum from 1st July 2016. The Facebook post replies are from several different students and callouts have been used to highlight important points.

Box   5.1

Friday Thinker question:	Is having a referendum a good way of deciding public policy?
Facebook post:	No especially when a lot of people are unaware on their decision and consequences
Facebook post:	The people should not vote unless they know fully what they're voting for. But saying that a referendum is not legally binding and shows where the people stand on issues. But those issues need to be explained fully before a vote and not just be hearsay. If we don't have the facts we shouldn't vote.

> Teacher is emphasising importance of facts. Also raising questions which encourage critical thinking

Friday thinker:	Referenda, on contentious issues, can be divisive. But they do record an opinion. A mood. Especially if having a high turnout. Last week saw the biggest turnout in a national election since 1992. Has parliament no option but now to respect the outcome

(continued)

Box 5.1   (continued)

	of the vote? And implement the decision to leave the EU?
Facebook post:	Referendums can't sit comfortably with representative democracy as sources of public policy. But only if the circumstances in which they're used, how they are triggered, by whom, the majority needed to settle policies and its duration are agreed in advance. The problems arise – such as tension with Parliament when these are absent
Facebook post:	Aren't the government still under investigation for election fraud .... if found guilty shouldn't that mean they had no legal right to implement the policies they did and wouldn't that mean this was an illegal referendum and on that basis ... all policies etc. overturned just cases that a judge found guilty are overturned?

Difficulty is the emotional nature of some topics and the informal style of interaction can lead to poor communication.

Facebook post:	Yes, of course it is! 1 man, one vote each. Fair & square
Facebook post:	Quite simply NO. A choice can only be democratic if it is an informed choice otherwise it is a matter of manipulation by one side or another which removes freedom of thought.
Facebook post:	A referendum can be effective if the campaigns of both sides are clearly set out and agreed by both sides, thus ensuring fairness and accuracy. In this instance, the huge disparities between promises and reality has only increased the "us and them" divide in the country.

This is a small extract from over 62 comments (many with subsequent conversation strings) on this issue, but it does provide a good example of the opportunities and limitations of using such social media for academic discussion and debate. The topics chosen by academics tend to reflect contemporary events and the ensuing discussions can range from carefully considered positions to emotional responses. Nevertheless, it demonstrates the potential for taking academic debate into the learners' online social milieu. Without stretching the comparison too far, it resembles the type of conversation a tutor might have if s/he was talking with students over a coffee in a social space such as a café. In other words, it is less a formal transfer of codified knowledge which will be assessed and more an opportunity to introduce the need for facts and critical questioning into discussions of everyday news items.

Although some responses are short, many are quite detailed and show elements of academic engagement. Over time the number of Friday Thinker responses has been gradually increasing, partially because practical lessons have been learned about how to set straightforward but engaging questions (pick a contentious contemporary issue and introduce it in lay terms) but also because there are more learners visiting the page. When facilitating discussions academics present evidence, build arguments and ask probing questions.

Something about informal learning, Wenger's agency – we are encouraging them to think …These can be seen as offering pedagogical depth to an aspect of informal learning.

Critique and Commentary

While there are clearly many strengths relating to using Social media in HE there are some important issues we have to reflect upon. These include the power imbalance between commercial companies and Universities, the possibility that algorithms narrow rather than broaden debates and that the flow of constant stimuli from the web detracts from deep learning. We finish this section by looking at how Universities might engage with these issues.

Power

Social media rely on the software, platforms and servers of technology companies. This gives such corporations tremendous power and raises questions as to the ethics of Universities increasing the profits of such companies by using social media in their teaching. For example, Weller (2013) has expresses concern about the extent to which using profit seeking platforms such as Facebook illustrates the OU is supporting commercial organizations. In fact, as we discussed earlier, in order to maximize the reach of postings the Faculty directly pays Facebook to reach News Feed accounts. In addition, use of Facebook will increase the company's advertising revenue. Veletsianos, drawing on the work of Boyd also argues that "While social in nature, the commercial nature of these technologies and the affordances they provide to observe and scrutinise others raises conundrums for individual scholars and academia alike" (2016: 4).

There are also lessons for education from other sectors of society. For example, the news industry, in which 44% of US citizens access news stories through Facebook (Pew Research Centre 2016), has found to its cost that social media companies are ruthless in following their own priorities. As media commentator John Naughton points out, organizations which rely on Facebook Instant Articles to generate readers, lose out when the company changes its algorithms to prioritise issues other than news feeds (Naughton 2016).

In terms of HE, as we argue elsewhere (Callaghan and Fribbance 2016), one of the methodological difficulties is that the algorithms which generate data and prioritise the sharing of postings are decided by Facebook. Universities have no control over the social media software associated with such companies. This means planning activities and analyzing data over the long term is difficult: at any time the commercial company can initiate change.

It's also the case that the transparency of the web has implications for the employment relationship between University managers and staff. A situation which has implications for academic freedom. While social media means academics can reach a large audience, any message seen as problematic, opens them up to censorship from their institution. In his book on digital scholarship Veletianos cites the case of Dr Steven Salaita, who in 2014 had a job offer rescinded, reportedly following Tweets he had made criticizing Israel. As Veletsianos writes "The capacity of networked speech acts to reach large and even viral audiences, particularly if in some way controversial, is an uncomfortable reality for institutions in an age of carefully controlled brand optics and communications. (2016: 55)".

Echo Chamber

Another issue which should be critically reflected upon is the potential for social media to create echo chambers; to narrow, not widen debate. One of the tools commercial organisations use to wield and express their power is through developing algorithms which decide the results of searches and the flow of data and information. Of course, one could see this as an aspect of customer service, in the sense that citizens are presented with the information deemed to be most useful; but control rests with the corporation.

The technology executives who develop and decide how to deploy algorithms decide on the flow of information. The possibility that this might lead to a tendency to control and shrink audiences is highlighted in Pariser's (2011) book The Filter Bubble: What the Internet is Hiding from You, which critically comments upon the power controlling information networks bestows on large corporations. Controlling the process of information flow provides companies such as Google and Facebook with tremendous power to push their values and priorities.

This leads to the ironic possibility that, rather than widen and broaden, social media might telescope the focus and flow of information. For if we are only Facebook "friends" with those holding similar values and sign up to the Twitter feed of those we agree with, then the terms of reference of any debate are considerably narrowed. There is evidence to support this position. For example, in a 2016 article Katherine Viner, the Editor in chief of Guardian News and Media, raises concerns about the use of algorithms and filter software. She goes so far as to argue that the process which tailors search results based upon what commercial companies think is of interest to a particular individual can "disrupt the truth". The logic here is that tightly controlled algorithms create "filter bubbles" where people might think they are co-existing with a free world wide web but in fact exist in an electronic ghetto; albeit a large one. She cites the following experience of a British internet activist following the UK referendum on leaving the EU:

> I am actively searching through Facebook for people celebrating the Brexit leave victory, but the filter bubble is SO strong, and extends SO far into things like Facebook's custom search that I can't find anyone who is happy *despite the fact that over half the country is clearly jubilant today* and despite the fact that I'm *actively* looking to hear what they are saying.

This echo-chamber problem is now SO severe and SO chronic that I can only beg any friends I have who actually work for Facebook and other major social media and technology to urgently tell their leaders that to not act on this problem now is tantamount to actively supporting and funding the tearing apart of the fabric of our societies … We're getting countries where one half just doesn't know anything at all about the other. (Viner 2016: 26).

This concern has been amplified and magnified with arguments around the role social media and "fake news" play in politics more generally, such as the 2016 election of Trump in the US (Lewis 2016). As Veletsianos argues the algorithms driving such processes reflect and reinforce the values of specific networks and may "… blind users to diversity and encourage uniformity (2016: 59)".

Deep Learning

A third concern is that the Internet is changing the way people think, read and remember (Carr 2010). This anxiety, shared by others (Bilton 2010), is that the capacity to read and interpret meaning from written text is more difficult when done electronically. The argument is that the

Web involves numerous stimuli: visual, moving images and auditory output which distract users from deep thinking where reflection and creativity are more likely to take place. Carr writes that "… when we go online, we enter an environment that provides cursory reading, buried and distracted thinking and superficial learning (2010: 115)." He draws on the work of developmental psychologists to argue the Web weakens the capacity for "deep processing" which is needed for "mindful knowledge acquisition, inductive analysis, critical thinking, imagination and reflection. (2010: 141)."

While Carr's main focus is more on the knowledge building associated with formal learning the potential for distraction associated with the web also has implications for social learning. For if over stimulation and distraction make reflective thinking and the development of agency more difficult, then such technology has the potential to impact upon informal as well as formal learning. For example, students might be flooded with too many channels of informal learning or seduced into a particular echo chamber. This requires thought and vigilance on the part of educationalists introducing social media to their teaching.

Engagement

Despite these important concerns, Universities must engage with technological developments. As Veletsianos writes, "… scholars are part of a complex socio-cultural system that is ever-changing in response to both internal and external stimuli, including technological innovations, political and economic climates, and dominant cultural values (2016: 109)". Higher Education must critically engage with this process, using new technology to enrich and add value to both informal and formal learning.

Part of this critical engagement means Universities, institutions which at their best offer a critique of and challenge to existing power structures, should be alert to the dangers of passively accepting the pressures, priorities and power of the current Web structure. Rather they must use social media as a critical teaching tool.

Through providing free access to learning materials and developing and deploying open teaching modules such as MOOCS, Universities are already using the Web to break down barriers to accessing knowledge. However, one area where more could be done is improving the study skills of staff and students in relation to using the Web for both informal and formal learning.

The work of Howard Rheingold (2010, 2012) has relevance here, particularly his argument that citizens need to develop digital literacies. His focus is on the importance of developing skills in attention, participation, collaboration, network awareness and critical consumption. On these he wrote: "Although I consider attention to be fundamental to all the other literacies, the one that links together all the others... They are interconnected...Ultimately, the most important fluency is not in mastering a particular literacy but in being able to put all five of these literacies together into a way of being in digital culture" (Rheingold 2010: 14). One could summarize his position as arguing that people need to learn how to demonstrate agency within a digital environment; a focus in keeping with the thoughts of Wenger and other social learning theorists.

Although his emphasis is on digital skills which are useful to all citizens, there are clear parallels with how Higher Education uses social media in its interaction with students and wider society. The emphasis on building networks, encouraging students to focus, be self-reflective and critical are core elements of both formal and informal learning.

One practical step which Universities could put in place is training in just these digital literacies – both for their teaching staff and their students. At present such study skills materials as there are tend to be in the domain of librarians (Walton et al. 2012), but given their importance these capabilities need to become part of mainstream Faculty learning. There also has to be an effort to ensure these are not just skills in using a particular piece of software or website, such as Endnote or Wikipedia, but also on how students approach and understand the web. Rheingold advises that web users be constantly mindful as to what they are doing and why. This recommendation is aimed at encouraging self-reflection and opens the way for critical agency. Universities might shift digital literacy training from the library into formal and informal learning.

Conclusions

This chapter argues that social media platforms, such as Facebook, are relevant and important channels of informal learning. The conceptual framing of the chapter draws on social learning theory, in particular the work of Wenger (2010, 2008) and his focus on informal learning. This theoretical viewpoint states that the knowledge and skills learned through informal channels and settings has pedagogic value. We argue that depth and value can be added to informal learning by encouraging students to be self-reflective, critical and to develop and deploy agency. Digital initiatives, such as the FASS Facebook page, offer case studies which can be built on by others.

While we acknowledge there are challenges and problems associated with social media, in particular the power of commercial companies and the potential for learners' attention to be diluted and distracted, we conclude that this is a space in which Universities must be active. In their role of fostering and encouraging learning Universities should aim to build relationships and to teach using formal and informal channels. Social media offers tremendous potential in this area, but Universities must retain their focus on criticality. This means at an institutional level they must acknowledge the power of technology companies and, when they see fit, to challenge this power directly through working with national Government's and regulators. It also means adopting new methods of and approaches to informal and formal learning, a process which will require input from both teachers and students. Both scholars and students need to continually reflect upon how learning takes place and there is, we argue, advantages in making digital literacy a core learning skill.

It's also the case that the data here is drawn from only one institution. One fruitful area of further research would be to examine the lived experience of students and academic staff with respect to social media and learning across a number of Higher Education institutions. In particular, we need to know more about how engaging with informal learning mediums such as social media impacts upon different aspects of teaching and learning. In what ways does behavior change, has it for example encouraged students (and staff) to become active citizens in other areas of their lives? Also, is it done at the expense of other learning activity, in particular deep reading and thinking? We also need to keep in mind that the flow of technical change and innovation – and the necessary interrelationships this involves between teacher and student – is constant. This means that all those involved in education need to continually challenge and change their approach to teaching and learning. Another constant is a concern with criticality, with Universities being active institutional citizens who encourage self-reflection and agency amongst staff, students and within broader society.

Tips and Discussion Points

* Purpose: think carefully about the reason for using social media. For example, it could be as part of an informal learning and strategy which seeks to build a community of learners or it could be a more formal element of a module.
* Critical awareness: the academic team working with Facebook needs to be aware that the power resides with the company. Such social media providers can change
* Rules without consultation, so the social media team must constantly monitor developments.
* Engage academics: to maximise pedagogical impact teaching staff need to be involved in the planning, implementation and review of social media strategy.
* Connections: the teaching team need to think carefully about how social media innovations connect to other learning activities. For example, how do they link to formal assessed course work?
* Mix content: one issue is to keep students engaged and with social media such as Facebook is to offer a changing mix of activities including photos, humorous posts as well as more formal teacher led discussions.
* Interact: given the centrality of encouraging critical reflection it is also worth including an element of communication between academic staff and students.

- Plan content: from a viewpoint of practical organisation it is advisable to use a content calendar with term dates, main exam periods, political elections and media events which link to postings.
- Resources: University management need to be aware of the costs of social media activity. These are likely to involve workload from both academic and academic related staff.

References

Bilton, N. (2010). *I live in the future & here's how it works: Why your world, work, and brain are being creatively disrupted*. New York: Crown, Random House.
Callaghan, G., & Fribbance, I. (2016). The use of Facebook to build a community for distance learning students: A case study from the Open University. *Open Learning: The Journal of Open, Distance and e-Learning, 31*(3), 260–272. http://www.tandfonline.com/doi/abs/10.1080/02680513.2016.1229176?journalCode=copl20 Accessed 27 Sept 2016.
Carr, N. (2010). *The shallows: How the internet is changing the way we think, read and remember*. London: Atlantic Books.
Chen, B., & Bryer, T. (2012). Investigating instructional strategies for using social media in formal and informal learning. *The International Review of Research in Open and Distance Learning, 13*(1), 87–100.
Dewey, J. (1916). *Democracy and education*. Pennsylvania State University. http://library.um.ac.id/images/stories/ebooks/Juni10/democracy%20and%20education%20-%20john%20dewey.pdf. Accessed 24 Aug 2016.
Guardian. (2015). *Social media overtakes entertainment as favorite online activity*. https://www.theguardian.com/media/2015/sep/02/social-media-overtakes-entertainmemt-as-favourite-online-activity. Accessed 26 Aug 2016.
Guy, R. (2012). The use of social media for academic practice: A review of literature. *Kentucky Journal of Higher Education Policy and Practice, 1*(2), 1–20. http://uknowledge.uky.edu/cgi/viewcontent.cgi?article=1015&context=kjhepp. Accessed 18Aug 2015.
Hung, H. T., & Yuen, S. C. Y. (2010). Educational use of social networking technology in higher education. *Teaching in Higher Education, 15*(6), 703–714.
Jakovljevic, M., Buckley, S., & Bushney, M. (2013). Forming communities of practice in higher education: A theoretical perspective. In *Management, Knowledge and Learning International Conference*, Croatia. http://www.

toknowpress.net/ISBN/978-961-6914-02-4/papers/ML13-368.pdf. Accessed 31 Jan 2017.

Kent, M., & Leaver, T. (2014). *An education in Facebook?* Croydon: Routledge.

Lave, J. (1988). *Cognition in practice: Mind, mathematics and culture in everyday life*. Cambridge: Cambridge University Press.

Lewis, H. (2016). Did fake news on Facebook swing the US election? *New Statesman.* http://www.newstatesman.com/world/2016/11/did-fake-news-facebook-swing-us-election. Accessed 24 Nov 2016.

Liu, Y. (2010). Social media tools as a learning resource. *Journal of Educational Technology Development and Exchange, 3*(1), 101–114.

Manca, S., & Ranieri, M. (2013). Is it a tool suitable for learning? A critical review of the literature on Facebook as a technology-enhanced learning environment. *Journal of Computer Assisted Learning, 29*, 487–504. https://doi.org/10.1111/jcal.12007.

Marsick, V. J., & Watkins, K. (1990). *Informal and incidental learning in the workplace*. London/New York: Routledge.

Marsick, V. J., & Watkins, K. E. (2001). Informal and incidental learning. *New Directions for Adult and Continuing Education, 89*(spring), 25–34.

Marsick, V. J., Watkins, K. E., Callahan, M. W., & Volpe, M. (2006). *Reviewing theory and research on informal and incidental learning*, online submission. http://files.eric.ed.gov/fulltext/ED492754.pdf. Accessed 8 July 2016.

Naughton, J. (2016, July 3). Few news providers with now by liking Facebook. *Observer.* https://www.theguardian.com/commentisfree/2016/jul/03/facebook-journalism-news-feeds-partisan-politics. Accessed 8 June 2016.

Pariser, E. (2011). *The filter bubble: What the internet is hiding from you*. London: Viking/Penguin Press.

Pew Research Centre. (2016). *News use across social media platforms 2016.* http://www.journalism.org/2016/05/26/news-use-across-social-media-platforms-2016/

Rheingold, H. (2010). Attention, and other 21st-century social media literacies. *EDUCAUSE Review, 45*(5), 14–24.

Rheingold, H. (2012). *Net smart: How to thrive online*. London: MIT Press.

Taylor, J. (2013). Learning journeys: The road from informal to formal learning – The UK Open University's Approach. *Journal of Interactive Media in Education*, 2. http://jime.open.ac.uk/articles/10.5334/2013-08/. Accessed 23 June 2016.

Tess, P. A. (2013). The role of social media in higher education classes (real and virtual) – A literature review. *Computers in Human Behaviour, 29*, 60–68.

Veletsianos, G. (2016). *Social media in academia: Networked scholars*. New York: Routledge.

Viner, K. (2016, July 12). How technology disrupted the truth. *Guardian*. https://www.theguardian.com/media/2016/jul/12/how-technology-disrupted-the-truth. Accessed 13 July 2016.

Walton, G., Gwyer, R., & Stubbings, R. (2012). *The road to information literacy: Librarians as facilitators of learning*. Berlin: De Gruyter.

Weller, M. (2011). *The digital scholar: How technology is transforming academic practice*. Bloomsbury Open Access. https://www.bloomsburycollections.com/book/the-digital-scholar-how-technology-is-transforming-scholarly-practice/. Accessed 7 July 2016.

Weller, M. (2013). The battle for open – a perspective. *Journal of Interactive Media in Education*, (3). http://jime.open.ac.uk/articles/10.5334/2013-15/. Accessed 24 June 2016.

Wenger, E. C. (2008). *Communities of practice: Learning, meaning, and identity* (18th printing, first published 1998). Cambridge: Cambridge University Press.

Wenger, E. (2010). *Communities of practice and social learning systems: The career of a concept*. http://wenger-trayner.com/wp-content/uploads/2012/01/09-10-27-CoPs-and-systems-v2.01.pdf. Accessed 9 Sept 2016.

Wenger, E. C., & Lave, J. (1991). *Situated learning: Legitimate peripheral participation*. Cambridge: Cambridge University Press.

6

Creativity, Criticality and Engaging the Senses in Higher Education: Creating Online Opportunities for Multisensory Learning and Assessment

Stefanie Sinclair

Introduction

This chapter considers why there is a need for a greater focus on creativity in higher education and critically explores how digital technology can be used to facilitate creative, multisensory learning and assessment in higher education, particularly, though not exclusively, at a distance. It introduces and critically appraises three forms of assessment used in Religious Studies and Philosophy modules at the Open University, including the assessment of digital audio recordings of oral presentations, presentation slides and a 'Take a picture of religion' activity involving digital photography.

S. Sinclair (✉)
Open University, Milton Keynes, UK
e-mail: stefanie.sinclair@open.ac.uk

J. Baxter et al. (eds.), *Creativity and Critique in Online Learning*,
https://doi.org/10.1007/978-3-319-78298-0_6

The Benefits of Creativity

Creativity is in demand. At all levels of education, creativity has been linked to increased levels of wellbeing, student engagement and depth of learning (Robinson 2011; Gauntlett 2011). Furthermore, creativity features highly amongst desirable graduate attributes as identified by employers around the world (Osmani et al. 2015; Rampersad and Patel 2014; Robinson 2011). As Gaspar and Mabic note, "in the last decade creativity has become a mantra which is used by politicians, businessmen, employees, teachers, professors, students and others. Creativity is seen as a cure for a wide range of [social, economic and educational] problems" (Gaspar and Mabic 2015, p. 598). It is widely acknowledged that creativity builds students' resilience (Gauntlett 2011, p. 20) by enabling them to find resourceful ways of dealing with challenges they may face in their studies and their personal and professional lives. Creativity can build students' capacity to work out "unprecedented highly complex problems, often termed 'wicked' problems" (Stefani 2017, p. 198) that contemporary and future societies face, linked to increasing rates of change, rapid globalisation of economic and social systems, environmental concerns and rising social and economic inequality. As Robinson points out, "the more complex the world becomes, the more creative we need to be to meet its challenges" (Robinson 2011, p. xiii).

From this point of view, it could be argued that creativity has an important *political* dimension. Gauntlett argues that even 'everyday creativity' – making things, including DIY or knitting – can lead "to a whole new way of looking at things, and potentially to a real political shift in how we deal with the world" (Gauntlett 2011, p. 19), due to "the fact that people have made a choice to make something rather than consume what's given by the big suppliers" (Gauntlett 2011, p. 19). Stefani argues that by fostering creativity and creative learning to unlock creative, critical capacity, higher education in particular can "play a profound role in contributing to socially responsible (in the sense of critically aware rather than socially compliant) citizenry" (Stefani 2017, p. 198).

What Is Creativity?

Creativity is a complex, multi-faceted concept. The literature on creativity and creative learning fails to agree on how exactly these terms can be defined (Watts and Blessinger 2017, p. 229). The term 'creativity' is derived from the Latin word *creare*, which means 'to make'. However, notions of creativity range from its understanding as an elite enterprise that is reserved for the talented and gifted few to the increasingly influential understanding of creativity as a powerful *collaborative* process that can and should be harnessed in everyone (Rampersad and Patel 2014, p. 1; Robinson 2011). Literature also distinguishes between the 'everyday creativity' of 'making things' (Gauntlett 2011) and "major creative achievements that *change a domain* and are recognised as such by the domain's experts" (Blessinger and Watts 2017, p. 3). Literature exploring the complex relationship between creativity and critical thinking skills (Watts and Blessinger 2017, p. 226), imagination (Blessinger and Watts 2017, p. 4) and intelligence (Kim 2011, p. 285) broadly agrees that these strengths are complementary and overlapping, but opinions vary on the extent to which they overlap.

There are also different views on what kind of environments or conditions can stimulate creativity and on the extent to which creativity requires novelty and originality or builds on existing knowledge or practices. Csikszentmihalyi argues that "an idea or product that deserves the label 'creative' arises from the synergy of many sources and not only from the mind of a single person" (Csikszentmihalyi 2013, p. 1). In other words, creativity does not come out of nowhere and can best be understood as part of a multi-faceted *process* embedded in a wider socio-cultural context, rather than confined to lightbulb moments of isolated individuals. As Blessinger and Watts note,

> Western cultures tend to associate creativity with novelty and originality. [...] But [...] in today's world there is no such thing as a completely novel and original work, since all works are to varying degrees built upon the works created before them, and all creativity is also a balance between tradition and invention. Each domain has its own established rituals, rules, cultural norms, symbols and the like. (Blessinger and Watts 2017, p. 9)

From this point of view, creativity is fundamentally understood as a socio-cultural concept (Jackson 2006, p. 201), and creative learning relies on effective communication and collaboration (Watts and Blessinger 2017, p. 222). If creativity is understood in this way, the formal education system, and higher education in particular, can play an important role in the transfer of existing knowledge and norms and in the development of students' communication skills (Blessinger and Watts 2017, p. 6).

Room to Grow: Fostering Creativity and Creative Learning in Higher Education

A growing number of educational experts argue that "creative learning – learning to be creative – is an orientation and capability that all students *could* and most importantly *should*, develop while they are studying in higher education" (Jackson 2017, p. ix). However, are higher education institutions living up to this premise?

Employers around the world report a 'broad mismatch' between the competencies graduates acquire in higher education and current and future workplace requirements, particularly when it comes to creativity (Osmani et al. 2015; Rampersad and Patel 2014; Robinson 2011). As Csikszentmihalyi notes, "one hears the same story in industry and the business world, in civil service and scientific research. Technical knowledge and expertise might abound, but originality and innovation are scarce" (Csikszentmihalyi 2006, p. xviii). While the benefits of creativity and creative learning are widely acknowledged, there is growing recognition that education could do more to nurture it (McLellan and Nicholl 2013, p. 165). In fact, it has been argued that "the dominant forms of education actively stifle the conditions that are essential to creative development" (Robinson 2011, p. 49; see also: Kim 2011), with their predominant focus "on teaching 'facts' and conducting lots of tests" (Gauntlett 2011, p. 227). Gauntlett blames the impact of neoliberal policies on education for this. He argues that:

in education, the influence of neoliberalism means that students become 'customers' who assume that their purpose is to purchase and extract qualifications as simply as possible rather than engage in the process of discovery, learning and growth. For their teachers, the work becomes a matter of handing over relevant 'packages' of 'knowledge' in a uniform manner – the practice which can be most simply unified, at the cost of individuality and creativity. (Gauntlett 2011, p. 229)

Stakeholders in higher education increasingly acknowledge that this situation is no longer sustainable and needs to change (Watts and Blessinger 2017, p. 215). Stefani concurs that "it is no longer enough to teach students all that we know. Rather it is time to explore, innovate and enable the co-creation of new knowledge" (Stefani 2017, p. 199).

However, teachers in higher education, who are keen to explore and develop ways in which creativity can be fostered in teaching and learning, face a wide range of significant logistical, financial and cultural challenges. Large workloads, funding cuts and demands for greater efficiency, personal accountability, quality assurance and student satisfaction put teachers in higher education under increasing amounts of pressure (Jackson 2006, pp. 4ff.). The current environment, determined by league tables and 'burdensome bureaucracies', encourages a risk-averse culture that is not conducive to innovative, creative learning and teaching strategies (Stefani 2017, pp. 198f.).

How can Creativity and Creative Learning Be Facilitated in Higher Education?

In spite of the challenges, Blessinger and Watts confidently predict that "it is safe to presume that creativity will continue to grow in importance and that creative learning will start to emerge as a major focus area in all disciplines and at all levels of education" (Blessinger and Watts 2017, pp. 3f.). However, how can educational environments be created within which creativity can develop and thrive? While there is a sizable body of research and literature on creativity in primary and secondary education, much less attention has been paid to the role of creative thinking and creative learning in higher education, though there is growing interest in this area (Blessinger and Watts 2017, p. 6; see also Jackson et al. 2006). There are also different views on how creativity can be nurtured and what conditions allow and inspire creativity to flourish. Csikszentmihalyi (2006, pp. ixf.) highlights the importance of rewarding and facilitating the love of learning among students and staff, and of a curriculum focused on joyful learning and student engagement as a bedrock for creative thinking and creative learning. Student engagement is a central theme here, and there are many different ways of engaging students more effectively in their learning: through the exploration of 'real-world questions and problems' (Gauntlett 2011, p. 238), through collaborative approaches to learning, through critical reflection (e.g. reflecting on 'mistakes' as opportunities for learning) and through active, multisensory and experiential learning.

Chatterjee et al. (2015) particularly emphasise the value of object-based learning in higher education. They argue that the engagement of multiple senses (i.e. touch, vision, smell, hearing and/or taste) in close interaction with objects can lead to more holistic learning experiences that engage a greater range of different learning styles (Chatterjee et al. 2015, pp. 2–5). Chatterjee et al. focus on students' hands-on engagement with artefacts from museum collections, but their findings highlight the benefits of object-based, multisensory learning in higher education in a much broader sense. Their research shows that a more engaging, active learning experience is likely to lead to a greater level of immersion, concentration and 'personal meaning-making', which – in turn – is more likely to facilitate students' innovative, creative thinking. From this point of view, creativity "captures the impulse to think innovatively, and to welcome, access and utilise the unpremeditated congruencies of multisensory exploration" (Morrison 2015, p. 215).

Digital technologies potentially offer exciting new opportunities for the development of creativity, creative learning and different modes of communication. They also offer new opportunities for the facilitation of multisensory learning experiences, particularly in distance learning settings, where multisensory learning experiences have traditionally been much harder to facilitate than in face-to-face classroom settings. However, the use and influence of digital tools in higher education (and other contexts) and changing pedagogies as a consequence of the digital age (Stefani 2017) require further critical appraisal. This includes the question of the extent to which digital technologies can support or stifle the development of creativity and creative learning – or learning per se – and how these technologies can be most effectively used in higher education (Losh 2014).

In the remaining sections of this chapter I will explore examples of how digital technologies have been used in the context of two Open University Religious Studies modules and one Philosophy module to facilitate multisensory, creative approaches to learning. Though the relevance of the findings of these case studies is not limited to these particular subject areas, it could be argued that as an inherently interdisciplinary subject, crossing the boundaries and thresholds of many different academic discipline domains, Religious Studies is in a particularly strong position to facilitate the development of creativity and of creative learning in higher education. As Stefani argues, multidisciplinary and interdisciplinary approaches play a particularly important role in the development of creativity and creative learning in higher education. She points out that creative solutions that are required to solve complex, 'wicked' problems often "lie in the 'liminal' spaces, the boundaries or thresholds of different academic discipline domains" (Stefani 2017, p. 206). Indeed, the *Employability* guide published by the Higher Education Academy's (HEA) Subject Centre for Philosophical and Religious Studies in the UK argues that "in an increasingly global economy, the skills of vision, *creativity* and religious sensitivity, which are developed through the study of TRS [Theology and Religious Studies], will be at a premium" (HEA Subject Centre for Philosophical and Religious Studies 2009, p. 4; emphasis added).

The Open University's mission, with its commitment to widening participation and accessibility, fits very well with inclusive ideals of creativity and creative learning as something that needs to be made available to *all* students (Jackson 2017, p. ix) and the understanding that "a culture of creativity has to involve everybody, not just a select few" (Robinson 2011, p. 3). Although the Open University offers some optional face-to-face tuition, the fact that many students study at a distance and are not in a position to attend face-to-face tutorials (for a range of good reasons) poses particular challenges to the facilitation of multisensory, experiential learning and the development of students' oral communication skills. However, digital technology has created new opportunities to address these challenges creatively in distance learning settings, and beyond.

Before I go into any further detail of each of the three case studies, I should explain that at the Open University, module materials and assessment strategies are designed by a small group of academics (referred to as the 'module team'), and modules are delivered and assessed by a larger group of tutors, who each teach small groups of about 20 students across the UK (and beyond). The modules that form part of these case studies each run over 9 months (from October to June) each year.

Case Study 1: Digitally Recorded Oral Presentations

Why is religion controversial? (A332), a Religious Studies module designed for students in their final year of undergraduate study (HE Level 6), was the first module in the Open University's Arts and Humanities programme that included the assessment of digitally recorded oral presentations. This innovative form of assessment, praised by the external examiner "both on grounds of transferable oral skills, and in breaking the perceived constraints of distance learning" (A332 External Examiner report, 2015), has since been introduced across a wide range of modules in the Open University's Arts and Humanities programme. This new form of assessment was created to support students' development of oral communication skills in recognition of the fact that that "most careers require [oral] communication skills; some require them far more than the kind of written skills fostered through written exams and essay assessments" (Higher Education Academy [HEA] n.d.). As part of this assessment, students are asked to make a three-minute long digital audio recording of an oral presentation. The topic of this presentation is closely related to that of a written assignment (an essay of 1500 words). It basically requires students to imagine that they are briefly explaining the content and main arguments of their written essay to a general audience who are not familiar with the topic. Students with relevant disabilities are offered the alternative option of submitting a written script for an oral presentation.

Supported by funding from the Higher Education Academy, I critically assessed the use of this form of assessment in the context of this module over the period of two years (2014–2015), through the analysis of 50 sample assignments and student and teacher questionnaires, completed by 233 students (sent out to 607 students with an overall response rate of 38%) and 17 tutors (sent out to 21 tutors with a response rate of 81%), and designed a toolkit for best practice in the design of this form of assessment in consultation with tutors and students. I drafted this toolkit on the basis of the survey findings and then invited students and tutors to comment on this draft on online forums (Sinclair 2014; Sinclair 2016). This toolkit has since been shared with other module teams across the Open University's Arts and Humanities programme and at a range of national and international conferences.

The findings of the critical evaluation of this form of assessment highlight the technical and logistical challenges of the introduction of a new form of assessment that heavily relies on the use of digital technology, but also stress the benefits of multisensory approaches to communication and the use of different media. The questionnaires sent out to students did not include any specific prompts or questions about creativity or the benefits of multisensory learning and assessment experiences. However, I was struck by spontaneous feedback that students included in their open comments, which highlighted how much approaching a similar task through both a spoken presentation and written essay can deepen their learning experience. Some students noted that their spoken presentation helped them with writing the related essay:

A benefit was that when I first did the sound recording [...] I discovered I'd missed an important point to be made in the essay conclusion. (A332 Student 2014)

and vice versa:

writing the essay gave me confidence with the subject matter so when I came to write my script [for the audio recording] I felt knowledgeable & comfortable with my talk. (A332 Student 2015)

Some students also said that they were inspired to consider changing their practice of writing essays in future, saying for example:

> I may now say my essay into a recorder, which will be more fluent when I write it down. (A332 Student 2015)

These findings very much reflect Thompson's (2014) and Elbow's (2012) views on the opportunities that multisensory approaches can bring to the development of sophisticated communication skills, and the mutually beneficial relationship between oral and written communication skills in particular. Survey responses also showed that this form of assessment can be of particular benefit to students who struggle to express themselves in writing, such as students with dyslexia, as they appreciated the opportunity to express themselves through a different medium. This is reflected in the following open comment from a student:

> As a dyslexic I really enjoyed this part [of the assignment], as I was able to express my ideas much better. (A332 Student 2015)

In fact, all student survey respondents, who identified themselves as dyslexic, specified that they would welcome the wider adoption of this form of assessment in the Arts and Humanities programme at the Open University.

However, the novelty of this form of assessment posed a number of challenges. Especially in the first year it was introduced, survey responses clearly reflected that some students felt very anxious about this new form of assessment. These anxieties were, for example, related to the fact that some students had little or no prior experience of delivering oral presentations or of using digital audio recording technology in this way. These difficulties were exacerbated by technical teething problems of the Open University's in-house audio recording tool. Furthermore, the analysis of tutor feedback revealed discrepancies in the quality and type of feedback that tutors provided in the first year this form of assessment was introduced. This indicated that tutors needed more support in the implementation of this new form of assessment, particularly since it was – at that point – not only new to students, but also to many tutors. This finding led to the further revision and clarification of the marking criteria the module team provides to both tutors and students for this assignment and highlights the challenges associated with supporting both students and tutors in the introduction of innovative assessments.

The findings of this study also highlight the limitations of a relatively isolated assessment of a particular skill or mode of communication in terms of its effect on the development of these skills. This is why a further range of preparatory activities and resources have since been included in this module to support students in the development of oral presentation skills as well as the technical skills required for making a digital audio recording. While this Religious Studies module pioneered this form of assessment in the Open University's Arts and Humanities programme, this form of assessment has since been included – in a variety of adapted guises – in a wide range of different modules at different levels of study across this programme. Collaboration between module teams in the development of this form of assessment and related assessment criteria has aided the formation of a consistent approach to this new form of assessment across the Open University's Arts and Humanities programme. This has enabled students to build on their tutors' feedback (and 'feed forward') in the development of their oral presentation skills across different modules (see also: Sinclair 2016). This highlights the need to carefully manage the implementation of new forms of assessment, particularly when a shared understanding of the aims and purpose of this form of assessment need to be reached across different modules and tutors.

Case Study 2: Offering Students a Choice Between the Assessment of Oral Presentations and Presentation Slides

Key questions in philosophy (A333), a Philosophy module for Open University students in their final year of undergraduate study (HE Level 6), further develops the oral assessment discussed in Case Study 1. It offers students a choice between submitting a digitally recorded four minute long oral presentation (using the same Open University in-house audio recording tool as the Religious Studies module discussed above) and presentation slides. Students who choose the option of a slide-style presentation are asked to create this using slide-presentation software or an ordinary word-processing package and to not exceed 500 words (including headings and notes). As with Case Study 1, this assignment is closely linked to an essay-writing task. Whichever style of presentation students choose for this assignment, they are asked to present the key points of their essay clearly and succinctly in the form of a brief summary aimed at a general audience who are not familiar with the topic.

To critically assess this form of assessment, I worked together with the A333 module team in the design of questionnaires which were sent out to 281 students in March 2016, of whom 81 students responded. 49% of the respondents had submitted an oral recording and 51% had submitted a slide-style presentation. Surveys were also sent out to all 14 tutors, of whom 10 (71%) responded.

The questions asked in this questionnaire focused more explicitly on creativity than the survey for Case Study 1 had done. "I thought that recording a spoken presentation would be more creative than putting together presentation slides" was, for example, part of a list of options students could select as reasons why they chose either form of assessment. Indeed, this was the second most frequently selected reason, chosen by 34% of the respondents who opted for the digitally recorded presentation, just after "My prior experience prepared me better for the oral recording than for the slide presentation" (which was chosen by 39%). Prior experience featured even more strongly as a motivation among those students who opted for the presentation slides (selected by 46%). However, creativity was also mentioned as an influential motivation among this group of students. "I thought that making presentation slides would be more creative than an oral recording" was the joint second most frequently mentioned reason for choosing the presentation slides, mentioned by 27% of the respondents who opted for this form of assessment, jointly with "I didn't feel confident in my oral presentation skills".

While the findings suggest that many students value opportunities to express and develop their creativity, a large majority of survey respondents (80% of respondents who opted for presentation slides and 71% of respondents who opted for the oral presentation) did not think that either the creation of an audio recording or the preparation of presentation slides was *more* creative than writing an essay. Some students even stressed in their open comments that "academic writing requires much more creativity" (A333 student 2016) and argued, for example, that a four minute oral presentation was too short to allow creativity to unfold. Others felt that "I wouldn't particularly say that the oral recording was more or less difficult or more or less creative than the essay, it just posed a different challenge" (A333 student 2016).

82% of respondents found it helpful that the topic of the oral presentation or presentation slides were based on the same topic covered in their essay (though aimed at a different audience). 49% of those respondents who had opted for the presentation slides and 39% of those who had opted for the oral presentation agreed that they had gained a deeper understanding of the topic by approaching the same topic through different media. While some students noted a sense of unnecessary repetition and duplication, others emphasised how engagement with the same topic through different modes of communication had enhanced their understanding of the subject matter, improved their communication skills and/or built their confidence.

70% of all students who responded to this survey welcomed the fact that they had been given a choice between an oral and a slide-style presentation. However, tutors were divided on whether or not giving students this choice was indeed a good idea. Some tutors felt that it was important to offer students this choice, especially since some students struggled with the technical aspects of making an audio recording. Others regarded the presentation slides as a much easier option and felt that the learning benefits of an oral presentation by far outweighed those of the creation of presentation slides. Some tutors also felt that some students struggled with preparing the presentation slides "because no one quite knows what is wanted" (A333 tutor 2016), which, in their view, also made it difficult to mark this task. As in Case Study 1, this highlights the importance of clear marking criteria.

Only 13% of all student respondents stated that they would have found it helpful if this assignment had required them to submit a combination of both an oral recording and presentation slides for this assignment. When asked whether they would have preferred making a video rather than an audio recording, not a single student expressed enthusiasm for this option. Furthermore, only 27% of respondents expressed interest in receiving recorded oral instead of written feedback on their assignment from their tutor, whilst 35% stated that they would not welcome this (the rest expressed no opinion on this matter).

What stood out for me was that the guidance this module provided in relation to the production of presentation slides exclusively focused on the production of written text for the slides, not images or graphs. Even though Open University teaching materials make sustained use of images, this was not transferred into this assessment task. However, this was not picked up as an issue by either students or tutors in their comments, which might be specific to the particular subject area of philosophy, where images are perhaps not considered to be as relevant or helpful as in other subject areas. Prompted by the project findings, the module team is now providing students with a sample slide show that clarifies expectations and illustrates how images, tables and speech bubbles can be used effectively.

Case Study 3: 'Take a Picture of Religion' Activity

Engagement with images and objects plays a much more prominent role in the subject discipline of Religious Studies. The new Religious Studies module *Exploring religion: Places, practices, texts and experiences* (A227), for Open University students in their second year of study (HE Level 5), therefore includes a range of assessed and non-assessed activities which aim to harness the benefits of multisensory learning experiences in order to foster student engagement and provide students with opportunities to apply and develop their creative and critical thinking skills. Multisensory learning experiences are of particularly great value here due to this module's focus on the study of 'vernacular' or 'lived' religion and material aspects of everyday religious places, practices, texts and experiences. This module will be presented for the first time in autumn 2017. This means that at the time of writing, there has not yet been the opportunity to critically appraise this approach in action. However, the module team has secured funding to conduct a scholarship project critically evaluating this module's multisensory approach to learning and assessment in the first year this module is offered.

This scholarship project will particularly focus on an assignment task, which asks students to engage critically and creatively with different understandings of the concept 'religion' and explore this concept in the context of their own locality. This assignment is divided into two assessed parts, linked to a preparatory 'Take a picture of religion' activity. This preparatory activity asks students to take a photograph of an object or place (human-made or natural) representing an aspect of 'religion' in their locality and post this image together with an image description on an online platform (called 'OpenStudio'), which is shared by small group of other students and moderated by a tutor. This activity also involves an interactive element as students are asked to comment on each other's photographs on the OpenStudio platform. Part A (50%, 500 words) of the associated assignment task asks students to explain why they chose a particular photograph, how it represents something 'religious' and why what is represented in this photograph might be worthy of further study. Part B of this assignment task (50%, 500 words) asks students to critically reflect on their experience of the 'Take a picture of religion' activity and comment on how their understanding of the concept of 'religion' (and of different theoretical approaches to this concept explored in this module) was enhanced, shaped or challenged by engaging with images shared by other students on the platform and with other students' comments. They are also asked to reflect on what they found challenging or interesting about the activity.

Multisensory learning experiences can open up opportunities to many students (such as those with dyslexia, as demonstrated by Case Study 1), as they engage a range of different senses and respond to a wider range of learning styles and modes of communication. However, they can also pose challenges to some students in terms of their accessibility. In order to address this, accessible alternatives are available for this assignment. For example, in the case of the 'Take a picture of religion' activity, students unable to take their own photographs are given the option to upload images from an image bank provided by the module team. All students are asked to include image descriptions as part of this activity, which will support the accessibility of their chosen image to students with certain disabilities. Students in secure environments (such as those studying in prison) are sent a print version of the bank of images.

While this is the only activity using the OpenStudio platform as part of its formal assessment, this module uses a number of other unassessed activities involving this platform. This includes, for example, a sound bank activity, which asks students to listen to, comment on and upload sounds associated with lived religion and religious traditions. Hopefully, the scholarship project will shed some further light on the value of the use of the OpenStudio online platform and of multisensory learning experiences in fostering student engagement and creative learning.

Conclusions

The benefits of fostering creativity in higher education are widely acknowledged, and so is the role that multisensory learning experiences can play in this. While it can be particularly challenging to facilitate multisensory learning experiences in distance learning environments, my three case studies provide examples of how digital technologies can be used to address some of these challenges. They also highlight that innovations in online technology and the use of digital technology in learning, teaching and assessment in higher education involve many challenges and potential risks in themselves, which require critical appraisal.

I have experienced the involvement of students and tutors in the critical evaluation of new forms of assessment (see Case studies 1 and 2) as extremely valuable. Students' and tutors' engagement in surveys and in the development of a relevant toolkit has led to the improvement of these particular forms of assessment and contributed to the establishment of principles of good practice. I would also argue that their involvement in the improvement of these new forms of assessment has helped to bring students and tutors 'on board' and encouraged them to feel more open to innovative and creative learning and teaching strategies and to being challenged in new ways. When it was first introduced, the digitally recorded oral presentation was initially met with a considerable amount of resistance by students and tutors (Case study 1). In turn, the surveys provided students and tutors with an important opportunity to voice their concerns around this new form of assessment, which – in this case – were particularly focused on anxieties around the use of new technology, and helped the module team to address these concerns and support students and tutors more effectively.

Collaboration with colleagues working on different modules (for example, through sharing good practice and co-led scholarship projects) has also been extremely valuable in the development of these new forms of assessment, not least as it has supported the development of a consistent programme approach. It also very much resonates with Csikszentmihalyi's (2013) understanding of creativity as a collaborative process – which is not only relevant to fostering creativity in students, but also to the creation and development of innovative forms of teaching, learning and assessment.

However, it is important to bear in mind that these three case studies are only examples of very small steps towards the injection of creativity in teaching and learning in higher education. Multisensory approaches to teaching, learning and assessment and the use of different media can play a role in facilitating creative learning, but there are many different routes and approaches to this. In order to create an environment that is more conducive to fostering creativity, change is required on a much more structural, fundamental level. This means moving away from a culture in higher education determined by league tables, 'burdensome bureaucracies' and students as customers purchasing qualifications, and a greater focus on teaching and learning as collaborative processes of discovery and growth.

Tips and Discussion Points

- A good way of creating learning environments, where creativity can develop and thrive, is to provide students with opportunities to engage different senses (i.e. touch, vision, smell, hearing and/or taste) and use different media in their learning and assessment.
- Digital technologies (such as audio and/or visual recording devices, including digital cameras and mobile phones) can offer new opportunities to engage students in multisensory learning and to develop and assess different communication skills. This applies particularly - though not exclusively- to distance or online learning settings.

- The use of digital technologies in higher education should primarily be driven by the intended learning outcomes, not by the technology as such. It is therefore particularly important to provide clear learning outcomes and, if an activity is assessed, clear and transparent assessment criteria.
- The use of digital technologies in higher education requires ongoing and thorough critical appraisal, especially since these technologies develop so quickly and in light of the fact that some students struggle with accessing or working with them.
- Be bold and try out new forms of learning and assessment. Consult colleagues and involve students in the critical evaluation of new forms of learning and assessment, and share and exchange learning and teaching resources with other colleagues as much as possible.

References

Blessinger, P., & Watts, L. S. (2017). History and nature of creative learning. In L. S. Watts & P. Blessinger (Eds.), *Creative learning in higher education: International perspectives and approaches* (pp. 3–13). New York/London: Routledge.

Chatterjee, H. J., Hannan, L., & Thomson, L. (2015). An introduction to object-based learning and multisensory engagement. In H. J. Chatterjee & L. Hannan (Eds.), *Engaging the senses: Object-based learning in higher education* (pp. 1–18). Farnham/Burlington: Ashgate.

Csikszentmihalyi, M. (2006). Foreword: Developing creativity. In N. Jackson, M. Oliver, M. Shaw, & J. Wisdom (Eds.), *Developing creativity in higher education: An imaginative curriculum* (pp. xviii–xvixx). London/New York: Routledge.

Csikszentmihalyi, M. ([1996] 2013). *Creativity: The psychology of discovery and invention*, First harper perennial modern classic edition. New York: Harper Collins.

Elbow, P. (2012). *Vernacular eloquence: What speech can bring to writing*. Oxford: Oxford University Press.

Gaspar, D., & Mabic, M. (2015). Creativity in higher education. *Universal Journal of Educational Research, 3*(9), 598–605.

Gauntlett, D. (2011). *Making is connecting: The social meaning of creativity, from DIY and knitting to YouTube and web 2.0.* Cambridge/Malden: Polity.

HEA Subject Centre for Philosophical and Religious Studies. (2009). *Employability: Where next? Unlocking the potential of your theology or religious studies degree* (2nd ed.). York: Higher Education Academy.

Higher Education Academy [HEA]. (n.d.). *Diversifying assessment 2: Posters and oral presentations in undergraduate history of science. Resources Centre.* Retrieved May 14, 2014, from http://www.heacademy.ac.uk/resources/

Jackson, N. (2006). Making sense of creativity in higher education. In N. Jackson, M. Oliver, M. Shaw, & J. Wisdom (Eds.), *Developing creativity in higher education: An imaginative curriculum* (pp. 197–215). London/New York: Routledge.

Jackson, N. (2017). Foreword. In L. S. Watts & P. Blessinger (Eds.), *Creative learning in higher education: International perspectives and approaches* (pp. ix–xxiii). New York/London: Routledge.

Jackson, N., Oliver, M., Shaw, M., & Wisdom, J. (Eds.). (2006). *Developing creativity in higher education: An imaginative curriculum.* London/New York: Routledge.

Kim, K. H. (2011). The creativity crisis: The decrease in creative thinking scores on the Torrance scale for creative thinking. *Creativity Research Journal, 23*(4), 285–295.

Losh, E. (2014). *The war on learning: Gaining ground in the digital university.* Cambridge, MA/London: MIT Press.

McLellan, R., & Nicholl, B. (2013). Creativity in crisis in design and technology: Are classroom climates conductive for creativity in English secondary schools? *Thinking Skills and Creativity, 9*(August), 165–185.

Morrison, E. (2015). Immersive and somatic learning: A summary of creative-based practices as a method for higher education. In H. J. Chatterjee & L. Hannan (Eds.), *Engaging the senses: Object-based learning in higher education* (pp. 207–224). Farnham/Burlington: Ashgate.

Osmani, M., Weerakkody, V., Hindi, N. M., Al-Esmail, R., Eldabi, T., Kapoor, K., & Irani, Z. (2015). Identifying trends and impact of graduate attributes on employability: A literature review. *Tertiary Education and Management, 21*(4), 367–379.

Rampersad, G., & Patel, F. (2014). Creativity as a desirable graduate attribute: Implications for curriculum design and employability. *Asia-Pacific Journal of Cooperative Education, 15*(1), 1–11. Available online at http://www.apjce.org/files/APJCE_15_1_1_11.pdf

Robinson, K. (2011). *Out of our minds: Learning to be creative* (2nd Rev ed.). Chichester: Capstone.

Sinclair, S. (2014). Assessing oral presentations in open and distance learning. In A. M. Teixera & A. Szűcs (Eds.), *Challenges for research into open and distance learning: Doing things better – Doing better things* (pp. 203–212). Oxford: European Distance and E-Learning Network (EDEN).

Sinclair, S. (2016). The introduction and refinement of the assessment of digitally recorded oral presentations. *Open Learning: The Journal of Open and Distance Learning, 31*(2), 163–175. Special issue on Assessment in Open, Distance and e-Learning: Lessons from Practice.

Stefani, L. (2017). Realizing the potential for creativity. In L. S. Watts & P. Blessinger (Eds.), *Creative learning in higher education: International perspectives and approaches* (pp. 196–209). New York/London: Routledge.

Thompson, P. (2014, May). What talking can do for academic writing. *patter.* [Blog] Available online at http://patthomson.wordpress.com/2014/05/22/what-talking-can-do-for-academic-writing/

Watts, L. S., & Blessinger, P. (2017). The future of creative learning. In L. S. Watts & P. Blessinger (Eds.), *Creative learning in higher education: International perspectives and approaches* (pp. 213–230). New York/London: Routledge.

7

That's Cheating: The (Online) Academic Cheating 'Epidemic' and What We Should Do About It

David J. Pell

Introduction

From their own experience, many UK academic practitioners may share my worry about the claimed 'epidemic' of cheating amongst students in higher education (HE) especially in the context of ever increasing online opportunities. My concern was first prompted by the 'puzzle' of why over 10 years (part-time) face to face teaching of mostly foreign international business masters students in a brick university, I detected typically online aided academic cheating, by approaching one third,[1] whereas during my 25 years of (part-time) Open University (OU) distance science and social science undergraduate teaching of many times more mostly UK students apparently only a handful of cases amongst them was detected by the University. Investigating this 'puzzle' in the context of a claimed cheating 'epidemic' led me to this wider enquiry into academic misconduct and especially that facilitated online.

D. J. Pell (✉)
Open University, Milton Keynes, UK
e-mail: d.j.pell@open.ac.uk

© The Author(s) 2018
J. Baxter et al. (eds.), *Creativity and Critique in Online Learning*,
https://doi.org/10.1007/978-3-319-78298-0_7

The chapter begins with an explanation of what is usually meant by academic misconduct in the UK context. It then outlines the apparent scale and context of the claimed cheating epidemic and in particular the online aspects. A focus on some aspects of the motivational and moral context of this follows. Providing an outline of some online cheating methods, the chapter concludes with a review of UK responses to them and an argument for what more should be done.

Defining Academic Misconduct or 'Cheating'

Bretag's (2016) comprehensive, edited 'Handbook of Academic Integrity' shows clearly that there is no worldwide consensus on what amounts to academic misconduct. 17 authors representing 39 countries explained different national/regional interpretations.[2] Fishman (2016), for example, presents higher education in the United States as a relatively young system underpinned by Judeo-Christian morality causing instructors to be educators and disciplinarians. In contrast Orim (2016) explains that the focus in Nigeria has been more narrowly on students' examination malpractice instead of other breaches of academic integrity by both staff and students. Chen and Macfarlane (2016) present academic misconduct in Chinese HE as widespread and entrenched in part as a result of guanxi (networks of influential relationships) and because, they say, the state has normalised certain unethical practices. Mohanty (2016) explains that in India academic integrity concern is in its infancy because there is no national policy, planning or implementation and organized efforts at institutional level have made insufficient progress.

The University of Edinburgh's (2016) definition of academic misconduct is typical of UK HE institutions, stating that it is: 'any type of cheating that occurs in relation to a formal academic exercise.' It lists examples as plagiarism, collusion, falsification (such as presenting fictitious or distorted data, evidence, references or citations), cheating (submitting work which is not one's own), deceit (such as 'resubmitting one's own previously assessed work') and personation.

This chapter is concerned especially with the online aspects of all such types of academic misconduct and takes a retributive justice understanding of misconduct.

The Nature and Scale of Academic Cheating

Increasing and sometimes dramatic UK media coverage has been given to this subject. A report of an investigation by the Quality Assurance Agency for Higher Education (2016), for example, found a 'growing threat to UK higher education from custom essay writing services' and received some attention (e.g. Havergal 2016). Its subsequent guidance to universities (The Quality Assurance Agency 2017a, b) on how to clamp down on this, however, received much more publicity. This was probably because the UK Universities Minister[3] Jo Johnson promised that the new regulator, the Government's Office for Students (OFS), will "ensure that the sector implements strong policies and sanctions to address this important issue in the most robust way possible" (Turner 2017). Turner claimed that institutions which fail to do this could be stripped of their powers to award degrees by the OFS.

Much publicity was also given to the report of an investigation for The Times newspaper by Mostrous and Kenber (2016) which claimed that 'Universities face [a] student cheating crisis' given that the previous three years saw close to 50,000 students at British universities caught cheating. They argued that the crisis goes well beyond 'copy and paste' type plagiarism from websites and includes other practices such as use of the 'digital paper mills' of the essay writing industry. They also note that collusion through the digital intimacy of social networks including assignment writing and impersonation for example by friends, parents et cetera with a vested interest in the student's success has become easier through online communication.

A similar investigation was reported a year earlier for a British television documentary for Channel Four (Dispatches 2015) and suggested that figures on the scale of academic cheating based on detected cheating are a significant underestimate. It found that over four years, almost 60,000 UK university students were accused of plagiarism and, citing Dr Thomas Lancaster, claimed that recorded plagiarism is "just the tip of the iceberg."[4]

Nevertheless, there are possible reasons for universities not to try too hard to detect or publicise incidents of cheating. Professor Alan Ware (2016), for example, Emeritus Fellow, Worcester College, Oxford and Senior Research Associate, UCL, made the following claim:

> Most forms of plagiarism are detectable and most academics want to penalise it …. However, universities do not do so because it is not in their interest, even when the evidence is irrefutable. They fear that both costly litigation and adverse publicity for student recruitment, especially from outside the EU, will ensue. Yet a university is accountable only to itself, and the practice of 'sweeping instances under the carpet' has been evident during the last two decades.

Similarly, Macdonald (2017, p. 8) pointed to '…the understandable reluctance of universities to prosecute students who are also paying customers…' and to a situation where 'Too little prosecution may cast doubt on academic standards: too much may deter the punters.' Further, he argues that academic staff can be sensitive to this strategy and thus be disinclined to take the personal risk of reporting plagiarism. Horncastle (2016) added the more reassuring point that a high number of cases at a university can suggest a better detection rate. Similarly, Martin (2017) pointed out that universities are often unfairly criticised when confidentiality requirements make it difficult to mount a public defence.

An alternative approach to the quantification of the actual incidence of academic cheating has been the (mostly US based) surveys of students. Stogner et al. (2013) for example point to the study by H. W. James as long ago as 1933 which found that 94% of high school students said they had allowed others to look at their answers during an exam. In their own study at a USA south-eastern university Stogner et al. used self-administered questionnaires of 544 undergraduate criminology students and reported a worryingly high proportion of two fifths of respondents admitting to specifically online-facilitated cheating. They related this finding to McCabe's (2005) much larger scale US study which involved 60 institutions and about 50,000 students and found that 70% of undergraduates admitted to cheating. McCabe's study also investigated 'internet plagiarism' and found that whilst only 10% of students confessed to 'cut and paste' in 1999 almost 40% admitted to it in surveys which collected data over 2001–2004. 77% of students considered that such plagiarism was not very serious. More recently McCabe et al. (2012) found that over two thirds of students reported that they had engaged in some form of cheating but that many students do not see plagiarism or colluding on tests as cheating at all.

The findings of studies beyond Western universities confirm that academic misconduct, in the terms outlined above, is a global problem. Coughlin's (2015) study for example examined 48 licenciatura theses and 102 masters theses from five of Mozambique's largest universities using text matching programmes. 75% contained matches over 100 word equivalents, and 39% over 500 word equivalents.

Figures for detected cheating at the OU are consistent with my own experience there. The average referral rate for academic misconduct from the beginning of 2011 to the end of September 2016 was 1.73% of the student population (ACQ 2016), although with a rising trend: 2011 – 1.06%, 2012 – 1.79%, 2013 – 1.67%, 2014 – 2.13%, 2015 – 2.16%, 2016 – 1.88%. In respect of assessment submissions rather than students, 0.61% of these referrals resulted in confirmed cases with 0.28% receiving disciplinary action and the other 0.33% receiving offers of help with study skills.

In summary then, the literature suggests that business and international students are the most likely student groups to cheat. The McCabe et al. (2006) large scale study of mostly MBA students in the United States and Canada found that '…graduate business students cheat more than their nonbusiness -student peer's.' (p. 294). Mostrous and Kenber (2016) found that 'Students from outside the EU were more than four times as likely to cheat in exams and coursework'. Perhaps therefore I already have part of the answer to the puzzle first prompting this enquiry. At a brick university teaching students who are in both the international and business categories, I might expect to experience the worst end of the cheating 'problem' – aided or not by online opportunities.

Motivations for and Ethics of (Online) Academic Cheating

Some scholars (see for example Kincaid, 1997, in Fishman 2016) have argued that originality is a relative rather than an absolute concept. Differing international perceptions add some weight to that proposition. Notwithstanding that, in the interests of the credibility of academia and its awards, we must strive for agreed standards of conduct by all involved. Moreover, many of the students we teach today will be the professionals and leaders of the future and their time in HE will be crucial for the formation of their ethical standards. McCabe et al. (2006) made this point in regard to then recent corporate scandals (see also Martin 2016, and Azulay et al. 2014, on academic integrity in the health sciences). Indeed, failure to bolster ethical standards across any and every disciplinary area is socially consequential.

Our efforts to manage online facilitated academic cheating need to take account of the motivations for student behaviour which include their attitudes and beliefs, and contextual aspects such as the teaching/learning environment and online opportunities. My experience of some justifications given by students, exemplify some of these motivations.

- **Moral relativism:** The behavioural sciences support the view that what others do has an impact on what we do, and, in a competitive society, as McCabe comments (cited in Blackburn 2013): "As long as they think others are cheating, students feel they have no choice but to cheat as well." Brimble (2016, p. 365) cites a perfect storm for encouraging academic cheating consisting of: 'commercialization, massification, disengagement, resource constraints, short termism, and increased (ease of) opportunity' which 'converge to influence student (and faculty) behaviour and attitudes'.
- **Injustice/disadvantage:** An example of this dilemma which is especially relevant to my enquiry is the case of international students studying in a second language. Competition for students can lead institutions to pay insufficient attention to students' readiness to study in a second language making those institutions complicit in the challenges their students face (Harris 2014; Macdonald 2017).

- **An unfair academic system:** Here, a student may feel that the system itself disadvantages them in some way. Barkan et al. (2015, p. 157) explain this claim that 'When anticipated ethical dissonance arises, people use pre-violation justifications to redefine unethical behaviors as 'non' violations.' This may indicate why some students cheat when they are unable to meet academic demands or are unwilling to because it involves unacceptable pain.
- **Acceptable risk:** For some students, their understanding of the teaching environment and their perceptions of the likely consequences from the regulatory circumstances created for them to work within will make a difference to their judgements of risk and the incidence of cheating.
- **Higher loyalties:** For many students, perhaps especially those from cultures where failure is viewed as shameful, or where parents are highly ambitious for their children (Twenge 2014), letting down their family is a huge worry which can far outweigh any perceived moral concern about cheating the (impersonal) system.
- **Unintentional:** As discussed by Barnhardt (2016), it can be argued that it is not immoral conduct or 'cheating' if the student is unaware of the rule which has been broken. The student might however be considered blameworthy as a result of culpable ignorance through an unreasonable failure to know the rule especially where previous warnings have been issued.

Opportunities for Online Academic Cheating

Perez-Pena (2012) claimed that 'generations of research has shown that a major factor in unethical behavior is simply how easy or hard it is'. According to Stephens et al. (cited in Stogner et al. 2013, p. 176) whilst at their best, technologies 'help us do our work more efficiently, accurately, and even creatively' they 'can also make it easier to steal and cheat, or otherwise deceive and defraud others.' Moreover, not only is it arguably easier but, as Waters (2013) suggests, this technology has enabled a paradigm shift to information sharing as a 'natural' way of working for digital natives which blurs the lines between what is cheating and what is not. This presents huge challenges for teaching and some examples follow.

Plagiarism

The best known form of online academic cheating is copy and paste plagiarism. It is very easy and tempting to present someone else's words from websites, articles, blogs, books, Wikipedia and other people's deposited dissertations etc. as your own. It is especially useful if you have difficulty with paraphrasing or expression in English perhaps because it is not your first language.

Put strongly, plagiarism is a failure of academic integrity first and foremost because the presenter of the work attempts to defraud the giver of credit by claiming the words of others to be his/her own. This attempted theft of credit risks devaluing the work of others who (have probably worked much harder to) earn credit by presenting only their own words. Much of the debate about why plagiarism is misconduct however focuses on the idea that it is theft from the original author. Sutherland-Smith (2016) for example discussed the traditional Romantic view of authors as having property rights over their words and how this 'criminal law' approach is arguably outdated whilst remaining fundamental to the plagiarism regulations of many universities.

Plagiarism also extends to recycling your own work, text re-use or 'double dipping' to gain more than one credit for the same work or aspects of it without acknowledging it. Arguably, this should be viewed and strongly discouraged as a 'fraud' in the same way that any other plagiarism should. In his detailed discussion of the subject Roig (2016) however pointed out how doing so in respect of those with limited language / writing skills may be questionable.

Collusion

Collusion can also be viewed as a form of plagiarism. It is work which is presented by students as their own but in fact is the result of varying degrees of help from others, often friends or family but wider social networks provide an even greater opportunity for such collusion. It is not easy to explain to students the difference between collaboration, which is often to be encouraged, and collusion, which is most certainly not; and while proofreading is acceptable it can easily stray into the reader rewriting chunks or all, of a piece of work. Moreover, advertisements posted around university campuses in the UK offer online 'proof reading' services and some of these are clearly business ventures which go way beyond proof reading.

Lancaster and Clarke (2016, p. 639) provided a useful overview of the increasingly common practice of 'contract cheating' or the 'outsourcing of student work to third parties' which is at the thick end of plagiarism (although equally this could be regarded as a form of impersonation, see below). This includes work purchased from the now huge number of online essay swap sites and essay writing 'mills'.

Essay swapping or trading sites are internationally diverse. They apparently include the Australian 'thinkswap.com', and 'allfreepapers.com' for which, like others, you must pay. The Chinese web search engine 'Baidu' provides a library where students and others can upload and download papers. Some of these will be picked up by plagiarism checking systems but 'Studymode.com' offers a variety of writing support services including the statement: 'Original Essays. Search our giant database of original essays classified by topic. We partner with Turnitin to make sure that there are no copies.'

Essay writing services are also internationally diverse. They apparently include 'Oxbridge Essays' which boasts on its website: 'Since 2005, we have written more than 60,000 completely original essays and dissertations.' The cost for an undergraduate essay from an essay mill is likely to be around £800 and available within 24 hours whereas an MA thesis in the same timescale will cost around £4,500 (PhD ten times that price). Bigsby (2015), who writes for an essay mill, claims earnings for essay writers of around £2000–£4000 per month are available (for justifications offered by essay writing sites see reports from Bateman 2013, and Sivasubramaniam et al. 2016). Work which is written to order by an essay mill cannot usually be detected by plagiarism checking systems.

In addition to commissioned writing, Rogerson and McCarthy (2017) drew attention to the ready availability of often free paraphrasing tools online and, studying two such sites (www.paraphrasing-tool.com and www.goparaphrase.com) concluded that whilst the quality of output from these algorithms is poor, students can use them without it being detectable by originality checking software such as Turnitin. They recognised however that the intent may not be to plagiarise and also the existence of a fine line between the use of these tools and de facto plagiarism.

Impersonation

This involves not just getting help with your online assignment or exam but getting someone else to pretend to be you. Where the only contact with the 'student' is online, impersonation can be hard to detect so it not possible to know how common it is. Protecting against this possibility thus presents a challenge especially for large providers of online education. To investigate what validation is being done and challenges to it, Amigud (2013) gathered data from administrative staff at Athabasca University, The Open University UK, Penn State University World Campus, University of Maryland University College and eConcordia, Concordia University's distance learning facility. Whilst the strategies reported were anonymized, they varied significantly. Using a Likert Scale, Amigud found that three of the five strongly agreed and one agreed that identity fraud had emerged as an issue for them. Also, four of the five 'neither agreed nor disagreed' that the identity control measures their institutions employ to authenticate the identities of online students are effective. Three of the five agreed that their authentication system has challenges. One administrator reported students sharing login details and hiring others to complete online assignments.

Falsifying Data

Students claiming to have carried out research such as interviews or questionnaire surveys are sometimes found to have fabricated parts or all of it by taking information instead from online sources and/or from their imagination.

What We Should Do About It

The European context was described by Glendinning (2014) in reporting the findings of the large, 2010–2013 study by the European Commission funded Impact of Policies for Plagiarism in Higher Education project which compared the academic integrity policies and procedures in higher education institutions (HEI) in the 27 European Union (EU) states focusing on bachelor and master's levels. It found that (p. 17): 'HEIs in many parts of Europe had poorly defined policies and systems for assurance of academic integrity.'

Five of the main responses to online aided academic cheating are outlined here. They are not mutually exclusive.

Prevention (Especially of Plagiarism) Through Teaching

Surprisingly, Davies and Howard (2016) denied that the Internet has increased cases of student plagiarism. Less surprisingly though, they argued that catching those who plagiarise and then teaching them how to cite does not work because 'writing without plagiarizing is an advanced skill.' They refer to a 'deep well' of 'rhetorical resources and knowledge' which good academic writers and researchers have but which most tertiary students do not yet have, through no fault of their own. In support of this claim Davies et al. refer to the Citation Project Study described by Jamieson (2013 in Davies and Howard 2016). In this study 174 US first year college students' researched writing was examined and it was found that 77.4% of all the 1911 references were to be found in the first 3 pages of the source regardless of its length suggesting (not always unreasonably) no engagement with the whole of the source. Davies et al. argued that this shortfall points to the need for 'in-depth, long term skills education' which cannot be achieved through computer programmes (such as plagiarism detection systems).

Other educators such as Pecorari, cited in Walden (2009), also argue that we should move away from the retributive justice model of detection and punishment in respect of plagiarism effectively advocating instead that we should teach our way out of the 'problem' by promoting the proper use of sources. Prescott (2016) suggests a collaborative approach to this. Following research using an OU Arts module which, as an early assignment, involved online collaborative writing, she presented this group work approach as an apparently promising way to help with the development of good academic practice and especially for the avoidance of plagiarism. She found that because the students are 'visible' (in the online sense) to each other they tend to become more effectively self-aware and self-monitoring when engaging with sources, not only when contributing to the collaborative writing but also in individual work submitted later in the module.

As argued above, some plagiarism will be intentional and some will result from a lack of understanding of what is required. In respect of the OU for example, Prescott (2016) argues that given its distinctive open entry policy where its new students need have no previous educational qualifications, we might think that such lack of understanding is more likely than elsewhere. The OU's recognition of the challenge of unintentional plagiarism however is shown through the emphasis on good academic practice in its teaching materials and by offering the very small percentage of students found to have plagiarised additional one to one tutorials.

Thomas and Scott (2016) claimed that in the UK there has been a clear shift from detection and punishment to prevention through the promotion of a culture of academic integrity. They pointed to a changed HE environment as a result of the challenges including widening participation, internationalisation, league tables incentivising universities to award more highly classified degrees and an 'arms race' between new ways to cheat and new ways to detect. They offer evidence for this shift away from 'big brother' type plagiarism detection including the changed language of the Quality Assurance Agency for HE in 2006 from requiring 'mechanisms to deal with breaches of assessment regulations' to measures to 'encourage good conduct' and then in 2013 to 'preventing and training for students'. This might include addressing language problems where, as Longman (2014) argues, the solution is for universities to test all their potential incoming students even if they already have recognised language qualifications. It is not fair on foreign students working in a second, third (or further) language, or other students or tutors to try to patch up serious weaknesses in the language of study once they have begun their studies. Trying to teach the relevant language at that point is too late.

In effect, getting better at teaching how not to plagiarise will reduce especially unintentional misconduct and new approaches to this should be tried. In the current educational context however, the temptation to intentionally cheat will still be too great for some to resist.

Prevention Through Honour Codes

McCabe (2005) investigated honour codes of conduct by universities to counter the temptation to cheat. Mostly a US approach, with roots in West Point military codes, they involve pledges not to cheat (amongst other things) and a duty for students to report anyone who they believe is doing so. In a modern version the codes sometimes include student judicial enforcement, an undertaking by the university not then to use plagiarism detection systems and in a few cases even not to invigilate exams. McCabe concluded however that such codes are not a panacea largely because of the cheating which students see in the world all around them as normal. Nevertheless McCabe et al. (2006) advocated the active and explicit development of ethical community building and the centrality of engaging students in that process. Forna (2012) was positive for similar reasons when reporting her experience of codes in the USA explaining how it seems that they work because the students buying into the communities are hard on each other for breaches because that is cheating your friends. Perhaps British universities could learn from that? Thomas and Scott (2016) argue that cultural differences between UK and USA universities make USA style honour codes unworkable in the UK.

'Gotcha', Punishment and Deterrence

In my experience the focus on plagiarism is probably because it is relatively common and because it is the most easily detected and evidenced type of academic cheating. It fits neatly within our standard retributive justice model which suggests that greater deterrence will derive from visibly greater chances of detection and greater punishments both of which are discussed here. Beyond the much relied on Turnitin, there are many checking systems ranging from Copycatch for collusion detection within a student group, Google which is free but does not always give the source of the plagiarism, use of 'statistically improbable phrases' (SIPs – credited to Amazon for its 'look inside' facility) and much more specialised crowd sourced plagiarism hunting websites such as VroniPlag for checking for example the theses of German politicians (BBC News, 27 September 2015). No matter which system is used it is important for academic practitioners to use plagiarism checking systems to best advantage. My experience is of two contrasting approaches.

The first is as used at the OU where neither students, nor their immediate tutors have direct access to the text matching software in use – in this case mostly Turnitin. Work submitted by students is run through the system by central staff. Tutors are then often advised if significant plagiarism or other apparent cheating is indicated. Centrally located academic conduct officers (ACOs) initiate action in accordance with the published policies on academic cheating. In addition, tutors suspecting plagiarism or other cheating (e.g., from the style of writing) may also make referrals for investigation. A range of penalties are available to ACOs including awarding zero for an assignment, disallowing part of an assignment and instructing a marker to assess what remains of a submission after plagiarised parts have been disallowed, and capping grades, typically at the level of a bare pass.

The second approach, as used at my brick university, allows students and teaching staff direct access to the plagiarism checking system. Students can submit their work to Turnitin in advance of the submission deadline and then if the result shows what the student considers likely to be unacceptable 'matching', s/he can produce an amended version and resubmit until satisfied there is no significant matching. Surprisingly even with this opportunity, much work is still submitted with Turnitin showing apparent plagiarism. The advantages of this approach are that teaching staff are directly involved with the problem and are perhaps therefore more likely to respond to it in their teaching practice as part of their professional responsibility. Also, it gives students the opportunity to learn about what is and is not acceptable. A disadvantage is that if so minded students can keep trying different 'cheats' until one shows no significant matching.[5] Another disadvantage is that under time and other pressures teaching staff will inevitably differ in terms of the amount of effort they will put in to the detection of cheating. The more successful the tutor is in detecting apparent cheating then the more work s/he will have in producing reports and attending, at best uncomfortable, 'judicial' academic conduct hearings etc. Detection rates will thus typically vary within departments, and between departments and faculties.

Consistent, comprehensive, reliable and thus fair treatment for students at a particular institution should be the paramount consideration and so on balance well managed, centrally led checking for plagiarism seems to offer the better approach.

Whatever the approach, unfortunately, there can be fundamental misunderstandings about what the checking systems in fact reveal. Students and some staff may focus too much on the size of the percentage 'match' rather than what it shows, a tendency that can be inadvertently encouraged by the way checking software reports are presented. The result is that some procedures / staff do not further examine any work which shows a match below a certain percentage. This may be seen as a practical imperative in response to the large scale of a particular student cohort. Unfortunately relatively low matches for example just 15%, can show blatant plagiarism which deserves to be followed up whereas high matches can sometimes be explained by long direct quotations which are properly referenced and can often suggest some good research albeit highlighting the separate challenge of a student failing to demonstrate understanding by not writing in their own words.

Coughlin (2015, p. 16) makes the vital point that it is not enough for an educational institution to rely entirely on text similarity recognition programmes because not all sources are online. Moreover, he points out that students and paper mills will: 'increasingly translate or paraphrase from foreign-language texts or invent new technical ruses to trick detection programs into overlooking similarities.' The tutor / student relationship is thus vital in this respect in that a tutor who has witnessed the other aspects of a student's work, for example class discussions (online or face to face), previous assignments, emails etc., can draw comparisons and often quite easily spot work which is not the student's. Weber-Wulff (2016, p. 636) goes further in her study of the strengths and the 'complex and deep' weaknesses of text matching software concluding that 'algorithms can be badly modeled or wrongly implemented'. She argues that they 'should not be used routinely on students' texts but only as an additional tool in the academic integrity toolkit' and that 'They can only deliver evidence that must be evaluated by a human being'. To support the tutor and to aid the student in developing good practice in that respect there would be advantages in a university's systems alerting a tutor to a new student's history regarding suspected or actual plagiarism. But this also risks producing bias in the tutor.

The apparently very low, albeit rising, rates of detected plagiarism at the OU described earlier, need some explanation. A significant (but by no means the only) likely reason is the nature of OU study materials. Students have typically not needed to go far beyond module materials provided because open distance learning could not assume local access to academic libraries. This recognition has underpinned the depth, integrated coherence, and excellence of OU learning materials and students have not needed to seek potential source material elsewhere as often as those at more traditional universities. This focus on working with provided materials (at one time mostly OU published books and OU/BBC programmes) seems likely also to have enabled OU tutors to recognise and teach out potential plagiarism problems more readily. The advent of online resources however has radically altered the nature of the teaching / learning environment and the OU has developed a comprehensive virtual (interactive) learning environment which still largely retains the use of OU books (and BBC videos and sound recordings). It is now easier for students to cut and paste from OU or any other material electronically available and the availability of online communication has also made the other forms of academic cheating easier to achieve. Nevertheless, the traditional nature of the student cohort, the quality of the provided materials and teaching at the OU backed up by centralised checking of work, seem to be the main reasons for the apparently low incidence of academic cheating. This provides another part of the answer to my 'puzzle'.

Combatting Impersonation

With technological advances and the relative economic advantages of online mass university education, face to face teaching seems likely to decline and so student authentication is likely to become increasingly important. Amigud (2013) reviews a range of technological methods for attempting to authenticate that the online student's work is his/her own. They include biometric authentication such as iris pattern or fingerprint scans, voice and keystroke recognition. He refers also to a remotely operated 360 degree online camera which sits next to the student all the time that s/he is writing an exam paper e.g. at home. Even if any of these are used as 'access keys' though, someone else could easily be lurking around the corner and use an online device to pull up answers to be signaled to the student.

On the one hand, it is arguable that online and distance learning institutions are vulnerable to impersonation due to meeting fewer students face to face than when students more routinely attended campus tutorials. On the other hand, because of the now often extensive email communication between students and tutors I have often got to know more students rather better than when some were put off communicating by having to 'disturb me' and speak on the phone or in front of others at tutorials.

Designing Out Cheating

In respect of online and distance institutions the QAA (2017a) noted that: 'Establishing authorship and authenticity of work is difficult enough for campus-based students, but there is an additional burden on an institution that offers distance learning/online programmes with no attendance requirements. It guides that: 'Providers' regulations should set out the additional processes for non-campus students to ensure that suspected contract cheating cases are identified and suitably managed.' Lancaster and Clarke (2016) conclude that for the prevention of contract cheating 'it is essential for institutions and academics to consider the ways that they formulate assessment.' One approach, emphasised by Thomas and Scott (2016), is to design out areas of potential cheating e.g. by testing higher level academic skills rather than factual content. Macdonald (2017, p. 8) also has a point in stating that: 'The path to essay mills has been made the more attractive by universities (and the QAA) eschewing examinations'. Arguments about the academic value of examination testing versus coursework are unresolved but real location examinations, whilst arguably not perfect for the purpose, if diligently administered and invigilated can help to add to the certainty that the registered student has achieved the appropriate standard for the award. Face to face viva voce's could similarly be used more frequently and well managed online Skype type oral examinations may also have a role.

In discussing the politics of the academic integrity movement, Drinan (2016) presented a strong if controversial argument that we should treat academic misconduct or cheating as corruption. If we then consider that it is part of the very nature of our education system, then we should say so and it can then be measured and assessed as are other important issues in education such as diversity and sustainability which receive political attention. It is certainly arguable that especially aided by online opportunities academic cheating now needs such wider political recognition.

The QAA's (2017b) guidance on combating essay mills seems to be moving albeit only quite gently, towards Drinan's position in requiring:

- 'clear information for students on the risks of cheating, including academic misconduct being reported to relevant professional bodies
- support for students to develop independent study skills, including academic writing
- using a range of assessment methods to limit opportunities for cheating
- blocking essay mill sites and taking action against essay mill advertising on campus
- smarter detection, including new software and greater familiarity with students' personal styles and capabilities
- appropriate support for whistle blowing – to protect accuser as well as accused
- student involvement on academic misconduct policies and panels.'

In response, the UK Universities Minister, Jo Johnson sounded stronger (QAA, 2017b): 'I expect the new regulator, the Office for Students, to ensure that the sector implements strong policies and sanctions to address this important issue in the most robust way possible.' Macdonald (2017) however, was far from optimistic about this, arguing that: 'essay mills are only an indicator of rot, and eliminating them – even were this possible – would do nothing to address the basic problem. Essay mills will survive, but they will be more discreet, less threatening to university reputation. Government and universities will be seen to have taken action, and nothing fundamental will have changed.'

Conclusions

Most of the research presented above as well as my own experience suggests that, much aided by online opportunities, academic cheating is a serious and growing problem which threatens to under-mine the credibility of the awards of our universities. Some possible prevention measures have been outlined, including a collaborative approach to face to face or online teaching of academic conduct, ethical community building, for example through honour codes, and the testing of all potential incoming students for language proficiency even if they already have recognised language qualifications. It seems that teaching to good quality, comprehensive, learning materials backed up by centralised checking of work as at the OU can also help us to teach out (online) academic misconduct. Impersonation presents as a threat to which online teaching institutions are apparently especially vulnerable. Ultimately the best, though not perfect, safeguard against this may well be to include a decisively weighted, comprehensively invigilated, real location, examination in the assessment mix.

My practitioner enquiry has answered my own 'puzzle' but I have also become persuaded that a great deal needs to be done in UK HE (and worldwide) in response to the challenges presented by (especially online facilitated) academic cheating. In arguing that much academic misconduct is a moral fraud, intentional or not, I have suggested that Drinan's (2016) proposition for gaining greater political recognition needs serious consideration. The QAA (2017a) recommendations and the response of the UK Universities Minister, suggests some such recognition.

Tips and Discussion Points

- Involve students more in developing their own solutions to maintaining academic credibility.
- Explore strategies for designing out opportunities to cheat in the way assessment is formulated.
- Revisit the role of examinations in academic assessment.
- Consider the value of raising the political focus on combatting academic cheating.

Notes

1. This was not typical of the overall rate for the modules which was informally estimated to be 10–15%. Explanations for this are likely to include the probability that I had more foreign students than some colleagues and that there will also have been some differences in how we each set about the detection of cheating. Both of these factors are discussed further in this chapter.
2. These include USA, Australia, UK, Europe, Indonesia, Malaysia, India, China, Japan, The Gulf, Egypt, Nigeria and Columbia / Latin America.
3. Minister of State for Universities, Science, Research and Innovation.
4. Such investigations and reports rarely present cases as percentages of all students at the given universities and it is likely that these would make for considerably less dramatic headlines than the absolute figures.
5. Even where the university does not allow students to have access to a plagiarism checking system this can be purchased for example 'Writecheck' (2016). This business will check a student's paper for plagiarism and grammar for less than $8 and undertakes not to sell the submitted paper which it claims other checkers do.

References

Allfreepapers.com., https://www.allfreepapers.com. Accessed 14 Nov 2016.

Amigud, A. (2013). Institutional level identity control strategies in the distance education environment: A survey of administrative staff. *The International Review of Research in Open and Distributed Learning, 14*(5), 128–143.

Assessment, Credit and Qualifications, Policy Exceptions and Academic Conduct Centre, The Open University. (2016). *Academic conduct statistics 1st Jan 2011 to 7th Oct 2016*, sent to D. J. Pell, 21 October 2016.

Azulay Chertok, I. R., Barnes, E. R., & Gilleland, D. (2014). Academic integrity in the online learning environment for health sciences students. *Nurse Education Today, 34*(10), 1324–1329.

Baidu.com., http://www.baidu.com/ English text: http://ir.baidu.com/phoenix.zhtml?c=188488&p=irol-irhome. Accessed 14 Nov 2016.

Barkan, R., Ayal, S., & Ariely, D. (2015). Ethical dissonance, justifications, and moral behavior. *Current Opinion in Psychology, 6*,157–161. http://portal.idc.ac.il/FacultyPublication.Publication?PublicationID=4540&FacultyUserName=cy5heWFs. Accessed 7 May 2017.

Barnhardt, B. (2016). The "epidemic" of cheating depends on its definition: A critique of inferring the moral quality of "cheating in any form". *Ethics and Behavior, 26*(4), 330–343. https://doi.org/10.1080/10508422.2015.1026595. Accessed 14 Nov 2016.

Bateman, P. (2013, August 1). Why I write for an essay mill: How a 'freelance ghostwriter' haunts the sector. *Times Higher Education* [online]. https://www.timeshighereducation.com/comment/opinion/why-i-write-for-an-essay-mill/2006074.article. Accessed 14 Nov 2016.

BBC News. (2015, September 27). German defence minister denies plagiarism [online]. http://www.bbc.co.uk/news/world-europe-34376563. Accessed 13 May 2017.

Bigsby, C. (2015, January 8). Some cheats are enterprising, if not moral. *Times Higher Education* [online]. https://www.timeshighereducation.com/comment/columnists/some-cheats-are-enterprising-if-not-moral/2017761.article. Accessed 14 Nov 2016.

Blackburn, M. (2013, January). Why college students cheat. *John Hopkins University Gazette* [online]. http://hub.jhu.edu/gazette/2013/january/cheating-in-school-no-easy-answers/. Accessed 14 Nov 2016.

Bretag, T. (Ed.). (2016). *Handbook of academic integrity*. Singapore: Springer.

Brimble, M. (2016). Why students cheat: An exploration of the motivators of student academic dishonesty in higher education. In T. Bretag (Ed.), *Handbook of academic integrity* (pp. 365–382). Singapore: Springer.

Chen, S., & Macfarlane, B. (2016). Academic integrity in China. In T. Bretag (Ed.), *Handbook of academic integrity* (pp. 99–105). Singapore: Springer.

Coughlin, P. E. (2015). Plagiarism in five universities in Mozambique: Magnitude, detection techniques, and control measures. *Journal for Educational Integrity, 11*(2), 1–19.

Davies, L. J. P., & Howard, R. M. (2016). Plagiarism and the internet: Fears, facts, and pedagogies. In T. Bretag (Ed.), *Handbook of academic integrity* (pp. 591–606). Singapore: Springer.

Dispatches. (2015). Channel 4, 15 June 8pm. '*Exams: Cheating the system?*', *Report available: Channel Four Television Corporation*, http://www.channel4.com/info/press/news/dispatches-investigation-reveals-extent-of-student-plagiarism. Accessed 13 Nov 2016.

Drinan, P. (2016). Getting political: What institutions and governments need to do. In T. Bretag (Ed.), *Handbook of academic integrity* (pp. 1075–1087). Singapore: Springer.

Fishman, T. (2016). Academic integrity as an educational concept, concern, and movement in US institutions of higher learning. In T. Bretag (Ed.), *Handbook of academic integrity* (pp. 7–21). Singapore: Springer.

Forna, A. (2012, May 20). Will a student lie, cheat, steal, or tolerate those who do? *The Guardian* [online]. https://www.theguardian.com/commentis-free/2012/may/20/us-universities-honour-code-exams. Accessed 15 Nov 2016.

Glendinning, I. (2014). Responses to student plagiarism in higher education across Europe. *International Journal for Academic Integrity, 10*(1), 4–20.

Harris, K. (2014, July 3). English language tests: Poor preparation? *The Times Higher Education* [online]. https://www.timeshighereducation.com/comment/opinion/english-language-tests-poor-preparation/2014248.article. Accessed 7 Oct 2016.

Havergal, C. (2016, August 18). Bar essay mills from advertising and search engines, says watchdog. *The Times Higher Education* [online]. https://www.timeshighereducation.com/news/bar-essay-mills-advertising-and-search-engines-says-qaa

Horncastle, B. (2016, January 4). Letters. *The Times* [online]. http://www.the-times.co.uk. Accessed 6 Jan 2016.

Lancaster, T., & Clarke, R. (2016). Contract cheating: The outsourcing of assessed student work. In T. Bretag (Ed.), *Handbook of academic integrity* (pp. 639–654). Singapore: Springer.

Longman, C. (2014, September 18). Test foreign students' English to ensure competency. *The Times Higher Education* [online]. https://www.timeshighereducation.com/comment/opinion/test-foreign-students-english-to-ensure-competency/2015741.article. Accessed 15 Nov 2016.

Macdonald, S. (2017, May 25). Of essay mills. (Full version of article published in *Times Higher Education)* [Online]. http://www.stuartmacdonald.uk.com/wp-content/uploads/2017/05/Of-Essay-Mills.pdf. Accessed 4 Nov 2017.

Martin, B. (2016). Plagiarism, misrepresentation, and exploitation by established professionals: Power and tactics. In T. Bretag (Ed.), *Handbook of academic integrity* (pp. 913–927). Singapore: Springer.

Martin, B. (2017). Defending university integrity. *International Journal for Educational Integrity, 13*(1), 1–14.

McCabe, D. L. (2005). Cheating among college and university students: A North American perspective. *International Journal for Educational Integrity, 1*(1), [online]. http://www.ojs.unisa.edu.au/index.php/IJEI/article/view/14/9. Accessed 12 Nov 2016.

McCabe, D. L., Butterfield, K. D., & Treviño, L. K. (2006). Academic dishonesty in graduate business programs: Prevalence, causes, and proposed action. *The Academy of Management Learning and Education, 5*(3), 294–305 [online]. Accessed 13 Nov 2016.

McCabe, D. L., Butterfield, K., & Trevino L. K. (2012). *Cheating in college: Why students do it and what educators can do about it* (pp. 1–37). Johns Hopkins University Press. Available at Google Books [online]. https://books.google. co.uk/. Accessed 12 Nov 2016.

Mohanty, S. (2016). Academic integrity practice: The view from India. In T. Bretag (Ed.), *Handbook of academic integrity* (pp. 93–98). Singapore: Springer.

Mostrous, A., & Kenber, B. (2016). Universities face student cheating crisis. *The Times Higher Education* [online]. http://www.thetimes.co.uk/tto/education/ article4654719.ece. Accessed 11 Nov 2016.

Orim, S.-M. (2016). Perspectives of academic integrity from Nigeria. In T. Bretag (Ed.), *Handbook of academic integrity* (pp. 147–160). Singapore: Springer.

Perez-Pena, R. (2012, September 7). Studies find more students cheating, with high achievers no exception. *New York Times.* http://www.nytimes. com/2012/09/08/education/studies-show-more-students-cheat-even-high-achievers.html?_r=0. Accessed 14 Nov 2016.

Prescott, L. (2016). Using collaboration to foster academic integrity. *Open Learning: The Journal of Open, Distance and e-Learning, 31*(2), 152–162. https://doi.org/10.1080/02680513.2016.1169162. Accessed 12 May 2017.

Rogerson, A. M., & McCarthy, G. (2017). Using internet based paraphrasing tools: Original work, patchwriting or facilitated plagiarism? *International Journal for Educational Integrity, 13*(2), 1–15.

Roig, M. (2016). Recycling our own work in the digital age. In T. Bretag (Ed.), *Handbook of academic integrity* (pp. 655–669). Singapore: Springer.

Sivasubramaniam, S., Kostelidou, K., & Ramachandran, S. (2016). A close encounter with ghost-writers: An initial exploration study on background, strategies and attitudes of independent essay providers. *International Journal for Educational Integrity, 12*(1), 1–14.

Stogner, J. M., Miller, B. L., & Marcum, C. D. (2013). Learning to e-cheat: A criminological test of internet facilitated academic cheating. *Journal of Criminal Justice Education, 24*(2), 175–199 [online]. Accessed 12 Nov 2016.

Studymode.com., http://www.studymode.com/. Accessed 14 Nov 2016.

Sutherland-Smith, W. (2016). Authorship, ownership, and plagiarism in the digital age. In T. Bretag (Ed.), *Handbook of academic integrity* (pp. 575–589). Singapore: Springer.

The Quality Assurance Agency for Higher Education. (2016, August). *Plagiarism in higher education: Custom essay writing services: An exploration and next steps for the UK higher education sector* [online]. http://www.qaa.ac.uk/publications/information-and-guidance/publication?PubID=3107#.Wdye1i-os2w. Accessed 9 Oct 2017.

The Quality Assurance Agency for Higher Education. (2017a, October). *Contracting to cheat in higher ducation': How to address contract cheating, the use of third-party services and essay mills'* [online]. http://www.qaa.ac.uk/publications/information-and-guidance/publication/?PubID=3200#.Wdyggy-os2w. Accessed 9 Oct 2017.

The Quality Assurance Agency for Higher Education. (2017b). *Cheating in higher education: New guidance on prevention.* Newsroom [online]. http://www.qaa.ac.uk/newsroom/cheating-in-higher-education-new-guidance-on-prevention#.WgDI4S-7KS5. Accessed 6 Nov 2017.

The University of Edinburgh. (2016, September 2). Academic misconduct: How the university defines academic misconduct, including plagiarism, and how it deals with suspected cases [online]. https://www.ed.ac.uk/academic-services/students/conduct/academic-misconduct/what-is-academic-misconduct. Accessed 19 Nov 2017.

Thinkswap.com, Thinkswap Pty. Ltd, https://thinkswap.com/. Accessed 14 Nov 2016.

Thomas, J., & Scott, J. (2016). UK perspectives of academic integrity. In T. Bretag (Ed.), *Handbook of academic integrity* (pp. 39–53). Singapore: Springer.

Turner, C. (2017, October 8). Lecturers paid to help students cheat in their essays. *The Sunday Telegraph* [online]. https://www.pressreader.com/uk/the-sunday-telegraph/20171008/281500751465130. Accessed 9 Oct 2017.

Twenge, J. (2014). *Generation me* [online]. http://www.generationme.org/. Accessed 14 Nov 2016.

Walden, K. L. (2009, January 15). Academic writing and plagiarism: A linguistic analysis. *Times Higher Education* [online]. https://www.timeshighereducation.com/books/academic-writing-and-plagiarism-a-linguistic-analysis/404953.article. Accessed 15 Nov 2016.

Ware, A. (2016, January 4). Letters. *The Times*, p. 28 [online]. http://www.thetimes.co.uk. Accessed 6 Jan 2016.

Waters, J. K. (2013, August 9). From texting to plagiarism, How to stop high-tech cheating. *T.H.E. Journal* [online]. https://thejournal.com/articles/2013/09/02/from-texting-to-plagiarism-how-to-stop-high-tech-cheating.aspx. Accessed 1 Aug 2016.

Weber-Wulff, D. (2016). Plagiarism detection software: Promises, pitfalls, and practices. In T. Bretag (Ed.), *Handbook of academic integrity* (pp. 625–638). Singapore: Springer.

Writecheck., http://www.plagiarism.org/. Accessed 16 Nov 2016.

8

The Challenges of Massive Open Online Courses (MOOCs)

Graham Pike and Hannah Gore

Introduction

Recognising some of the challenges of engaging and retaining learners in online courses, this chapter considers issues of learning design and audience engagement in the development of Massive Open Online Courses – MOOCS. We outline the rapid evolution of this field and note some of the tensions around concepts of openness and engaging and retaining learners. Drawing on our experiences of designing a Forensic Psychology MOOC specifically with learner retention in mind, and our analysis of retention patterns, we consider the positive impact of a serialised storytelling approach to maintaining learning engagement for the duration of an eight week course.

G. Pike (✉) • H. Gore
Open University, Milton Keynes, UK
e-mail: Graham.Pike@open.ac.uk; Hannah.Gore@open.ac.uk

© The Author(s) 2018
J. Baxter et al. (eds.), *Creativity and Critique in Online Learning*,
https://doi.org/10.1007/978-3-319-78298-0_8

A Brief History of MOOCs

Massive Open Online Courses (MOOCs) are online courses which do not restrict admission, either in terms of the number of learners that can be recruited or the educational qualifications of those learners. Although no definitions or quantification exist that allow a precise categorisation of which courses might be designated as a MOOC, broadly speaking the term is considered to involve an educational experience which is:

- Massive – due to uncapped registration (the number required to be considered 'massive' is subjective and widely debated).
- Open – in that registration is available to anyone and does not require previous study or existing qualifications; in addition, most MOOCs are free, although some do charge for entry and many charge for certificates.
- Online – with no requirement for face-to-face attendance, though some MOOCs conduct meet-ups or are used as part of flipped classrooms where students view lecture materials at home prior to taking part in activities and discussion; (unlike more conventional 'homework' which takes place following class activity, hence the description 'flipped').
- Course – the concept of a pedagogically designed learning journey.

Although they have had significant appeal, as we will explain, the challenges involved in creating a successful MOOC have arguably been even more significant.

The history of MOOCs has been one of rapid evolution that has yet to stabilise (Mackness et al. 2010). The term was first used in 2008 by educational researchers Dave Cormier (University of Prince Edward Island) and Bryan Alexander (National Institute of Technology in Liberal Education) in reference to a course called "Connectivism and Connective Knowledge/2008" (often referred to as CCK8). Created by two researchers in the field of online learning, Stephen Downes and George Siemens (see Downes 2007, and Siemens 2005), CCK8 was based on a standard campus course at the University of Manitoba and was taken by a combination of Manitoba students and online learners from the general population. Drawing on the authors' expertise in learning based on connectivism theory, the course used a variety of online educational (e.g. Moodle) and social platforms (e.g. FaceBook) and encouraged learners to create content collaboratively through the use of forums, wikis and other tools (Downes and Siemens 2011). This resulted in a large, organic, but interconnected community of over 2,200 learners each with their own personal learning environment (Siemens 2013) and pushed the boundaries of connectivism through 'knowledge distributed across a network of connections' (Downes 2007).

This approach to MOOCs, using a connectivist approach whereby content was co-created by learners, was labelled by Downes as a cMOOC, whilst MOOCs following a more traditional learning approach, in which expert teachers provide a set syllabus of learning material to students, was labelled an xMOOC (Prpic et al. 2017). As well as there being different types of MOOCs, there have also been a plethora of different styles of open online course, and associated acronyms, including:

- TORQUE – Tiny, Open-with-Restrictions, focused on Quality and Effectiveness
- DOCC – Distributed Online Collaborative Courses
- SMOC – Synchronous Massive Online Courses
- SPOC – Small Private Online Courses
- BOOC – Big Open Online Courses
- Corporate MOOC – developed solely for the Continuing Professional Development market
- MOCC – Massive Online Closed Course

Regardless of the acronym, these courses share commonalities in that they are all open (albeit in various forms), online and adhere to a course-like structure.

MOOCs arguably entered into mainstream higher education in 2012, when Sebastian Thrun and Peter Norvig, two professors from Stanford, presented a free online course titled "Introduction to Artificial Intelligence". The course globally attracted over 160,000 learners (many from within the academic community) and was described by Mehaffy

(2012) as the first *truly* 'massive' open online course. From this course Thrun and Norvig built the foundations of their MOOC platform, Udacity.

Further MOOC platform announcements from Stanford continued in 2012, with the launch of Coursera by Daphne Koller and Andrew Ng, and the University itself launching two further platforms; Class2Go and NovoEd. In the same year Stanford also announced an alliance with the not-for-profit MOOC platform edX (launched in 2013 by Harvard and MIT). In 2012 the United Kingdom entered the MOOC platform arena with an announcement from The Open University regarding the launch of FutureLearn. This was an initiative led by The Open University, but conducted in partnership with the British Library, British Council, British Museum and over 20 UK universities. Such initiatives were not confined to America, Canada and the United Kingdom, as further MOOC platforms were soon launched in Australia (Open2Study) and Germany (iversity) (Lewin 2013). It was unsurprising, therefore, that 2012 was soon dubbed "The Year of the MOOC" (Pappano 2012).

The development of so many different MOOC platforms, each operating different business and pedagogical models, along with the absence of any agreed and decisive specification for a MOOC, led to a rather organic evolution of the concept. In addition, each platform differed in terms of what was offered, leading to different experiences, goals and outcomes for the learner, including: subject content; methods for completion; assessment and examination; certification, badging, and for-credit options. The fundamental look and operation of each platform was also quite different, built as they were on different frameworks and scripting languages. In effect, the development of MOOCs has not adhered to any universal principles. Furthermore, many additional platforms emerged within a similar timeframe to those mentioned previously, including Saylor Foundation, Khan Academy, Google Course Builder, Peer-to-Peer University (P2 PU), Udemy and ALISON, but were labelled as 'quasi-MOOCs' by Siemens (2013), as their offerings were outside of the university system and because courses were offered through self-paced, perpetual presentation cycles.

Designing MOOCs Based on Available Data

Even with such a complex landscape to navigate, the appeal of MOOCs is clearly a global one that transcends many of the boundaries, such as those associated with location, time (with options for perpetual or repeated presentation cycles), nationality, age, and professional and educational prerequisites, that are a common feature of more traditional approaches to delivering higher education. Although such openness appears to challenge concepts of access and selection based on prior achievement that are commonplace throughout the global university sector, it is important to note that whilst MOOCs do not place mandatory conditions on entry, many state that knowledge to a certain level or in a specific academic field is beneficial prior to registering for a course.

So, although the only requirement to register for a MOOC is that the learner has access to the internet, it is not the case that all learners will be able to follow or cope with the material presented post-registration. This problematizes constructions of openness for MOOCs, and it is important to distinguish between a course being open simply in terms of allowing anyone to register, from being open in a way that also allows any learner, or at least a non-specialist one, to be able to complete the course successfully. Even if the level and complexity of the material presented is a limiting factor to how truly open a MOOC might be, one important element relating to openness that is offered by MOOCs is that they provide learners with a means of engaging with learning materials asynchronously. This means it is possible for the learner to progress at a pace according to their own schedule, so that the course can be fitted around other demands that might prevent the learner from engaging with more traditional forms of education. In many ways, this latter feature of MOOCs is as important in making them open as is the removal of formal entry requirements. Indeed, if one thinks in terms of learners being able to complete a course rather than simply being able to register for it, then it may be an even more important feature of openness.

As a result of having an open registration policy and allowing the learner to schedule their own learning, MOOCs have an obvious place within a social mission for the advancement of widening participation in the education sector. In addition, there is also a place for MOOCs within other parts of the socio-economic hierarchy. This includes, for example, middle class families embarking on learning through MOOCs as a method to offset the rising costs of education (Thrift 2013). As a result, the population of MOOC learners is truly a heterogeneous one on a large scale.

Despite the large investment in MOOCs and their platforms by the various providers, MOOCs have not yet evolved enough to provide a number of important pedagogical elements, including thorough peer assessment methodologies and tools for dealing with plagiarism and online cheating. In addition, MOOC platforms have generally failed to provide high, stabilised retention rates, robust business models, resoundingly engaging learning design or presentation without technical difficulty. These problems led Creed-Dikeogu and Clark (2013) to conclude that "MOOCs are not an educational panacea" and have, so far at least, failed to live up to earlier expectations that they would be the vanguard of a revolution in higher education provision and funding.

Additional problems can arise as a result of MOOCs being both massive and open. For one thing, although MOOC platforms originated in the West, learners from across the globe can register for the courses. Whilst this produces a richly diverse learner population it does pose additional challenges to those noted above:

- Learners can access content and post discussions 24 hours a day with no barriers to time zones, which can cause issues with facilitation and group work,
- Learners have varied digital and information literacy skills so the ability to read, understand, search, analyse, and discuss content can be considerably more problematic than amongst a traditional cohort of students
- MOOCs are generally presented in English, though this may not be the learner's first language
- Learners may have different cultural viewpoints regarding the content presented that can make the discussions generated more complex and harder to navigate.

Unfortunately, and even though the number of learners who take MOOCs is certainly in a multiple of millions, the data available on MOOC learners that could be used as the basis from which to attempt to address the challenges outlined above are limited. Relevant data are not widely shared across the MOOC community due to the different business models of each of the various platforms and because the platforms are financial competitors. This results in a heavy reliance on academic papers where data are referred to, such as Kolowich (2012a, b), even though the data may have changed in subsequent years. This poses an additional challenge for MOOC authors in gaining insight into the demographics of such a large heterogeneous population and in assessing rates associated with engagement and completion.

Due to the continuing competitive nature of MOOCs, it is not expected that large quantities of data will be released in the near future. The lack of available data compounds the ongoing challenge that the learning designs of MOOCs, and MOOC platforms, are continually evolving, which means any study of the status quo can quickly become outdated.

Data are limited not only in terms of the demographics and behavioural patterns of the learners registered for each MOOC, but by the variety of platforms (each having their own learning style) and the number of presentations of each MOOC which make comparisons across courses a complex affair indeed. Despite such limitations, data are available and analysis has demonstrated that MOOC learners tend to be university educated, to have attempted or completed higher level academic study at some point in their lives and may well have an affiliation to their chosen subject area prior to registering (Zhenghao et al. 2015).

Importantly, and a point that is central to the case study we will be looking at in this chapter, the available data have also revealed that although registrations for MOOCs often number in the tens (if not hundreds) of thousands, the number of learners *completing* the courses tends to be just a few percent of those who start (Onah et al. 2014). In other words MOOCs appear to suffer from very poor retention and completion rates.

Analysis of retention and completion rates is hampered because (as stated above) data are not widely shared between MOOC providers, making it difficult to determine rates across the sector. As a result, individual providers can explore factors such as individual and group motivation, learner behaviours in discussions and forums, and the uses (both positive and negative) of the impact of technological and pedagogical design, but these data will inevitably be isolated to just one provider. This leads to a limited understanding of the "levers of change" (Kraut and Resnick 2010) of the wider MOOC community, and can act as a barrier to designing alternative tools likely to be more engaging, using varying forms of communication, and employing different systems of rewards and feedback (Kraut and Resnick 2010).

Understanding learning design and its impact on the learners may assist in fostering a culture of commitment to learner engagement in the MOOC community. It is theorised that committed learners are more active, leading to healthier social learning communities (Blanchard and Markus 2004; Rodgers and Chen 2006; Fisher et al. 2006). However, it is possible for a learner to be just as committed and engaged without being active socially, through reading and reflecting on course content and the interactions of others.

Regarding the future of MOOCs, some notable commentators have proclaimed that the MOOC is "dead" (Charbonneau 2013; Weller 2013), but it could be that the future of open online courses is one of shape-shifting rather than one of demise. MOOC content providers and platform hosts continually adapt their MOOCs and their platforms depending on the statistics that they have. With the movement towards MOOCs for-credit by a number of institutions including Georgia Institute of Technology, University of Illinois, University of Colorado, MIT, The Open University and the University of Leeds to name but a few, the evolution of MOOC offerings continues. For example, Udacity has launched a range of professionally endorsed nanodegrees (a short, 6–12 month, online degree) with Google, Amazon Web Services, GitHub, Facebook and Mercedes Benz.

MOOC Engagement

One of the largest challenges facing MOOCs is undoubtedly engagement, with poor engagement undoubtedly contributing to poor completion rates. The majority of studies focusing upon learner engagement have taken place within a classroom setting, and engagement is normally based on class attendance, interaction with discussion and grades achieved (Ramesh et al. 2013). Such factors are not easily observable in open courses so it is difficult to use these traditional markers in evaluating engagement rates with MOOCs.

Ramesh et al. (2013) classify learner engagement into three categories: Active Engagement, Passive Engagement and Disengaged. Though the classification for a disengaged learner is identified by a decrease in their level of posting, viewing, voting and assessment submission, it may be that the learner is not disengaged per se, but is instead developing a 'lurking' or passive engagement approach by following activity rather than engaging personally in visible learning activity (Milligan et al. 2013) or is becoming a strategic learner by applying 'surface-level processing' (Biggs et al. 2001; Tagg 2003). In situations such as this, data based on page analytics are not enough to clarify whether the activity is 'clicking or learning' (Reich 2015) without actually making contact with learners to understand more.

It is also possible that learners may be displaying the characteristics of 'uncourse' (Hirst 2009) whereby they are not learning in the linear path set out by the course and therefore not engaging in the forums and discussions as and when expected. The learner may not see themselves as being disengaged, but rather adapting the course to suit their needs as a self-directed learner (Belz and Muller-Hartmann 2003). As open courses attract such high numbers and have diverse learner populations, the development of autonomy in approaches to learning is to be expected (Mackness et al. 2010). Therefore, not all learners can be expected to learn the course exactly as the educator had planned it. This creates an additional problem because the data frequently used to analyse MOOCs are taken at the course start and end dates. If a learner does not complete the course within these dates then they are deemed as disengaged, but may of course go on to complete it later. As MOOCs are a form of informal learning, it must be considered that learners have a more relaxed view as to the importance of the end date and therefore they can create an 'engagement gap'. In addition, learners may find the embedded conversations disparate and overwhelming due to the large volume of learners (Lau 2014), which again can cause problems in determining engagement through data relating to active posting.

Research has been conducted on the use of videos and forums in open courses (Sinha et al. 2014; Ramesh et al. 2014; Rosé et al. 2014; Wen et al. 2014a, b; Yang et al. 2013), however, little research has been conducted into how learners view all component parts of a course collectively (e.g. forums, videos, articles, transcripts, quizzes, and activities) or which they prefer to engage, or not engage, with. This causes problems if an approach assumes there is consistency across learners as one size does not necessarily fit all (Sinha et al. 2013; Lie et al. 2014; Sinha 2014). Understanding what learners perceive to be disengaging is just as important as what they perceive to be engaging as the motivation to learn can be fragile (Barnett 2007). As demonstrated through the literature currently available, engagement is an outcome often used to evaluate open online courses (Ahn et al. 2013; Yang et al. 2013; Yuan and Powell 2013; Glance et al. 2014). However, it is a term that is not clearly defined and the entity of engagement itself is not tangible as it tends to be measured primarily through course completion data which, as discussed above, is subject to other contributing factors.

Improving Engagement in a MOOC

As Creed-Dikeogu and Clark (2013) concluded, MOOCs do not seem to have turned out to be a panacea for widening participation in higher education and, moreover, suffer from serious problems with regards to learner engagement and retention. Although it is easy to be dismissive of the potential of MOOCs as a result of these problems, it is also the case that MOOCs are still a relatively new concept and that the design of many initial MOOCs did not sufficiently take account of the wealth of previous research findings related to effective online learning. This raises the question of whether it is possible to design a MOOC with significantly better retention, and it is this question that we will now explore in relation to the design of one particular Open University FutureLearn course. A number of factors are likely to impact retention, including the length of the course and also the topic covered. As both these factors were determined as part of an institutional strategy and were not under our control, we will instead focus on the elements, most notably relating to learning design, over which we did have control.

The course was on Forensic Psychology, and the original plan was to base it on existing Open University distance learning material, particularly footage from an Open University/BBC 2 coproduced TV series called 'Eyewitness', which followed Greater Manchester Police as they investigated mock crimes that had been staged by the producers in front of volunteer witnesses. The course was to last 8 'weeks', with each week consisting of material taking 3 hours to study. Although the suggestion to learners would be that they work through the course a week at a time (so that a course 'week' equated to a calendar week), as with other FutureLearn courses the entire course would be available the day it was scheduled to begin.

The initial learning design for the course very much followed the standard format for xMOOCs, and was to begin each week with a video introduction setting the scene, followed by largely text-based units introducing key theories, research, principles and concepts from forensic psychology relevant to obtaining information from eyewitnesses. Footage from the TV series, in the form of short videos, would then be used to illustrate the points being made in the text. Learners would be able to test their understanding of the material using multiple choice quizzes. This design was largely an online reproduction of the format used in many face-to-face lectures and seminars, and also mirrored the approach taken on other online courses.

As an example, one section of the course was to explore the use of the cognitive interview, which is employed by many police forces and based on psychological techniques for maximising the accuracy of recall (Fisher and Geiselman 1992). This would be done through text describing the procedure and the research that had been conducted to evaluate it, and then showing footage from the Eyewitness series in which an officer uses the cognitive interview.

Nearing the end of the learning design process it became apparent that copyright issues would restrict the amount of footage that could be used from the TV series, which necessitated replanning the course. At this point, and as a result of research highlighting poor engagement and completion rates (see, for example, Kizilcec et al. 2013) it was decided to focus more upon possible mechanisms that would improve learner retention and engagement across the eight weeks of the course. As a result the course was reconceptualised as a 'whodunnit' style story, in which learners would follow (fictional) detectives as they investigated a crime. The psychological theory and research would be introduced at relevant points throughout this story in a similar fashion to DVD extras which offer a behind-the-scenes look at a feature film.

Much research has been conducted into the role that narrative structure can have in learning and memory for information. For example, Kulkofsky et al. (2008) found that narrative cohesion was linked to accuracy of remembering in children aged 3–5, and Wang et al. (2015) showed that encoding information in a narrative form helped improve accuracy when memory for a story was tested 6 months later. However, in relation to MOOCs, it is the retention of learners rather than the learners' retention of information that is the key challenge. Although a narrative structure could make information easier to learn, and this might positively impact retention, there are other elements of narrative structure that could be more directly beneficial.

In this case a story was constructed about two fictional detectives, one (DI Jake Bullet) to represent an old fashioned style of policing based on hunches, and one (DS Lara Sund) to represent a more modern, evidence based form of policing that incorporates findings from psychological research. Each detective investigated an armed robbery that had been staged for the Eyewitness TV series, interviewing witnesses and obtaining evidence according to their own distinctive approach.

This is illustrated in the example of the cognitive interview. In the redesigned course witness interviewing was initially introduced by audio material following DI Bullet as he interviewed the witnesses. Learners then evaluated the evidence gained, before learning about the dos and don'ts of interviewing based on psychological research, before being introduced to the cognitive interview. They then heard DS Sund use the cognitive interview, before evaluating the evidence gained and comparing the techniques used by Bullet and Sund. Thus, teaching the cognitive interview was based within an overall narrative relating to the ongoing investigations, as well as using a specific narrative device of showing the 'wrong' way to do something, before showing the benefits of an alternative approach, that also mirrored the development of police interviewing techniques in the real world.

Although the provision for self-paced and scheduled study is undoubtedly a feature of MOOCs that is important in supporting a widening participation audience, particularly in that it makes study amenable to those with employment and carer responsibilities, it is not without its disadvantages as a pedagogic tool. The issue is primarily one of motivation (see Littlejohn et al. 2016), notably that self-motivation is acknowledged as a key problem for learners in all types of education, but perhaps particularly in distance/correspondence education. As progression through the course is entirely learner-paced and no deadlines are imposed, motivation to continue is undoubtedly one of the factors that has caused the low retention and completion rates in MOOCs for which there are zero barriers to exit.

Although imposing deadlines and study rates would unpick one of the fundamental elements that makes a MOOC a MOOC, and be problematic for those with demanding employment and carer responsibilities, it is possible to change one aspect of MOOC delivery that could impact motivation and engagement whilst avoiding these downsides. The standard approach to presenting a MOOC is to allow learners access to the entire course once they have registered. Even if later elements of the course cannot be accessed until earlier sections have been navigated, it is possible for a learner to complete the entire course immediately once it has been released. An alternative approach involves the serial release of discrete learning units, even if completion of each unit remains learner-paced. The advantage of such an approach is that new points of engagement/re-engagement are introduced that could act to motivate/re-motivate learners, whilst the obvious disadvantage is that it would stop a learner keen to complete the course in a reduced timeframe and potentially require learners to engage with the course over a much longer time period. This is a similar distinction, with similar issues regarding retention, to that of box-set binge watching compared with the weekly release of TV show episodes.

The serialisation approach seemed particularly apposite given the narrative elements used in the learning design, which also provided a rationale for holding back later weeks so as to avoid plot spoilers. Thus, each week revealed a little more about the ongoing investigations of the two detectives and focused on different types of evidence and the psychology behind these. The hope was that learners would get caught up in the stories in a similar fashion to reading a crime novel, and that wanting to find out whodunit would keep them engaged to the end of the course (at which point they would get to watch the crime as it had been committed and also see whether a team of detectives from the Greater Manchester Police had been able to solve it).

Evaluating the Forensic Psychology MOOC

As discussed above, there are a number of ways of evaluating the success of a MOOC in terms of engaging learners, but as the main aim of utilising a narrative approach to learning design was to attempt to retain the engagement of learners throughout the course, evaluation here will focus on the number of learners completing each week of the course.

In Fig. 8.1 data are presented regarding the percentage of learners who completed the first and last 'steps' (a FutureLearn term equating to activity) in each of the eight weeks.

As can be seen from Fig. 8.1, there was a large loss (34.32%) of learners during week 1, but a much reduced rate of loss with each subsequent week so that comparatively few learners dropped out once they reached week 4.

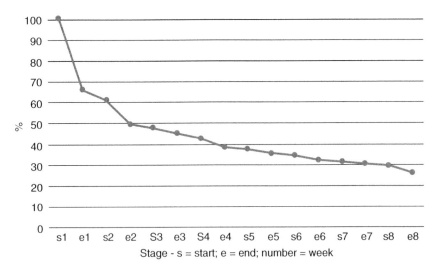

Fig. 8.1 Retention of learners over the eight weeks of the course

The apparent drop at the end of week 8 which does not quite follow the pattern from previous weeks could be an artefact of learners completing the entire course, but not the very final step which contained information about further courses rather than being a substantive part of the course itself.

Further analysis of the data presented in Fig. 8.1 revealed that on average 3.87% of learners who completed the previous week (or started the course with respect to week 1) did not study the subsequent week; whilst 11.96% of learners who began studying a week did not complete that week. In other words, mean drop-out of learners was 3.87% between weeks and 11.96% within weeks, indicating that learners are more likely to drop out mid-week than between weeks.

As can be seen from Fig. 8.1, there was a particularly large loss of learners within week 1. Removing this atypical week and repeating the above analysis on the data from weeks 2 to 8, revealed the mean drop-out of learners between weeks was 3.27%, whilst the mean drop-out within weeks was still higher at 8.77%.

These results are somewhat surprising, as it may have been expected that a higher proportion of learners would drop out between weeks than within. To stick with the TV series analogy, it would seem logical to expect comparatively few viewers to stop watching mid-episode than to finish one episode but not start the next. Explaining this counter-intuitive result is problematic without comparable data from a course that did not use narrative devices and was not released in a serialised fashion, and this could be a useful focus for future research and evaluation. One possibility is that the story-like structure and desire to find out what happened next did act to motivate learners to come back to study each week. Some evidence for this was apparent in comments posted from learners who were keen to begin the next week once they had completed the present one.

Although further research and analyses, particularly comparison with other, differently structured courses, are needed, the relatively low drop-out rate between weeks does suggest that the narrative approach to learning design was successful in engaging, and in continuing to engage, learners. Indeed, it may be possible to use such narrative techniques to improve engagement further, particularly the use of devices such as cliffhangers that have been used to great effect in other media. Although no formal data are available for presentation here, the narrative design of the course did seem to impact positively the way in which learners engaged through active posting. This was apparent in the number of comments and amount of discussion that focused upon the ongoing story and the two detectives within it.

While the largest drop-out of learners is always likely to be at the start of the course, it is also the case that for the Forensic Psychology MOOC described here, the start of the course focused on demonstrating the real world importance of eyewitness evidence and as a result did not contain as many narrative elements and devices as later weeks. Capturing the attention of learners and getting them caught up in a story right from the start of the course might be one way to combat the retention issue that is clearly a significant problem at this stage.

Conclusions

MOOCs offer an intriguing vehicle for widening participation in higher education, but although the available data has shown MOOCs to be very successful in terms of registration rates, they have been far less successful in terms of completion rates. It is critical, therefore, that their open nature is conceived as not simply as allowing anyone to register, but in constructing a learning environment and content that supports anyone who does register to complete the course. In this chapter we explored possible avenues for increasing learner's engagement with, and thereby completion of, the course by using a narrative structure, narrative devices and a serialised release of each week. The results showed a generally positive impact of this approach, and a much higher completion rate than has generally been reported for MOOCs, but also a counter-intuitive finding that learners were more likely to drop-out during a week than between weeks.

Tips and Discussion Points

- Spend time considering the learner audience of the MOOC prior to learning design.
- Work with the features of the online platform to develop an effective learning design.

- Develop an engaging narrative for the course to encourage retention and completion.
- Don't be disheartened by learners dropping out of the course. Just because a learner doesn't complete every stage doesn't mean the course wasn't engaging, and it doesn't mean learners didn't achieve what they set out to do. Completion isn't the sole purpose of learning.
- Review data after a presentation to see where changes can be made and share findings.

References

Ahn, J., Butler, B. S., Alam, A., & Webster, S. A. (2013). Learner participation and engagement in open online courses: Insights from the Peer 2 Peer University. *MERLOT Journal of Online Learning and Teaching, 9*(2), 160–171.

Barnett, R. (2007). *A will to learn*. Maidenhead: Open University Press.

Belz, J. A., & Muller-Hartmann, A. (2003). Teachers as intercultural learners: Negotiating German-American telecollaboration along the institutional fault line. *Modern Language Journal, 87*, 71–89.

Biggs, J., Kember, D., & Leung, D. Y. (2001). The revised two-factor study process questionnaire: R-SPQ-2F. *British Journal of Educational Psychology, 71*(1), 133–149.

Blanchard, A. L., & Markus, M. L. (2004). 'The experienced sense' of a virtual community: Characteristics and processes. *The DATA BASE for Advances in Information Systems, 35*(1), 65–77.

Charbonneau, L. (2013, June 12). The MOOC is dead, long live the MOOC. *Margin Notes*. Web. 18 Jun. 2013. http://www.universityaffairs.ca/margin-notes/themooc- is-dead-long-live-the-mooc/

Creed-Dikeogu, G., & Clark, C. (2013). Are you MOOC-ing yet? A review for academic libraries. *CULS Proceedings, 3*, 9–13.

Downes, S. (2007, January 3). What connectivism is. *Half an Hour*. http://halfanhour.blogspot.co.uk/2007/02/what-connectivism-is.html. Accessed 3 Apr 2015.

Downes, S., & Siemens, G. (2011). *The MOOC guide*. Online at https://sites.google.com/site/themoocguide

Fisher, R. P., & Geiselman, R. E. (1992). *Memory enhancing techniques for investigative interviewing: The cognitive interview*. Springfield: Charles C. Thomas.

Fisher, D., Smith, M., & Welser, H. T. (2006, January). You are who you talk to: Detecting roles in usenet newsgroups. In *System Sciences, 2006. HICSS'06.* In *Proceedings of the 39th Annual Hawaii International Conference on* (Vol. 3, pp. 59b–59b), IEEE.

Glance, D. G., Barrett, P. H. R., & Hugh, R. (2014). Attrition patterns amongst participant groups in Massive Open Online Courses. In *ASCILITE Conference*, Dunedin. Retrieved from http://ascilite2014.otago.ac.nz/files/fullpapers/16-Glance.pdf

Hirst, T. (2009). *Non-linear uncourses – Time for linked ed?* http://ouseful.word-press.com/2009/01/30/non-linear-uncourses-time-for-linked-ed/. Viewed 04 Feb 2015.

Kizilcec, R. F., Piech, C., & Schneider, E. (2013). Deconstructing disengagement: analyzing learner subpopulations in massive open online courses. In *Proceedings of the Third International Conference on Learning Analytics and Knowledge* (pp. 170–179), ACM.

Kolowich, S. (2012a, September 12) The MOOC survivors. *Inside Higher Education.* Web. 6 Jul. 2013. http://www.insidehighered.com/news/2012/09/12/edx-exploresdemographics-most-persistent-mooc-students

Kolowich, S. (2012b, June 5). Who takes MOOCs? *Inside Higher Education.* Web. 6 Jul. 2013. http://www.insidehighered.com/news/2012/06/05/early-demographicdata-hints-what-type-student-takes-mooc

Kraut, R. R., & Resnick, P. (2010). *Evidence-based social design: Mining the social sciences to build online communities.* Cambridge, MA: MIT Press.

Kulkofsky, S., Wang, Q., & Ceci, S. J. (2008). Do better stories make better memories? Narrative quality and memory accuracy in preschool children. *Applied Cognitive Psychology, 22*(1), 21–38.

Lau, T. (2014, July). Engagement or alienation? Reflections on MOOC design, facilitator role, and context. *Journal of Global Literacies, Technologies, and Emerging Pedagogies, 2*(3), 236–240.

Lewin, T. (2013, February 20). Universities abroad join partnerships on the Web. *New York Times.* Web. 6 Jan. 2013. http://www.nytimes.com/2013/02/21/education/universities-abroad-join-mooc-course-projects.htm

Lie, M. T., Debjanee, B., & Judy, K. (2014). Online learning at scale: User modelling requirements towards motivation and personalisation. In *Learning Innovations at Scale CHI'14 Workshop.*

Littlejohn, A., Hood, N., Milligan, C., & Mustain, P. (2016). Learning in MOOCs: Motivations and self-regulated learning in MOOCs. *The Internet and Higher Education, 29*, 40–48.

Mackness, J., Mak, S., & Williams, R. (2010). The ideals and reality of participating in a MOOC. In *Proceedings of the 7th International Conference on Networked Learning 2010,* University of Lancaster.

Mehaffy, G. L. (2012). Challenge and change. *Educause Review, 45*(5). Web. 6 Jan. 2013. http://online.tarleton.edu/fdi/Documents/EDUCAUSE_Mehaffy.pdf

Milligan, C., Littlejohn, A., & Margaryan, A. (2013). Patterns of engagement in connectivist MOOCs. *MERLOT Journal of Online Learning and Teaching, 9*(2), 149–159.

Onah, D. F. O., Sinclair, J., & Boyatt, R. (2014, July 7–9). Dropout rates of massive open online courses: Behavioural patterns. In *6th International Conference on Education and New Learning Technologies*, Barcelona. Published in: EDULEARN14 Proceedings pp. 5825–5834.

Pappano, L. (2012, November 12). The year of the MOOC. *New York Times.* Web. 6 Jan. 2013. www.nytimes.com/2012/11/04/education/edlife/massive-openonline-courses-are-multiplying-at-a-rapid-pace.html

Prpić, J., Melton, J., Taeihagh, A., & Anderson, T. (2015). MOOCs and crowdsourcing: Massive courses and massive resources. First Monday, 20(12). doi:http://dx.doi.org/10.5210/fm.v20i12.6143

Ramesh, A., Goldwasser, D., Huang, B., Daumé III, H., & Getoor, L. (2013). Modeling learner engagement in MOOCs using probabilistic soft logic. In *NIPS Workshop on Data Driven Education* (Vol. 21, p. 62).

Ramesh, A., Goldwasser, D., Huang, B., Daume III, H., & Getoor, L. (2014). Learning latent engagement patterns of students in online courses. In *Twenty-Eighth AAAI Conference on Artificial Intelligence*.

Reich, J. (2015, January 2). Rebooting MOOC research. *Science, 347*(6217), 34–35.

Rodgers, S., & Chen, Q. (2006). Internet community group participation: Psychosocial benefits for women with breast cancer. *Journal of Computer-Mediated Communication, 10*(4), np.

Rosé, C.P., Carlson, R., Yang, D., Wen, M., Resnick, L., Goldman, P., & Shere, J. (2014). Social factors that contribute to attrition in MOOCS. In *Proceedings of the First ACM Conference on Learning @ Scale Conference* (pp. 197–198), ACM.

Siemens, G. (2005). Connectivism: A learning theory for the digital age. *International Journal of Instructional Technology* 2.1. Web. 6 Jan. 2013. http://www.itdl.org/Journal/Jan_05/article01.htm

Siemens, G. (2013) *Massive open online courses: Innovation in education?* (Open Educational Resources: Innovation, Research and Practice). Vancouver: Commonwealth of Learning and Athabasca University.

Sinha, T. (2014). Together we stand, together we fall, together we win: Dynamic team formation in massive open online courses. In *Applications of Digital Information and Web Technologies (ICADIWT), 2014 Fifth International Conference on the* (pp. 107–112), IEEE.

Sinha, T., Banka, A., & Kang, D. K. (2013). Leveraging user profile attributes for improving pedagogical accuracy of learning pathways. *In Proceedings of 3rd Annual International Conference on Education and E-Learning (EeL 2013),* Singapore.

Sinha, T., Jermann, P., Li, N., & Dillenbourg, P. (2014). Your click decides your fate: Inferring information processing and attrition behavior from MOOC video clickstream interactions. *arXiv preprint arXiv*:1407.7131.

Tagg, J. (2003). *The learning paradigm college.* Boston: Anker.

Thrift, N. (2013, February 13). To MOOC or not to MOOC. *Chronicle of Higher Education.* Web. 6 Jan. 2013. http://chronicle.com/blogs/worldwise/to-mooc-ornot-to-mooc/31721

Wang, Q., Bui, V. K., & Song, Q. (2015). Narrative organisation at encoding facilitated children's long-term episodic memory. *Memory, 23*(4), 602–611.

Weller, M. (2013, May 30). You can stop worrying about MOOCs now. *The Ed Techie.* Web. 18 Jun. 2013. http://nogoodreason.typepad.co.uk/no_good_reason/2013/05/you-can-stop-worrying-about-moocs-now.html?utm_source=feedburner&utm_medium=feed&utm_campaign=Feed%3A+TheEdTechie+%28The+Ed+Techie%29

Wen, M., Yang, D., & Rosé, C. P. (2014a). Linguistic reflections of student engagement in massive open online courses. In *ICWSM.*

Wen, M., Yang, D., & Rosé, C. P. (2014b). Sentiment analysis in MOOC discussion forums: What does it tell us? In *Educational Data Mining 2014.*

Yang, D., Sinha, T., Adamson, D., & Rosé, C. P. (2013). Turn on, tune in, drop out: Anticipating student dropouts in massive open online courses. In *Proceedings of the 2013 NIPS Data-Driven Education Workshop* (Vol. 10, p. 13).

Yuan, L., & Powell, S. (2013). MOOCs and open education: Implications for higher education. *Cetis White Paper.*

Zhenghao, C., Alcorn, B., Christensen, G., Eriksson, N., Koller, D., & Emanuel, E. (2015, September 22).Who's benefiting from MOOCs, and why. *Harvard Business Review.* Retrieved from https://hbr.org/2015/09/whos-benefiting-from-moocs-and-why

9

Student Connections: Livestreaming and Creating Community via an Annual Student Conference

Karen Foley and Ian Fribbance

Introduction

A wide body of literature supports the relationship between student engagement and student success (Trowler 2010). Despite differences in definitions and measures, there is general agreement that dimensions of learning which promote emotional engagement are important to developing a sense of belonging (Trowler 2010). This is particularly important in distance education where communities are less physically evident (Thomas 2012). This chapter focuses on how Student Connections, an initiative consisting of livestreamed interactive conferences and podcasts that were developed by the Faculty of Social Sciences at the Open University (OU) in 2014, has contributed to bringing academics and students together to help foster an academic community.

To give an idea of the scale of student engagement, the 2016 annual conference attracted almost 2000 students, more than doubling the number of attendees from the previous year. The success of the initiative

K. Foley (✉) • I. Fribbance
Faculty of Arts and Social Science, Open University, Milton Keynes, UK
e-mail: Karen.foley@open.ac.uk

© The Author(s) 2018
J. Baxter et al. (eds.), *Creativity and Critique in Online Learning*,
https://doi.org/10.1007/978-3-319-78298-0_9

showed the attraction of engaging students beyond the individual module, and also that live interactive events can be a successful addition to asynchronous collaborative work that is sometimes included as part of the module.

Student Connections has had an impact at the OU, with the university now running regular livestreamed interactive events, for example those aimed at induction and the development of students' academic skills. Such activities provide pointers for other institutions who are offering 'blended' learning approaches. They will also be of interest in Universities where students are taught at a distance and therefore cannot engage with traditional face to face activities.

This chapter will outline how these platforms have assisted in providing another thread of support in the construction of an academic community. After initially outlining the theoretical context, the Student Connections platforms and data will be explored. The extent to which Student Connections has developed a sense of academic community will be considered, and the use of this format for other higher education settings discussed.

Theoretical Context

There is an increasing interest in student engagement because of the relationship between engagement and student success, progression and retention, and the teaching excellence of the institution (Trowler 2010). Since it has been established that some engagement activities and platforms can be developed by the institution, steps have been taken to establish emotional engagement through encouraging students to participate in co-curricular activities and peer to peer support.

Despite historical contestations about its definition, student engagement includes widely agreed components, and has been described by one author as;

> The interaction between the time, effort and other resources invested by both students and their institutions intended to optimise the student experience and enhance learning outcomes and the development of students and the performance and reputation of the institution. (Trowler 2010 p. 3)

There have been many models and proposed measures of engagement, predominantly focused on normative populations of students in full time, brick universities. Initially these centred on the interaction between the student and the learning activities of the institution, so measures such as attendance, on time task completion and grades were key indicators of engaged students (Ashwin and McVitty 2015).

Although behavioural and cognitive aspects are important to student success and institutional reputation, emotional interaction is seen as a third of these dimensional components, and Trowler explains why it is such an important element;

> Acting without feeling engaged is just involvement or even compliance: Feeling engaged without acting is dissociation. (Trowler 2010 p. 5)

This is echoed by Coates, who makes the point that the term engagement takes on different meanings when it is used as a noun and a verb (Coates 2006). The emotional aspect of student engagement offers a different insight into students' levels of engagement, and whilst it can be individual, there are links to co-curricular activities which may include learning communities or social learning.

Whilst communities may naturally occur on campus at brick universities, for distance learners, communities are potentially inaccessible, abstract concepts. Coates (2005) argues that institutions should scaffold opportunities for interactions and that this cannot just be left to emerge organically. Indeed, as was argued by Callaghan and Fribbance in Chap. 5 Wenger advocates that learning communities can be both designed and supported. He writes that after designing events, some sense of leadership (formal and informal), connectivity and membership aspects are important. Furthermore, he argues that connecting with others in a variety of media formats can establish meaningful connections (Wenger 2000). Scale of community membership is also important, and whilst critical mass is important in establishing a community, it should not be too wide or "grab people's identities" (Wenger 2000 p. 232).

The theoretical background to Student Connections is in the student engagement arena, particularly emotional engagement, and the idea that it is possible, and perhaps even beneficial to scaffold community building initiatives. The Student Connections events are co-curricular, covering student from across a number of Social Science disciplines. While we argue that such interactions are an example of informal learning, we recognise that it can only play a small part in building learning communities. However, we believe that even in institutions (such as the OU) with a geographically dispersed student population, it is possible for a number of threads to combine to create a bond of connection and community.

Methods

Measuring the effectiveness of an abstract concept such as "belonging" is obviously difficult. However, if we assume that choosing to participate in Student Connections signals a desire to be part of an academic community, then the numbers of participants and nature of their interaction can be seen as a reasonable measurement of engagement. It is, in theory, simple to calculate the number of people logging onto an event, but there are a range of complexities to do with the forms of data that are available, and the inferences we can make. The ongoing evaluation of these types of events is a work in progress, but our methods of analysis and range of data sources have developed considerably. Despite these developments, emotional aspects of engagement remain difficult to measure and point to an area for future research.

The first Student Connections conference had limited evaluation resource and limited data was gathered. Much of the development of the concept from the first event to the second was heuristic, and because the events were very different year on year comparisons are made with caution. Formal evaluations became a part of the Student Hub Live events which were established by the OU's Institute of Educational Technology (IET) after the first Student Connections conference. In addition to developing a framework for evaluation, resources were available to support the second Student Connections conference.

IET used both quantitative and qualitative data in evaluating impact. Analytics, (google analytics) were used to measure participation during the live event. Like most conferences, attendance is a key indicator of success, and the quantitative data included measures of traffic and attendance, however because there are a range of data points (from the website and from livestream) it is difficult to combine these to create a clear and accurate picture of the audiences' participation.

Substantial amounts of qualitative data were also generated. This related to the experience of participating from the perspective of the online audience and also the panellists who delivered live sessions. Data included online surveys, chat logs (the comments that were made in the chat boxes) and feedback forms from live panellists.

The complexities of these data sources and the insight they are able to provide us with will be discussed in the data section.

Student Connections in the Context of Student Engagement and Social Learning

The primary aim of Student Connections was to enhance an academic community for Social Science students at the Open University. The concept of the conference was initially proposed to invigorate the Social Science qualifications website – a space that supported students within their wider qualification, and that supplemented their individual module or course. The rationale for this was that students at traditional brick universities have access to community networks, but these are less available to students studying in a distance learning environment. The aim was to develop an extracurricular space that was also wider than the module.

Returning to the theoretical concept of community that was introduced earlier, although community can be interpreted in different ways, common definitions in the student engagement literature centre on aspects such as belonging and feeling included in a collective group (Ashwin and McVitty 2015). Belonging in this sense might contribute to improving retention, particularly in a part-time distance learning environment (Thomas 2015).

Community is of particular relevance to OU students who are studying at a distance with no access to the organic community that students at brick universities have as standard (Thomas 2012). This lack of identification with an academic community can be exacerbated because part time students tend to identify less with the label of 'student'; they often study part-time and combine being a student with many other roles and responsibilities (Butcher 2015). As a result, students in distance learning environments can feel isolated and disconnected, often assuming that they are performing less well than others. Establishing a community can not only facilitate dialogue about subjects that students are passionate about, but the protective factor of reducing isolation and normalising problems can allow students to seek support in addressing study issues (Butcher 2015; Butcher and Rose-Adams 2015). This echoes the importance of comparison to others that Wenger outlines in social learning (Wenger 2000).

In addition to the challenges in facilitating community in a distance learning environment, the OU experiences issues with retention and progression due to its long-standing open access policy (Butcher and Rose-Adams 2015). Whilst the curriculum has been designed to upskill students throughout their qualification, the part-time and distance nature can impact on progression and retention. Indeed, many students study with the OU because of the flexibility it offers; integrating well with other commitments or because of accessibility. However, these aspects can also act as barriers to progression if there is a fluctuation in demands on time.

Within this coverage of the literature it is important to also include the area of technology as a facilitator of community. To date there is little published research on the use of livestream technologies or online interactive conferences. There is only one published similar study involving streaming and synchronous chat, although this was to deliver curricula and was with a small group of students (Teng and Taveras 2004). Although livestream technology is increasingly used in Higher Education to provide remote access and assets of live lectures, few people have used the technology as a platform for teaching and helping to develop a sense of community. Livestream lectures are part of mainstream curricula, whereas the Student Connections initiative is co-curricular, optional and informal. Webinars and podcasts are traditionally used to deliver lectures to an online audience, but the literature around the pedagogy of this format is in its infancy.

As previously outlined, the concept of identity is important in both the student engagement literature and when looking at social learning, for example Wenger's framework includes the idea of connectedness, and shared experiences (Wenger 2000). These themes are evident in the survey feedback from the Student Connections 2015 conference. Digital innovations like Student Connections might offer a contribution to the creation of learning communities, although the extent of the contribution, taken in isolation, may be limited. But together with other informal learning approaches and other Open University driven events such as the Student Hub Live, it helps strengthen the case that a community is developing in both the faculty as and for many OU students.

The format of the Student Connections conference could also be applied to other contexts, including Higher Education and also as an alternative to webinars. The absence of any similar online interactive events in the literature and indicates that Student Connections initiated something new in terms of research and application.

Data Description and Analysis

Student Connections 2014

The first Student Connections conference, which was also the OU's first online conference of its kind, was held in July 2014 during five days and evenings from Monday 30th June – Friday 4th July 2014. The platform that was used, Stadium Live, was developed by the Knowledge Media Institute (KMi) at the OU, and is a technology enhanced learning interface that integrated livestreamed video with a chat function and interactive voting tools (widgets). Throughout the conference, the online participants used the chat to comment on aspects of the video content, and interactive voting tools (widgets) were used during the keynote talks that were scheduled in the evening.

The Student Connections conference was a conference in the descriptive sense, where students and academics came together, and discussing general areas of the Social Sciences. All presenters were offered support from the conference organisers, but most notable was the support offered to student presenters. Calls for expressions of interest for student presenters were advertised on module (course) websites and on the faculty's social media channels. Students were invited to come to "Activate" sessions;

online workshops held in the synchronous conferencing suite BlackBoard Collaborate. Conference organisers and presenters led these workshops, beginning with generating ideas, planning presentations and actually presenting at the Student Connections conference.

The programme represented an even spread of the Faculty's six disciplines and live and pre-recorded video content was alternated. Keynote speakers (such as Meg-John Barker from Psychology, author of the popular self-help book Rewriting the rules), had evening slots when it was assumed that a greater number of students would be able to participate (based on the scheduling of the majority of online tutorials and the increase in students in full time employment). These keynote talks were an hour in length, longer than standard 30 minute sessions, and included bespoke interactive voting tools (widgets).

In terms of the venue, two spaces were used for both the pre-recorded presentations as well as the live ones; a lecture style setting and a more private interview area. The production team vision-mixed, manually selecting the live feeds from the selection of static, cameras to give multiple views of the setting. Backstage, a team of students (who were presenting at the conference) managed the "social media" for the event. This included acting as moderators in the chat discussion, and drawing the presenter's attention to questions and observations from the remote audience.

Whilst the Student Connections conference and Activate sessions formed the key visible outputs in terms of the online conference, the initiative was promoted by the faculty Facebook page and the audio news magazine The PodMag, this was also promoted in the two series of "This Student Life", a weekly audio drama detailing the lives of OU students and their journey to presenting at the Student Connections conference.

The Student Hub Live

Student Connections directly influenced another university initiative; The Student Hub Live (SHL) which was shortlisted by the Times Higher Education awards 2016 in the "Best Outstanding support for Students" category. Since its inception it has been used to deliver live, online interactive events for Induction, module choice, Faculty conferences and study skills boot camps. The Student Hub Live extended the Student Connections platforms and also offered new insights into aspects such as evaluation and effective content programming. Like Student Connections it uses Stadium Live and livestream, and the Faculty of Social Sciences have been involved in many of the programmes, both in terms of academic contributions and participation from students.

2014 Evaluation

The 2014 conference had a very basic evaluation plan and limited analytical resource. Available data was gathered and the practioners reflected on what additional data would be useful. Much of the evaluation was heuristic, with the team reflecting on the lived experience of the event.

The attendance levels and numbers of students who accessed the website were recorded with attendances recorded at 400 people over the five-day period, many of them attending daily. Pre-registrations were also advertised, and over 1,200 people registered. It was expected that there would be a greater number of people pre-registering compared to actual attendance, although on reflection there could have been more correspondence with those who had expressed an interest. The live chat function had over 1800 individual entries a day, and over 3000 individual users have since logged on to the catch up service. Feedback from students who took part was overwhelmingly positive with all expressing the wish that the event should be repeated and that they want to remain involved.

The qualitative aspect was of more interest. The opportunity for students to integrate with their academic institution has led to some long term relationships. Three years later nine of the ten students who presented are still in contact with each other, the researchers, the faulty (mainly through Facebook) and the livestream initiatives which developed from the Student Connections conference.

Equally, the opportunity for students to engage in the chat appeared to be valued. It had been assumed that the chat would be used in a similar way to the use of Twitter at academic conferences, to ask questions of the live presenters or to reflect on the contribution. However, there was more discussion than had been expected, and the dialogue varied from content related to the presentation to conversations of a social nature.

Another surprising aspect was that students did not engage with the programme in the way that was anticipated. Time convenience, not subject, appeared to be the most important explanatory variable. It was assumed that students would select sessions from the programme that were relevant to their subject area, and that we would see different names in the chat (there is not yet a way of measuring the specific participants at this point). Instead it appeared that participants logged on when it was convenient and they stayed because they enjoyed talking to other participants. Furthermore, it was expected that academics with high profile publications or a lot of followers on social media would attract larger viewing figures, and that the audience would be more interested in academic presentations compared to student presentations, but again this was not the case. Despite keynote talks being scheduled in the evening, the daytime saw more traffic in terms of student numbers, a finding that has been replicated on numerous occasions with the SHL. Interestingly, the distinction between live and pre-recorded content was not a key factor in predicting attendance and participants appeared engaged with the chat in a similar way during both formats.

Student Connections 2015

Student Connections 2015 was a two-day event, from Friday to Saturday afternoon on the 29th and 30th September 2015. The event incorporated many improvements based on the Student Connections 2014 and also the Student Hub Live events. Initially, the 2015 conference was planned for March 2015, but there were various staffing issues that made this unachievable. The impact of this meant that the conference was rescheduled to coincide with the majority of module starts, and budgets were signed off one month before the event. Whilst many of the lessons from the previous event were incorporated, the significant reduction in preparation time impacted on what was possible.

Based on the experience of the 2014 conference it was agreed that a five-day event was too long. This was because of staff resource and a judgement that there was a limit to the additional audience reach that five days represented. Therefore, a two-day event was proposed, and this reduced costs.

By this time, and through developments at the Student Hub Live, the "social media desk" (where two students, in the live studio, moderated the chat forum and fed dialogue into the studio) had become an integral part of the programme format. The use of interactive tools (widgets) also developed and became increasingly used to promote audience participation. These included word clouds, multi-choice questions and balance scales. One of the benefits of the inclusion of the social media desk and the display of audience interaction is that the voice of the audience is seen as part of the process when the recording is viewed after the live event.

There were some differences and similarities in the construction and promotion of the first and second conference. A consequence of the short preparation time for the 2015 event was that it was not possible to engage student presenters. It was also not possible to record and edit sessions. This reduced the cost substantially, but also enhanced the live and interactive nature of the event.

Some aspects of the first conference were repeated; the 2015 Student Connections conference was promoted by the PodMag, a monthly audio news magazine, and on social media channels (such as Facebook and Twitter). It was also promoted on module and qualification websites and on the students' home page of the virtual learning environment. On the basis that many curricular activities (online and face to face tutorials) were planned for students in the evenings and on Saturdays, the conference was scheduled from Friday to Saturday. Due to time constraints, pre-registration did not feature for the 2015 event. There were more students at the second conference; the 2015 Student Connections conference attracted 2000 participants, an increase of 500% compared to 2014. There are a number of factors that this can be attributed to, and the impact is discussed further in the evaluation section.

2015 Evaluation

The evaluation for the second conference was more sophisticated, partly because of assistance in the gathering of data from the Institute of Educational Technology (IET) at the OU, and partly due to developments in the evaluation plan for the Student Hub Live. The 2015 Student Connections conference evaluation included a participant survey, panellist feedback, google analytics on the website, livestream views of the event, and the chat log. These methods for generating feedback were based the SHL evaluation plan and a focus on developing good practice, and the survey was designed by specialist in IET who had resource for design and analysis.

Although more data is available for the 2015 conference, there are limitations about what inferences can be made. There are obvious issues with measuring underlying key issues such as emotional engagement based on viewing figures. However, it is possible to identify trends and understand how participants experience these events from their contributions to the live chat. This points to the value of complementary methodologies, both qualitative and quantitative to understanding the value of participating in live events.

Analytics: Website Traffic and Participation

One of the measures of participation is the conference website traffic. This tells us how many people have visited the website, either to attend the conference, or for information. The majority of participants need to access the conference website to access the event. The website includes all the event information including the programme, abstracts, biographies and FAQ's (Table 9.1).

A session is the period of time a user is actively engaged with the site.

Page views are the total number of pages viewed on the website, which includes repeated views of a single page

Bounce rate: the percentage of visitors who only view one page before moving on

Table 9.1 Student Connections 2015 Live engagement: 25–26 September 2015

Measure	Conference website	Livestream
Sessions: total	1848	1219
Sessions: new visitors	853	649
Sessions: returning visitors	995	570
Users	1105	705
Page views	5615	3051
Session duration (mean)	4′46″	6′22″
Pages viewed per session (mean)	3.0	2.5
Bounce rate	26%	55%

In a similar display of behaviour to the 2014 conference where there were more registrations than participants, more people visited the website than attended the live event. The conference website had more traffic (52% more) than livestream and more page views (84% more). The livestream views included those who accessed the event in any format (watch and engage or watch only). It can be argued that the there is a different pedagogical value in knowing that there is an opportunity to connect with others, and actually attending the event. Knowing that a community exists can be seen as supportive, even if students choose not to engage.

As previously mentioned, the conference website showcased conference information and linked to the event. When the total page views are considered in detail it was the homepage that attracted the most website traffic. The "watch now" page was a link to the event. The popularity of the home page is unsurprising; it is common for people to be interested in attending a live event that they then do not engage with, or that they visit the home page more than once.

Table 9.2 shows that for the period 25th–26th September, the three most-viewed pages were:

It is also possible to measure the attendance over time and compare the types of interaction with the live event and also the traffic to the website. Figure 9.1 below shows the types of interaction at various times throughout the day. Replay footage was shown during the non-live times each day between 15:30 and 18:00. All other times included live content.

Viewing participation over time offers an insight into the times of day that events like this may be popular for students. It is natural to see peaks

Table 9.2 Most-viewed pages

Page	% age of views	No. of views
Website home page	34.9	1962
Watch-now page	22.6	1269
Programme page	15.1	848

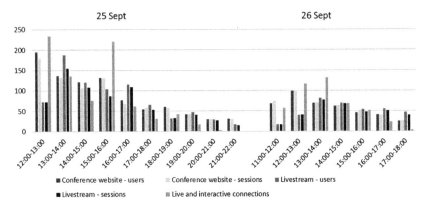

Fig. 9.1 Conference attendance during the live event

at the beginning of an event, and this was the case for the conference. Compared with data from the Student Hub Live, there is a similar trend which is that the second day has lower levels of participation.

Social media was a key driver in terms of acquisition, which refers to the source that was used to access the website. Facebook has been a very important part of the promotion, partly because it has included video trailers, and also because it facilitates a community of students, as was argued in Chap. 5. In this case, social media includes Facebook, Twitter, and LinkedIn, and the main OU accounts were used in addition to the OU Social Science accounts.

From the tables below it can be seen that over the period 25–26 September 2015 the majority of sessions resulted from direct traffic but with nearly a quarter coming from Facebook or Twitter. This demonstrates the importance of the faculty Facebook page and of social media more generally in generating interest in the event. It may also be the case that the type of student who engages in live interactive events also uses social media (Tables 9.3 and 9.4).

Table 9.3 Number and proportion of visits by channel to the Student Connections Website

Channel	% age of sessions	No. of sessions
Direct	57.6	1065
Social media	22.8	421
Referral	14.0	259
Search	5.6	103

Table 9.4 Top social referrers

Referrer	% age of sessions	No. of sessions
Facebook	12.6	232
Twitter	10.2	189

After the conference had taken place there were 580 sessions when visitors returned to the website to watch videos of the conference. This indicates the usefulness of leaving digital assets on-line for some time.

The Nature of Participation: Contributions to Live Chat

As previously discussed, the numbers of participants interacting give an indication about how many people engaged in the event, but it is also possible to consider the experience of some participants from the contributions that they made in the chat log, a stream of chat posted by participants who chose to watch and engage.

Over 4,000 chat messages were posted during the 2015 Student Connections conference. While this is a large number there are important points to make about them that relate to nature of the contributions. The level of engagement is not reflected in these data. For instance, a user may have read the chat without engaging, or demonstrated a very low level of interaction for example a single chat message saying 'hi'. On the other hand, some participants may have been very active, for example the top contributor (a moderator on the Social Media desk) posted 384 messages, which was 9.3% of the total chat contribution.

The majority of messages were of a social nature, often unrelated to the discussion. Whilst this points to the value of building and developing community, it could be seen as peripheral if students wanted to engage entirely with the content of the session. One attendee commented:

I did find it hard to read the chat, reply, write something in it and at the same time pay attention to what was being said. I would suggest, for a next time, that the chat sessions only open after the subject has been presented and then people can discuss over it. Mainly I found that people were trying to find others to meet and feel connected but not much (while I attend it) was being said on the matter in discussion.

Survey

In addition to the chat, more detailed questionnaire responses were received from participants who had engaged with the event. There were 36 returned questionnaires, with 24 fully completed.

The questionnaire included motivations for attending and the perceived benefits. The main finding here is that whilst gaining knowledge about their subject area was a driver, an outcome was that they felt engaged in the OU student community. The key drivers were subject related (75%), whereas 28% took part specifically to meet other students.

Participants were also asked about the most useful thing they experienced during the conference, and answers ranged from connecting with other students to knowing more about their subject. These four quotes from different students pick up on some of the benefits;

"The experience of an online conference increased my confidence a little more in regards to online tutorials etc."

"Feeling connected to academics and students, not alone"

"An additional way of learning outside of the course study materials. A more real-world approach to discussing topics"

"How studies are different from when I was younger. Nowadays, one can be at home and attend a seminar/conference, participate and feel connect. That's awesome!"

Overall the September 2015 Student Connections conference engaged over 2000 participants in real time or after the event. Over ten hours of video assets were created. These digital assets can also have a number of uses, for example many are used on qualifications websites. Most importantly, the format of the event and use of technology enhanced the study skills of the teaching team and also the learning experience offered to students.

Evaluation of Student Connections

Part of the aim of Student Connections was to help develop a greater sense of community amongst students, and this was done in a new virtual space that was unlike any other platform that students had previously experienced within the OU. Although we do not know whether students who attended the first conference came to the second one, the large increase in participants indicates that that the development of a sense of community is of increasing value. Student Connections has in turn inspired the creation of a new platform (Student Hub Live), now used regularly for live events. There are regular contributors to Student Hub Live and one indication of relationships being built is that students who recognise each other virtually are engaging in chat log dialogue.

This project has also highlighted issues with measuring the effectiveness of online live events – which will be important as experiments in this area continue to develop – and also the extent to which community matters. In terms of lessons learned evaluation has to be built into the initial project planning and costing – the 2014 Student Connections conference, for example, did not include data which allowed depth of analysis around pedagogy.

There was better quality data from the 2015 conference, which allowed us to assess the different types and nature of student engagement. The synchronous chats, a synchronous video views (catch up) and repeat visits to the website indicate that a great number of students were interacting with the university and fellow students in a new way. This type of activity within a university represents a form of social or informal learning and also, for the most involved students, also represent what Kuh has identified as "high impact" activities. (Kuh 2009)

As would be expected in the first event of its kind, there were many aspects that varied from the organisers expectations. These included the way that students attended and interacted with the event in terms of the programme, the use of interactive aspects and the role and participation of the remote audience. This has led to the concept being developed to create an interactive academic community in the form of the Student Hub Live.

Critical Reflection

The evidence we have gathered and analysed points to events like this being of value for students who want to engage in community activities, access extracurricular material and engage in informal learning. There is evidence that these events facilitate a sense of belonging which is valuable to some, but not all students. There is a dual function to these events; the live interaction and the recording that is available afterwards. It can also be argued, based on the greater number of website visits compared to attendance, that for other students the option to connect with a community of learners can be useful, even if they are not able or do not want to take part in the full spectrum of options. Behaviour of the online audience indicates that convenience is a key driver for participation in live events, but presumably those choosing to watch on catch up may be more influenced by the topic. This area also warrants further research.

There is a benefit to the Open University in running these events and in the ongoing learning process about how these are best delivered and executed. The process of evaluation is also conceptually developing, and in time the aspiration is that we can link participation in such events to student progression and retention. But due to challenges in identifying particular student participants, we cannot attribute benefits in terms of retention or progression or even student success on particular modules. Further initiatives such as longitudinal research, matched designs, analysis of the chat log and interviews are in development.

These online interactive events are used for the OU in distance learning, but there are clearly potential applications beyond the Open University, for example to all institutions experimenting in 'blended' learning. Examples include the workshops that were run on Blackboard Collaborate, the OU's online classroom. Although some of this is specific to the OU, our understanding of the relationship between interaction with social learning opportunities and student success is being developed. This is particularly important to learning environments with atypical student populations. Although the interface (Stadium Live) is owned by the OU, concepts of interactivity can be used in other settings. For example, the format offers an alternative way to produce accessible video resources of live discussion amongst students.

There are substantial costs and the need for specific skill sets in producing events like the Student Connections conference. It is also likely that when compared to the costs per person for a physical event, on-line initiatives can be seen to offer good value for money.

The pedagogical advantages related to such "impact" events include a contribution to the development of social learning communities (Kuh 2012). In addition, there is value in the content, in terms of the discussion topics and the opportunity to connect with other students. Finally, the environment is inclusive, where all participants, students or members of staff are able to engage on equal terms.

The downsides are that these events take time and effort to organise and can require specialist skills. The interface, Stadium Live, is used to collate the interactive aspects and this is owned by the Open University, however developments in software may mean that similar platforms will be available to other HEI's. Another consideration relates to access, as only those with access to the internet and sufficient bandwidth can participate.

Conclusions

In summary we can conclude that events such as these offer students and staff an innovative way to interact and are a useful addition in the process of building connections between the university and its students. Such connections are particularly important within a distance learning environment, where one of the most important challenges is to overcome isolation. In time, as technology, develops there may be other manifestations of these events, and there will be greater sophistication in terms of how we evaluate the effectiveness of these. At their best they offer a portal for communication, allowing students to meet with others and in so doing help to build a learning community. As one participant says;

> Feeling part of a community was immensely important. Loved the live chat aspects and will now actively look out for OUSA [Open University Students Association] events and try and be more involved (was rather nervous of those before). Also I now want to study EVERYTHING! All the subjects seemed so interesting!

Tips and Discussion Points

- There are a variety of benefits to students in actively participating in an academic community. For some, the opportunity to interact is invaluable, however it may not be a key driver in their attendance (especially if they haven't been to an event of this kind before)
- Such events carry staff costs and these must be built in at the start
- Similarly a plan for evaluation should be made
- Once assets have been created, think through how they might be used in other settings
- Live programmes are easier to deliver than ones with pre-recorded content, but replaying live sessions during "non-live" programme time can also be of value

References

Ashwin, P., & McVitty, D. (2015). The meanings of student engagement: Implications for policies and practices. In A. Curaj, L. Matei, R. Pricopie, J. Salmi, & P. Scott (Eds.), *European higher education area*. Cham: Springer.

Butcher, J. (2015). '*Shoe-horned and side-lined'?: Challenges for part-time learners in the new HE landscape*. HEA. https://www.heacademy.ac.uk/resource/shoe-horned-and-side-lined-challenges-part-time-learners-new-he-landscape#sthash.8yaeSuak.dpuf

Butcher, J., & Rose-Adams, J. (2015). Part-time learners in open and distance learning: Revisiting the critical importance of choice, flexibility and employability. *Open Learning: The Journal of Open, Distance and E-Learning, 30*(2), 127–137.

Coates, H. (2005). The value of student engagement for higher education quality assurance. *Quality in Higher Education, 11*(1), 25–36.

Coates, H. (2006). *Student engagement in campus-based and online education: University connections*. New York: Routledge.

Kuh, G. D. (2009). The national survey of student engagement: Conceptual and empirical foundations. *New Directions for Institutional Research, 141*, 5–20.

Kuh, G. (2012). *What matters to student Success*. https://www.youtube.com/watch?v=TrJPHKL6AH4&t=1946s. Accessed 27 Feb 2017.

Teng, T. L., & Taveras, M. (2004). Combining live video and audio broadcasting, synchronous chat, and asynchronous open forum discussions in distance education. *Journal of Educational Technology Systems, 33*(2), 121–129.

Thomas, L. (2012). *Building student engagement and belonging in Higher Education at a time of change.* Paul Hamlyn Foundation, 100.

Thomas, K. (2015). Rethinking belonging through Bourdieu, diaspora and the spatial. *Widening Participation and Lifelong Learning, 17*(1), 37–49.

Trowler, V. (2010). *Student engagement literature review.* Higher Education Academy. https://www.heacademy.ac.uk/resources/detail/evidencenet/Student_engagement_literature_review. Accessed 1 Nov 2017.

Wenger, E. (2000). Communities of practise and social learning systems. *The Organ, 7*(2), 225–246.

10

Supporting Team Teaching of Collaborative Activities in Online Forums: A Case Study of a Large Scale Module

Paige Cuffe and Jean McAvoy

Introduction

Against the backdrop of a growing need to offer more teaching online in higher education and the particular challenges of working with high population courses, this chapter explores the mechanisms put in place for supporting a group of over 200 tutors delivering team teaching of pre-set online collaborative activities, in small teams, to over 3000 students studying one first-year Open University undergraduate psychology module. It describes the development of resources in support of this team teaching, from the perspective of the module team chair with overall responsibility for the module at that time (Jean), and that of the

P. Cuffe (✉)
Psychology Department, Open University, Milton Keynes, UK
e-mail: p.a.cuffe@open.ac.uk

J. McAvoy
School of Psychology, Open University, Milton Keynes, UK
e-mail: jean.mcavoy@open.ac.uk

© The Author(s) 2018
J. Baxter et al. (eds.), *Creativity and Critique in Online Learning,*
https://doi.org/10.1007/978-3-319-78298-0_10

consultant tutor (Paige) who co-authored supporting resources and oversaw a forum provided for the tutor team to raise questions, discuss implementation, and seek advice on issues arising. The chapter presents a summary of the feedback gathered from the tutor forum along with student feedback and we discuss how this informed the next iteration of the module. The chapter concludes with a summary of recommendations for effective support of tutors conducting online team teaching of collaborative working by students.

Moves to Online Collaborative Learning

With over 180,000 students the Open University is one of the largest Higher Education providers in Europe. It provides distance learning across the UK and internationally. The central tenet of tuition at the Open University is one of Supported Open Learning. Supported Open Learning encapsulates a number of key principles. In line with its mission to be Open, the majority of undergraduate provision at the Open University requires no formal entry qualifications or prior educational credit. Comprehensive multiple media study materials, assuming no prior subject knowledge, are specifically designed for students studying at a distance. All students are supported by Associate Lecturers (tutors), who offer a range of tutorial support either online or face-to-face with additional guidance provided via email or telephone, and online forums. Individual feedback on students' learning and progress is provided through extended personalised feedback on assignments through a process of continuous assessment. Extended teams offer further pastoral and organisational support covering module choice, study intensity (full or part-time), skills development, and careers information. Supported Open Learning is a key concept which has underpinned the university's determination to remain open to students from all backgrounds, often studying alongside multiple other commitments and therefore frequently needing flexibility in study. Flexibility is key particularly in regard to *when* students are able to study and *where* they might happen to be when they are able to study. Maintaining this flexibility generates some challenges when it co-exists with a determination to provide expert tuition, one to one feedback on study progress, and significantly, access to opportunities for collaborative learning with other students also needing flexible and varying schedules. When this process is scaled up to hundreds or indeed thousands of students as in the case study here, the challenge of ensuring quality provision for all takes on additional complexity.

Distance education has been at the forefront of adopting online learning as an obvious progression in the format of 'knowledge' sharing from postal to mass media to interactive technologies (Anderson and Dron 2011). But, the report by The High Level Group on Modernisation of Higher Education (2014) talks of higher education more generally being on the brink of transformation and that "traditional providers must diversify their offering and provide more courses online". The appeal of doing so, against a backdrop of increasingly squeezed budgets and the presumption of greater efficiencies in costs of delivery, especially if scaled up, has increased interest in these conversations.

Alongside this move to digital platforms, the development of collaborative skills within a student's academic or professional community has become widely prized (Adams et al. 2017; European Commission 2012) and is claimed to aid greater learning gains (Siemens et al. 2015). Indeed, even face to face campuses are re-designing and moulding learning spaces to better enable digital interaction and collaboration between learners (Adams Becker et al. 2017). Within psychology education in the UK, the professional body – the British Psychological Society (BPS) – also requires that the opportunity to develop collaborative skills be a part of any university programme seeking BPS accreditation, which is an important mark of quality for students and employers.

The move to online education necessitates the development of new pedagogies and an ongoing examination and expansion of a teacher's repertoire (Rivers et al. 2014). For instance, online forums using highly structured activities for discussion, with support from fellow learners and a tutor, are regarded as the most successful means of supporting online learning (Darabi et al. 2013; Rovai 2007). Therefore, they need to be a core part of learning design for the future and skill development for teachers. In addition, incorporating teaching through more varied collaborative activity requires further skills. Moreover, collaborative learning in an online environment requires a larger time investment by lecturers, and this has led to increasing suggestions for academics to work with teams of teachers to support online learning (Siemens et al. 2015). However, adding a requirement to teach not just collaborative activity, but to teach collaboratively with other tutors, brings further challenges.

The annual *Innovating Pedagogy* report which scans the education horizon has, every year since 2012, noted new pedagogical innovations in response to or facilitating scaling up online courses (Sharples et al. 2015). There is, however, a growing realisation that maintaining learners' engagement with online study and achieving completion is challenging (see for example Jordan 2014) and this challenge increases as student numbers increase. But, as several Open University modules routinely have student registrations in the thousands in a single cohort, our experience of supporting distance learning, incorporating online learning, is also one of teaching at scale. Maintaining a strong teaching presence as we scale-up may seem unnecessary in the age of MOOCs – Massive Open Online Courses – which have been making front page news since 2012 (Department for Business 2013). However, tutor support in online courses in HE in general (Sieminski et al. 2016; Baxter and Haycock 2014) and during collaborative activities in particular (Ernest et al. 2013), is considered by many to be essential in ensuring student retention. This stance appears vindicated when typical MOOC completion rates of 13% or less (Onah et al. 2014; see also Chap. 8) are compared with those for large cohorts on OU modules, such as the 54% completion rate of an initial 9,500 students on a Level 1 technical module led by Martin Weller, or the 77% completion rate for the psychology module in this case study (Lane 2013; Weller and Robinson 2002; see also Chap. 8 for a discussion of the positive impact of adding engaged forum moderators to MOOC presentations). Note again, that these are open entry modules requiring no prior educational credit and where scaffolded learning is a core design expectation of module materials and activities. While frameworks have been developed to help with the transition to online teaching (for example, Baran and Correia 2014), these are not aimed at large teams all delivering a course together. There is thus an urgent need to identify elements that might be included to successfully support teams of teachers co-delivering online collaborative activities designed by others, and to offer experience of how this is done in a given context.

The Open University, Large-Scale Learning and the Tutor Role

The Open University currently comprises around 1200 academics and around 5000 Associate Lecturers (ALs) who also offer academic support in the form of tutoring. All students are allocated to a tutor group with an assigned named tutor, typically at a ratio of one tutor for twenty students, but for some modules, such as the Level 1 module in this case study, this is reduced to one tutor to fifteen students. The tutor will mark and give personalised feedback on assessments during the year in addition to preparing and delivering tuition. Within the literature, a variety of terms are used for roles that are similar to those of the OU tutor role, such as facilitator, emoderator, and online teacher (Baran et al. 2011), but that of the OU tutor also includes these tuition and assessment dimensions. The ALs who undertake tutoring are contracted on a part-time basis for a module, with some developing a portfolio of contracts for various modules and other work within the OU, and others teaching on one module a year and possibly holding positions within other universities and organisations.

Qualifications and component modules are designed by a Module Team, led by one or more academics, with members of faculty co-authoring the module materials and learning designers and technologists supporting production of content, including multimedia and interactive material hosted on the module website. Materials are delivered to students by a mix of printed books and/or online materials including interactive activities, audio-visual resources and extensive online library provision. The module website is accessed by staff and students and has a module calendar which each week guides activity through the range of materials assigned to that week. Most modules adopt a blended tuition approach combining a small number of optional face-to-face events such as tutorials or day schools, and online tutorials distributed throughout the module calendar. Further support and learning are offered in a variety of online discussion forums. Working to achieve online collaborative learning within forums has been part of the OU's Learning and Teaching Strategy since 2004, and the OU adopted an integrated Virtual Learning Environment (VLE) digital platform in early 2008, embedding various online tools for easier access and use. Acknowledging the presence of the technology in learning is important for understanding both the material and skills demands that learning places on learners and tutors alike. Indeed tutors' ability to manage the technology and their attitude to technology-supported learning is recognised as a significant influence on the effectiveness of learning in this environment (Kirkwood and Price 2016).

The OU tutor role now has a strong focus on the tutor as an online forum moderator; understanding and critical argument are progressively developed in discussions with peers, and the greater dependence on peer conversation in online collaborative learning necessitates tutor support to achieve this (Baran et al. 2011). Faculties may offer different guidance on what 'good' tutoring is held to be (Jelfs et al. 2009), but the importance of a dual academic/pastoral role has long been known (Price et al. 2007) as a counter to the affective issues and concerns about self-presentation which many students experience in online forums (Ferguson 2010). Tutor support is also known to make a key contribution to the learning improvement particularly for students achieving close-to-failing grades on the first assessment (Sieminski et al. 2016). In short, the importance of the role of the tutor in successful learning is both well established and complex.

Designing Innovation in a Module

Alongside environmental shifts and changing demands the OU's psychology programme also underwent comprehensive revision, producing new modules at all levels, and a suite of new qualifications. The module discussed here, *Investigating Psychology 1*, is a first-year 60-credit component in the new programme, designed to contribute to a range of accredited psychology degrees and combined honours qualifications. It is also an optional module undertaken by students following programmes in the social sciences more broadly, as well as an array of business, computing, legal, healthcare and science programmes. The module anticipated around 3000 students in its first presentation, rising to over 5000 students in subsequent presentations, with each student receiving individualised support and feedback. In a predecessor module of similar size, online forums had been included as additional support and discussion spaces for students and tutors at a group level although there was no explicit learning activity designed for these. Moreover, forum membership had been organised in various ways based either around a single tutor group (around 15 students), paired tutor groups (30 students) or clusters of tutor groups sharing a single forum space (upwards of 45 students). Consequently, a variety of approaches to using the forums emerged. A range of activities was tried, some successfully and some not. Student uptake was variable, and not just by tutor group but by cohort. Student and tutor satisfaction was mixed and inconsistent.

Against this backdrop, the role of the online forum in distance education was put under particular scrutiny by the production team in the design phase for the new module. Attention was given to the value of online forums for socialising, giving and receiving support and furthering learning and professional discussion skills. Considerable variability of practice, approach and skill in facilitating online forum discussion activities was noted in Barnes and Sainsbury's (2014) review of OU forums. For example, the promptness and style of opening posts in forums (supportive/content-focused/undirected) appeared to determine the forum 'climate' for the duration of the module. Furthermore, students themselves have identified a need for opening posts and for tutors to "initiate and shape discussion" (Baxter and Haycock 2014) and students are more likely to read – and return to – structured activity threads than more social threads (Attar et al. 2012). As OU Level 2 (second year) and Level 3 (third year) psychology research project modules delivered online require a greater degree of independence in students, developing those skills and experience from Level 1 is a priority. Indeed, the growing experience of the Open University in online learning, forums and module design suggested that structured activities embedded within the module which draw on and are interwoven with the module content would improve engagement and depth of discussion (Thorpe 2008). Recent work confirms the greater effectiveness of structured, moderated and guided online discussions for learning (Darabi et al. 2013) and student retention (Rienties and Toetenel 2016). Moreover, having module teams design the activities to be used in the discussion forums and embedding these activities in the curriculum material also removes one of the primary activities and responsibilities identified by Ernest et al. (2013) as most burdensome for tutors supporting collaborative learning in asynchronous forums.

For these reasons the module team embedded collaborative activities (CAs) in the study materials in order to provide clear structure and purpose to the discussion in forums, with a dedicated forum established for each CA. There were twelve such CAs in the initial design of the new module, distributed over 30 weeks. Although embedded in the curriculum, for this Level 1 module no individual activity was mandated other than the timely submission of required assessments wherein students must demonstrate their knowledge, skills and understanding of module content. In effect, students engage with the CAs if they choose to.

Attracting and retaining students to non-mandated activity generates particular challenges, including placing an additional burden on tutors tasked with stimulating and maintaining student engagement. Pre-designing and embedding activities aimed to alleviate some of this burden. However, use of prescribed activities around which forum discussion was to be structured was nevertheless a change in practice for most ALs tutoring on psychology modules. A further feature was that tutors were required to work in clusters of around four to six tutor groups. This meant not only that students were required to work collaboratively, but tutors too were required to teach collaboratively. For many this was a departure from previous ways of working, and for some an unsettling development. The reason for clustering in this way was to create a 'critical mass' of students (Kear 2010), in this case around 60–90, and to allow tutors to share the demanding work of leading 12 online asynchronous CAs with students mostly unfamiliar with the practice, mostly new to Higher Education, and many lacking in confidence as learners.

The design of the CAs commonly requested more than one action by students, with instructions for some CAs given in one week allowing students to prepare, and postings in the forum scheduled for the following week. Activities ranged from socialising students into the community of learners with an Icebreaker post, through both learning and professional skills development. Separate student forums were set up for each CA for each group, so as to limit the content to manageable proportions for students and tutors, aid good internal organisation of forum discussion threads, and encourage moving progressively through the module. Equally, if a student was unable or unwilling to join in with one particular activity, they could start afresh with a subsequent activity. A single module-long Cluster/Tutorial Group Forum was also created for more general notices, chat and queries (Fig. 10.1).

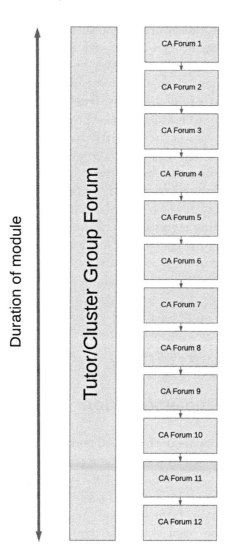

Fig. 10.1 Student Forums – Each student has access to their group's Cluster/Tutor Group Forum of around 60 students for the duration of the module, with a separate clustered forum space for each weekly or two-weekly Collaborative Activity (CA) of which there were originally 12 in all

The potential workload involved in successful moderation of discussions was altered by this new design, as forum discussion had shifted in importance to a more central position as part of the pedagogy of the module. In addition, given the volume of online content with which tutors would rapidly need to become familiar, the module team judged that proactive support for tutors was appropriate. This took the form of providing an overview of the objectives for each activity and suggested text and themes for developing forum posts and to encourage discussions, as well as points to consider about any particular student groups' engagement with the material. Furthermore, from the perspective of the module team, such a large tutor body engaged in a new module and new ways of working required sensible oversight, and appropriate support in order to ensure consistency in learning opportunity, whilst also allowing tutors flexibility and individual creativity within the contracted tuition time. Indeed, a core aim was to structure consistency but explicitly encourage individual tutor responsiveness to the particular dynamics of each student group, as this adaptation by tutors is a key mechanism for achieving personalisation in very large scale modules (MacDonald and Campbell 2012).

Supporting Implementation

Support and development of newly appointed ALs teaching on an OU module is underpinned with a nine-hour part-time online training course in online teaching, and the allocation of a peer mentor for the tutor's first presentation of a module. In addition, when a new module is launched, the ALs appointed to tutor it attend an extended module briefing at which the Module Team academics who designed and produced the module introduce the key elements of the module, its approach, assessment and tuition plan, as well as noting any potentially difficult aspects which need discussion. For large registration modules such as the one in this case study, these sessions are face to face, last most of a day, and to accommodate the number and geographical dispersion of ALs involved, are generally offered on more than one date and generally at two or more different locations across the UK. These briefing sessions usually include opportunities for small group discussion exercises. These might focus on standardising marking on coursework assessments during the module or considering best practice for managing particular components of the module.

To support tutors with the new CA Forum approach, a dedicated session was provided briefing them on the learning motivations for including collaborative learning, outlining the essence of the activities, and how they linked to the module content and calendar. Tutors were introduced to some of the supporting resources that would be made available to them, such as sample texts to post at the opening of the forums, and additional, adaptable, model responses which could be deployed as each CA progressed. Tutors were advised that for the first presentation of the module the resources for each CA were scheduled to become available a few months ahead of each activity. (This staggered release was not a design feature, but rather an artefact of scheduling module team workload to cover all the materials required for the launch of a new, large, module.)

For a further exercise during the briefing, tutors were encouraged to sit with colleagues from their geographical region in order to provide them with an opportunity to begin or renew relationships with the larger team from which clusters would be established. The exercise was firstly to consider tutors' queries and concerns, but also invite tutors' suggestions for good moderating practice for these CA forums. The intention was threefold: to raise issues which needed to be addressed in further support for tutors, to use the process of vocalising concerns to cue suggestions which might address these, and to allow an opportunity to develop trust in the competence of their co-teaching colleagues. A second exercise to formulate scenario statements such as 'if this happens, then we will …' developed tutors' strategies further.

Because of time constraints in module production, the first briefing day took place prior to tutors having access to the module website, meaning they had had no opportunity to explore it ahead of the event. Throughout the day, uncertainty and unhappiness about various innovations and activities in the module were expressed and these culminated in some resistance vocalised in the final CA briefing and exercises. The second briefing took place a week later, with access to the module website and materials having been achieved in the interim. In this instance, much less unhappiness was expressed. Concerns raised were discussed and explored in the dedicated sessions as planned, and ideas and suggestions for best practice and problem solving realised. These were gathered and used to inform decisions as the module ran (Table 10.1).

Once a module begins, attention shifts to supporting students and it becomes difficult for tutors to find time to become familiar with and draw together the parts of a module design for themselves. For this reason,

Table 10.1 Examples of issues raised as a concern in exercises at the briefing day

Issues raised	Strategies generated
That students would need help to make early sense of the different forums, their purpose and potential difficulties navigating between them.	*Tutors developed strategies of hyperlinking the Cluster/Tutorial Group Forum (running throughout the module for general discussion and support) and CA1 forum to each other in opening posts so the students became aware of both. Tutors used their introductory emails to explain the function of each forum type.*
That the wording of CA1 in the module materials created inappropriate student expectations by implying a 24/7 tutor presence by saying 'your tutor will be there to welcome you'.	*How often the moderating tutors would be present could be stated in their Introductory email and the opening post of CA1.*
That there was lack of clarity concerning how far in advance CA forums should open to avoid students beginning without direction.	*Tutors should have access to all forums ahead of students in order to post an opening message providing appropriate direction for the activity.*
That there was uncertainty around deciding how to arrange tutor rotas and responsibilities in managing the forums given that tutors would be working in clusters rather than individually.	*This was a function to be overseen by tutors' line mangers in consultation with tutors.*
That the number of CAs would potentially be too time consuming for students and for tutors.	*This was addressed in later presentations where some collaborative activities were amalgamated and reduced to eight in total.*

The strategies to address these are a mix of suggestions generated by tutors and the module team who produced and oversee the module supplementary supporting tutor resources were written by the team and further resources commissioned so that tutors would have a starting point. These resources included an overview of every CA within the module, and sample text for tutors to post to forums, either verbatim or adapted according to their preference (Fig. 10.2).

A single document containing an overview for each CA:

- Summarises in a few hundred words the module team's intention, key student actions and the linkage of the CA to other module material;
- Includes a central description of all the CAs scattered through the module's week by week schedule.

Tutor briefing resources:

- Slides used in the briefing session to introduce the CA. Includes explanatory diagrams of the relationship between the different types of student forums, the online activities and the module schedule which can be shared with students.

Example of an email for tutors to introduce themselves to their student group:

- Outlines the nature of the tuition plan and the forums in the module and invites students into the first CA.

Detailed resource for each CA includes:

- Example posts that might be used to open that discussion;
- Points to be aware of, including what difficulties students might encounter;
- Suggestions for ways to structure the discussion in the forum, such as threads topics to pre-populate the forum and strategies for dealing with issues arising.

Fig. 10.2 CA forum resources housed on dedicated webpage for Tutor Resources for this module

Support for a new, unfamiliar design element as complex as collaborative activities, taught collaboratively, by large numbers of tutors for yet larger numbers of students, can rarely be concluded effectively in a single session: it is not possible to predict and provide for everything that might arise for each tutor. It was expected that continued collective learning and exploration of ideas would be needed for sustained support (Boud and Hager 2012). This is particularly so when the teaching workforce is home-based and geographically dispersed, and therefore where much of the informal and incidental learning opportunities which happen in co-located contexts are not available (Campbell 2016). Furthermore, as Comas-Quinn (2011, p. 8) observes:

> There is also a tension, … to reconcile the provision of adequate training with the amount of time that part-time teachers are prepared to invest in training for a job that often accounts only for a small proportion of their income.

New modules ordinarily include a module-wide online forum for tutors to use as a space for discussion of various issues and aspects of the module and this was installed as usual. Our prior experiences on high population modules made us appreciate the value of a Tutor Module Forum, but also how busy and dynamic it can be. So in addition to the central 'meeting space' of the Tutor Module Forum, a further Collaborative Activities Tutor Forum was also established. This module-wide CA Tutor Forum was set up explicitly for support on the implementation of the new CAs and to explore strategies to moderate and guide the forums.

From previous modules we were aware of how differently student group dynamics may manifest in the forums from one cohort to the next. These are not cohort wide changes but reflect the sensitivity of interaction in forums to a range of factors (Thorpe 2008). Thus the learning gained as a moderator in one presentation does not necessarily prepare tutors for the next group. The sharing of experience within forums considerably expands the repertoire of practice and learning available to each individual tutor, whether they participate by posting or by quietly reading. In keeping the CA Tutor Forum and the general Module Tutor Forum at a module-wide level this maximised the range of experiences being offered in discussion.

Patterns in Conversations in the CA Forum

The value of a forum to its members is proven in the usage of the space. Within the first months of the module a little under a half of the ALs accessed this forum, most returning within the first weeks, and more than 60 ALs had within five days read any message posted. This is a much higher rate of participation than is customary for online forums and – in the initial implementation – is at approximately the same level as the more general Module Tutor Forum. The pattern of usage differed, however, as the posts were largely query-focussed initially, with a limited amount of general discussion, and tended to unfold as each CA drew closer. Much as with any student or community forum, approximately 50% of the tutors on the module never post to the Tutor Module Forum and only about 20–25% in the CA Tutor Forum. Interestingly, while the core posters are the same tutors in both tutor forums, additional posters do not overlap as clearly, suggesting there may a different value in the two forums for different tutors.

There was a range of ways that tutors used the CA Tutor Forum (Table 10.2), but they notably focused on raising issues around how to interpret the Module Team's intention in an activity, and adapting opening posts to a CA forum. Sharing of practice was evident from the early weeks, though initially this was limited to a few experienced tutors who brought a long history of working together and who formed a core of active posters that continued through successive presentations of the module.

A recurring conversation arose from some tension about the Module Team's dual desire of offering support and striving for consistency which a small number of tutors experienced as a reduction in their own professional autonomy and a drive to uniformity. This may suggest a need for explicit action to reinvigorate and support individual agency (Chetwynd and Dobbyn 2012) within structured activity so clear postings were needed from the moderator (Paige):

> My understanding is that the MT [Module Team] are happy for you to use the provided example posts exactly as they are, or not, <emoticon> as they are looking to lessen the workload, but not looking to prescribe and limit our ability to modify our opening post using our knowledge of our groups or local circumstances. If you'd like to copy across the CA instructions as your opening post, that would be fine too….

Table 10.2 Topics raised in the CA Tutor Forum indicate tutors sought affective support, clarification and ideas for practice and also offered (conflicting) views on and suggestions for practice and design

Key categories	Type of points noted by tutors
Student participation in CA activities	Low forum participation in some clusters
	Higher forum participation than prior modules in some clusters
	Activity patterns varying through the module in relation to the activity type or point in the calendar
	Students' reflective responses to participating in CAs required in the first assessment point for the module
Student feelings about CA activities	The size of the cluster having an effect on student participation
Effects of cluster structure	How different clusters might be sharing the team-teaching Rota
	How changes in the cluster size affected co-teaching
Use of supplied forum resources	Wanting greater individualisation of style or voice
	Not wanting to individualise or amend or adapt resources, but wanting a single, fixed post of CA instructions in all forums
	Wanting an "official" (module team) view on "correct" responses (such as providing a definitive grade for an activity requiring students to assess a mock essay)
The actual, as opposed to the intended, duration of activity on a particular CA	When to time an opening post to a forum if it should be posted in advance of a CA officially starting
	Managing continued activity in a CA forum after its official end
	Adapting the Icebreaker CA to fit individual cluster structure
Design	Suggesting which CA need re-design
	Suggesting how CA might be added to/ re-designed
How to respond to specific issues or queries	Exploration of how other tutors were responding to issues
Practical and technical issues	Managing difficulties created by design or software features (such as monitoring which students had contributed data to a shared data table)
	Broken hyperlinks

Thus one of the functions of the Tutor CA Forum was to include support for tutors in the change in working practice which for some challenged professional identity, and also to encourage tutors to adapt resources in line with their own pedagogical approach and in the process affirm the goal of personalisation of learning for their students over uniformity of practice. The Tutor CA forum was also used to affirm tutors' creative strategies for emerging issues in implementing the activities, as they contributed information about their various practices. Valuing "variation and diversity" of practice allows innovation to emerge from these differences (Ellström 2010). One of the key roles of the dedicated CA Tutor Forum is then giving space and place for comparing difficulties and sharing practice to find the variations. It is in this that the scale of the tutor body becomes an asset rather than a problem to be managed.

Within the CA tutor forum, moderation therefore attempted to follow a supportive approach with a focus on eliciting solutions and suggestions from the tutor body to address issues raised rather than impose and instruct, an approach successfully used by Ernest et al. (2013) in designing a formal programme to assist tutors in the transition to teaching in online collaborative projects. The interchange of experienced tutors and the moderator in this forum was seen also as an opportunity to model the different role and position of the tutors in online environments wanting to encourage collaboration, as compared with traditional face-to-face or hierarchical teaching settings. Transitioning to this approach can be challenging for tutors new to online forums (Comas-Quinn et al. 2012).

For the first few presentations of the module the number of students in each Cluster, and how the teaching hours available were arranged across face to face tutorials and day schools, and online tutorials, varied across the different parts of the UK as they were determined by the regional or national management in that area. The nature of the teaching pattern and cluster size were largely decided by the density and distribution of students within that area. Thus less densely populated areas were more likely to arrange tutors to work in small clusters or pairs so that students did not need to travel further for face to face Cluster day schools. This also meant a variation in the workload for moderating the CA forum activities, with some Clusters sharing this between four tutors and some between eight. This variation also occurred from cohort to cohort as the number of students registered in an area varied. These Cluster variations were ameliorated by tutors sharing strategies for different size clusters and how to divide up the work in ways that produced manageable patterns of workflow. Crucially, taking into account tutors' hands-on experience was vital in organising this effectively.

In addition to the practice sharing, the key categories of conversation emerging in the CA Tutor Forum (and similarly in the general Module Tutor Forum) coalesced around the difficulties encountered by students and/or tutors during the running of the module. Raising these during the presentation means they can be addressed by the Module Team, who have overall responsibility for initiating any changes, more speedily than if only surfaced in post-module student feedback surveys. In addition, through raising these in these forums where other tutors could respond and report the situation in their groups, it makes it possible for the module team to more rapidly establish how widespread any problem might be, and intervene with advice or instructions if required. Finally, with between 200 and 300 tutors and 2500 to over 5000 students on a presentation it would not be possible to capture and respond to individual reporting and queries; the Tutor Forums allow instead for these to be amassed and summarised to make the task of addressing them practically achievable. In this way, tutors also have agency within the module.

As can be seen from the main topic categories in the CA Tutor Forum (Table 10.2), this was a content and practice focused space. Developing threads according to the content and practice for particular CAs had the advantage of making it easier to maintain structured discussions, which in turn made subsequent searching for and finding discussions much simpler. It also decreased the reading load, as tutors could rapidly scan posts in a thread and threads in the CA forum tended to be shorter and more focused than in the general Tutor Forum.

It is recognised that social presence and the sharing of personal information in forums makes an important contribution to building the trust needed to share ideas openly (Booth 2012) but it is also recognised that this is not universally enjoyed. For example, during a period of increased anxiety and information flow from university senior management with the implementation of a major new policy during the 2016 presentations (see below) some tutors within the main Tutor Module Forum expressed frustration with the level of social chat embedded within 'content' threads discussing assessment and tuition queries. There was a call from some to clearly separate out banter and personal chat in a separate thread which was clearly labelled as such. In our experience this is a common concern but a delicate balance.

Implementing Changes

At the OU every module is systematically evaluated after its initial presentation, with the views of both students[1] and tutors sought. An emailed invitation to tutors on the first two presentations to fill in an online questionnaire produced 100 returns of which 72 were complete.

The quantitative and qualitative data were analysed and the key points to emerge were that tutors were generally happy with the module design, however, more concerns were raised about the collaborative activities than other elements. Suggestions included reducing the overall number of CAs and in particular removing three CAs viewed as not helpful and with which students were not engaging. Variations in levels of engagement were reported with some noting very low levels despite their attempts to address this, and one reported that the CAs were depressing to moderate. There was however considerable consensus amongst the tutor group and the module team responsible that some adjustment was needed with a consequent reduction of the number of CAs to eight and removal of the CAs which tutors recommended.

Clustering and co-teaching arrangements varied for tutors across the module, and difficulties with the planning, administration and coordination of teaching were raised in many of the responses and some noted difficulties working with peers whom they considered slow to respond, incorrect in their understanding or non-collaborative. A significant minority of tutors noted that clustering – in effect sharing the teaching of CAs – had resulted in the loss of a clear view of the student trajectory through the module with less individual student-tutor contact. A small number of respondents noted issues around loss of autonomy. Overall, however, clustered co-teaching was valued for a variety of reasons including the opportunity to learn from other tutors' experience and expertise, to share workload, to become part of a community of tutors, to share good practice and ultimately to work collaboratively.

As the planned revisions to the CAs were implemented, the tutor resources made available at the start of the module were also revised to match the reduced CA pattern and to incorporate some of the strategies and suggestions that had emerged in the CA Tutor Forum in prior presentations. A question arose regarding the continued necessity for the dedicated CA Tutor forum given that tutors were then more familiar with the module, design principles and objectives. It would have been possible to archive the forum which would have rendered it 'read-only' but nevertheless a source of information for later newly appointed tutors. Indeed the forum moderator (Paige) had thought the CA Tutor Forum would not be needed beyond the initial presentation, believing the queries raised in each thread could be summarised once each CA had been completed, and this used as a fixed resource, possibly in the form of a web-based set of 'Frequently Asked Questions' (FAQ). The module chair (Jean) saw value in maintaining it as a space for discussion until the customary module review and re-design had been completed and implemented, and until such time as tutors no longer considered it useful. Maintaining the CA Tutor forum throughout these – and other – changes proved to be a productive resource. The CA continued to be visited by new and experienced tutors and continued to act as a valuable information exchange between tutors and the module team having overall responsibility as further refinements were discussed and developed. Surprisingly though, subsequent developments and contributions from tutors pointed to a precarious balance in team teaching through clustering the CA forum.

The clustering arrangements on this module had been an elective innovation by the module team. The CAs had been designed to give students access to a wide range of collaborative working at Level 1 as preparation for more consequential collaborative working as they progressed through their undergraduate studies. But the wide range of CAs placed additional demand on tutors. Clustering tutors and their students allowed sharing of workloads for tutors, shared problem-solving, good practice innovations, and associated skill development. For students, clustering allowed a critical mass of participants in an attempt to ensure lively active forums. Tutor feedback indicated broad approval for the moves, after a period of familiarisation.

However, subsequent to the development of clustered working on this module, the university introduced a much wider policy of clustered teaching, which went considerably further. Under the new policy all tuition on the module was required to be managed within a clustered approach. So, what had been a feature primarily for teaching just online collaborative activities was now rolled out to all aspects of module tuition. Moreover, just as the module team had designed the CAs, they were now required to set the focus of all tutorial sessions with a resultant perception of further losses to teaching autonomy amongst tutors. At the same time some cluster sizes increased, so while most areas used Clusters of six to eight tutor groups, which is approximately 90–120 students, one Cluster comprised 14 groups, thus approximately 210 students. Baxter and Haycock (2014) advise that clusters should remain small enough for some meaningful tutor-student interaction and this increase in size was challenging to that principle, despite the wealth of experience amongst the tutors affected. Scaling up the size of discussion in a threaded discussion forum altered the flow of conversation, made it difficult to keep up with the rate of posting and quickly threatened to overwhelm both students and moderators. Opportunistically, and fortunately, the existing CA Forum was used to give space for tutors to share and develop strategies to deal with larger forums and potentially offer feedback to the module team on the implementation of the new university-wide policy, and to offer a source of affective support for tutors experiencing substantial changes to their working environment.[2]

Conclusions

A number of observations emerged from our review of the support put in place for tutors teaching collaborative activities collaboratively. The nature of the support tutors might require varies over the life of a module, and even ongoing support available from peers in the forum changes in terms of the issues which are addressed. Figure 10.3 captures some of these passages. Early design, tutor briefings, and the provision of supplementary resources give way to practical insights from implementing the activities designed; which in turn informs design revision; and then invites revisiting in the context of organisational shifts which bring implications for tutor practice.

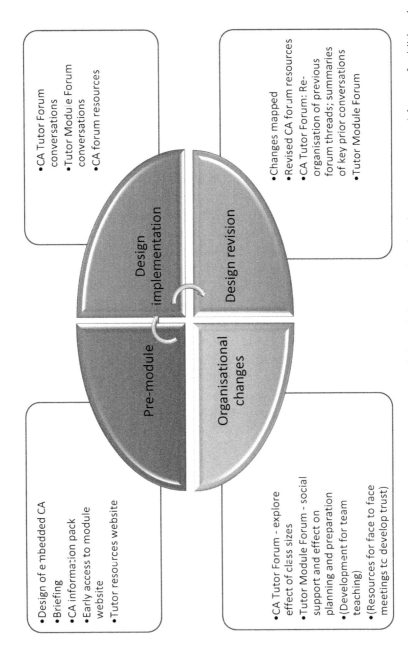

Design implementation

- CA Tutor Forum conversations
- Tutor Module Forum conversations
- CA forum resources

Design revision

- Changes mapped
- Revised CA forum resources
- CA Tutor Forum: Re-organisation of previous forum threads; summaries of key prior conversations
- Tutor Module Forum

Pre-module

- Design of embedded CA
- Briefing
- CA information pack
- Early access to module website
- Tutor resources website

Organisational changes

- CA Tutor Forum - explore effect of class sizes
- Tutor Module Forum - social support and effect on planning and preparation
- (Development for team teaching)
- (Resources for face to face meetings to develop trust)

Fig. 10.3 The phases and conditions arising in a module and the associated actions, resources and forms of additional support needed for tutors

What is signalled throughout is the importance of teaching relationships. For example, creating a suite of forum resources in addition to the curriculum is intended to support the achievement of particular learning outcomes for students, and minimise the preparatory time needed by each individual tutor multiplied, in the case of this modules, by more than 200 times over. But, providing tutorial resources can threaten role identities and creative autonomy so needs to be carefully framed. Tutors need space and time to work with those with whom they are co-teaching; to undertake tuition planning and explore their individual teaching philosophies, which may not always be an easy fit; and to build the trust to feel comfortable with the sense of exposure which co-teaching in an online environment can produce. Online teaching, and teaching of CAs in particularly, especially with a student body which may lack confidence, or even just time, is a highly skilled endeavour: tutors quite reasonably need time and resources to develop those skills in a supported environment. Amongst those resources, peer support can be invaluable: the sharing of experience and ideas produces a collective knowledge base that cannot be replicated easily in other ways. Providing a dedicated online space for discussion of new innovations in early presentations of a module ensures that knowledge base can be captured as a continuing resource – and not just for the tutors, but for the module team with overall responsibility for monitoring the quality and effectiveness of the module they have produced. In practical terms, tutors' forum discussions, valuable for how they trace out problem-solving, also benefit from being summarised regularly for ease of later access, particularly for incoming members to the teaching team. Moreover, when a support network is working, as the CA forum described here, maintaining it for as long as tutors are using it provides an effective and productive ongoing resource enabling tutors to work collectively and collaboratively in what is a complex and skilled endeavour.

Tips and Discussion Points

- Arrange a briefing day with all tutors. Use this to allow tutors to identify and discuss possible issues and jointly develop strategies for these.

- Focus on supporting relationships between tutors who will share clustered team teaching, including enabling opportunites for tutors to meet online and face to face where practical to explore teaching approaches.
- Create materials for tutors to use in online forum tuition when introducing innovations to the curriculum.
- Maintain a dedicated online space for tutors to share peer support during and beyond the introduction of an innovation.
- Utilise the feedback offered by tutors in forum discussions – and the feedback they report from students – to more immediately address issues arising and to re-visit the module design.

Notes

1. Student feedback varied from citing positive engagement with CAs, to valuing being able to read other students postings even if not posting themselves, to finding CAs unhelpful and unwelcome.
2. Concomitant with these changes were significant regional and administrative structural changes and faculty mergers, which all contributed to an increased anxiety and some loss of clarity about role identity and divisions of labour.

References

Adams Becker, S., Cummins, M., Davis, A., Freeman, A., Hall Giesinger, C., & Ananthanarayanan, V. (2017). *NMC horizon report: 2017 higher education edition*. Austin: The New Media Consortium.

Anderson, T., & Dron, J. (2011). Three generations of distance education pedagogy. *The International Review of Research in Open and Distributed Learning, 12*(3). Available at: http://www.irrodl.org/index.php/irrodl/article/view/890/1663. Accessed 11 Sept 2017.

Attar, D., Goodman, S., Hewings, A., Monaghan, F., Rhys, M., & Sinka, I. (2012). The effectiveness of interventions to support greater participation in and more purposeful use of online forums on undergraduate English language studies modules. In *Open University scholarship exchange*. Milton Keynes: Open University.

Baran, E., & Correia, A. P. (2014). A professional development framework for online teaching. *TechTrends, 58*, 95–101.

Baran, E., Correia, A. P., & Thompson, A. (2011). Transforming online teaching practice: Critical analysis of the literature on the roles and competencies of online teachers. *Distance Education, 32*(3), 421–439.

Barnes, F., & Sainsbury, K. (2014). *Clusters: An investigation into creating and sustaining effective online learning environments on K101. Open University Scholarship Exchange.* Milton Keynes: Open University.

Baxter, J. A., & Haycock, J. (2014). Roles and student identities in online large course forums: Implications for practice. *The International Review of Research in Open and Distributed Learning, 15*(1). Available at: http://www.irrodl.org/index.php/irrodl/article/view/1593/2763?utm_content=buffer81686&utm_medium=social&utm_source=twitter.com&utm_campaign=buffer. Accessed 30 Apr 2017.

Booth, S. E. (2012). Cultivating knowledge sharing and trust in online communities for educators. *Journal of Educational Computing Research, 47*(1), 1–31.

Boud, D., & Hager, P. (2012). Re-thinking continuing professional development through changing metaphors and location in professional practices. *Studies in Continuing Education, 34*, 17–30.

Campbell, A. (2016). Talking point – Flexible targeted online staff development that works. *Journal of Interactive Media in Education, 1*, 1–10.

Chetwynd, F., & Dobbyn, C. (2012, April 12–13). *Consistency v autonomy: Effective feedback to a very large cohort.* STEM annual conference 2012: Aiming for excellence in STEM learning and teaching, Imperial College London, London.

Comas-Quinn, A. (2011). Learning to teach online or learning to become an online teacher: An exploration of teachers' experiences in a blended learning course. *ReCALL* [Online], 23. Available: http://oro.open.ac.uk/32111/

Comas-Quinn, A., De Los Arcos, B., & Mardomingo, R. (2012). Virtual learning environments (VLEs) for distance language learning: Shifting tutor roles in a contested space for interaction. *Computer Assisted Language Learning, 25*, 129–143.

Darabi, A., Liang, X., Suryavanshi, R., & Yurekli, H. (2013). Effectiveness of online discussion strategies: A meta-analysis. *American Journal of Distance Education, 27*, 228–241.

Department for Business. (2013). *The maturing of the MOOC: Literature review of massive open online courses and other forms of online distance learning.* Department for Business, Innovation and Skills, Report 130. London. Available at www.gov.uk/bis.

Ellström, P.-E. (2010). Practice-based innovation: A learning perspective. *Journal of Workplace Learning, 22*, 27–40.

Ernest, P., Guitert Catasus, M., Hampel, R., Heiser, S., Hopkins, J., Murphy, L., & Stickler, U. (2013). Online teacher development: Collaborating in a virtual learning environment. *Computer Assisted Language Learning, 26*, 311–333.

European Commission. (2012). *Communication from The Commission to The European Parliament, The Council, The European Economic and Social Committee and the Committee of the Regions*. Rethinking education: Investing in skills for better socio-economic outcomes. Luxembourg City, Luxembourg: Publications Office of the European Union. Available at cedefop.europa.eu/files/com669_en.pdf. Accessed 09 Sept 2017.

Ferguson, R. (2010). Peer interaction: The experience of distance students at university level. *Journal of Computer Assisted Learning, 26*, 574–584.

High Level Group on the Modernisation of Higher Education. (2014). *Report to the European Commission on new modes of learning and teaching in higher education* (p. 65). Luxembourg: Office for Official Publications of the European Communities.

Jelfs, A., Richardson, J. T. E., & Price, L. (2009). Student and tutor perceptions of effective tutoring in distance education. *Distance Education, 30*, 419–441.

Jordan, K. (2014). Initial trends in enrolment and completion of massive open online courses. *International Review of Research in Open and Distance Learning* [Online], *15*. Available: http://www.irrodl.org/index.php/irrodl/article/viewFile/1651/2813. Accessed 08 Dec 2016.

Kear, K. (2010, 3–4 May). Social presence in online learning communities. In L. Dirckinck-Holmfeld, V. Hodgson, C. Jones, M. De Laat, D. Mcconnell, & T. Ryberg (Eds.), *Proceedings of the 7th International Conference on Networked Learning 2010*. Aalborg: University of Aalborg.

Kirkwood, A., & Price, L. (2016). *Technology-enabled learning implementation handbook*. Burnaby: Commonwealth of Learning.

Lane, A. (2013, October 23–25). *The potential of MOOCs to widen access to, and success in, higher education study: An historical comparison*. Open and flexible higher education conference, Paris, France. European Association of Distance Teaching Universities (EADTU), pp. 189–203.

Macdonald, J., & Campbell, A. (2012). Demonstrating online teaching in the disciplines. A systematic approach to activity design for online synchronous tuition. *British Journal of Educational Technology, 43*, 883–891.

Onah, D. F. O., Sinclair, J., & Boyatt, R. (2014, July 7–9). *Dropout rates of massive open online courses: Behavioural patterns*. 6th international conference on Education and New Learning Technologies, Barcelona. Published in:

EDULEARN14 proceedings, pp. 5825–5834. http://wrap.warwick.ac. uk/65543/1/WRAP_9770711-cs-070115-edulearn2014.pdf. Accessed 30 June 2017.

Price, L., Richardson, J. T. E., & Jelfs, A. (2007). Face-to-face versus online tutoring support in distance education. *Studies in Higher Education, 32*(1), 1–20.

Rienties, B., & Toetenel, L. (2016). The impact of learning design on student behaviour, satisfaction and performance: A cross-institutional comparison across 151 modules. *Computers in Human Behavior, 60*, 333–341.

Rivers, B. A., Richardson, J. T. E., & Price, L. (2014). Promoting reflection in asynchronous virtual learning spaces: Tertiary distance tutors' conceptions. *The International Review of Research in Open and Distributed Learning, 15*(3), 215–231.

Rovai, A. P. (2007). Facilitating online discussions effectively. *The Internet and Higher Education, 10*, 77–88.

Sharples, M., Adams, A., Alozie, N., Ferguson, R., FitzGerald, E., Gaved, M., McAndrew, P., Means, B., Remold, J., Rienties, B., & Roschelle, J. (2015). *Innovating pedagogy 2015:* Open University innovation report 4. Milton Keynes: The Open University.

Siemens, G., Gašević, D., & Dawson, S. (2015). *Preparing for the digital university: A review of the history and current state of distance, blended and online learning.* Available: http://linkresearchlab.org/PreparingDigitalUniversity.pdf.

Sieminski, S., Messenger, J., & Murphy, S. (2016). Case study: What supports students to improve their grades? *Open Learning: The Journal of Open, Distance and e-Learning, 31*, 141–151.

Thorpe, M. (2008). Effective online interaction: Mapping course design to bridge from research to practice. *Australasian Journal of Educational Technology, 24*(1), 57–72.

Weller, M., & Robinson, L. (2002). Scaling up an online course to deal with 12 000 students. *Education, Communication and Information, 1*(3), 307–323.

11

Values, Identity and Successful Online Teaching Relationships

Michelle Oldale and Madeleine Knightley

This chapter reflects on the experience of communicating values and identity in online teaching environments. Richardson and Alsup (2015) define teacher identity as the sense of self, "that results from productive combination of key personal and professional subjectivities or beliefs." (p. 142). What is of great interest to us here is how we maintain and express genuine identity rooted in our personal value systems in the increasing shift from face to face delivery (Baxter 2012). We report the findings of our action research using an Appreciative Enquiry model and discuss themes and implications in the light of pre-existing contemporary literature. After discussion of the findings we invite a pause for reflection. We summarise findings, posing questions we have frequently asked of ourselves and provide examples of best practice we have used (or observed

M. Oldale (✉)
Open University in the East Midlands, Nottingham, UK
e-mail: m.a.r.l.oldale@open.ac.uk

M. Knightley
Open University, Milton Keynes, UK
e-mail: madeleine.knightley@open.ac.uk

© The Author(s) 2018
J. Baxter et al. (eds.), *Creativity and Critique in Online Learning*,
https://doi.org/10.1007/978-3-319-78298-0_11

our colleagues utilising). As you engage with the chapter we would encourage you to think of your own examples, continue to raise these questions and others, and to carry on these discussions in the contexts of your own teaching practice. This is representative of what Baxter (2012, p. 102) describes as "drawing laterally on … ongoing experiences in order to shape and form … online interactions." Our hope is that this supports you towards making the experience of online teaching as effective and rewarding as possible. Although the chapter was written by both of us the practical research element was carried out by one author. This is reflected in the narrative.

Initial Reflections

Before you read on, and before we introduce ourselves as authors, take a moment to reflect on your first impressions of who we are. You have limited information so far and we are separated, from you the reader, by potentially huge physical distances. We have only the words on this page to communicate who we are and what our interests may be. You may gather that each of us is interested in online identity by virtue of the fact that we are writing this chapter in the first place! What more do you imagine we bring to the table as teachers and as human beings? What do you imagine are our values, motivations and passions? What would you want us to know about your own motivations and values, for reading the chapter and undertaking the role you do?

You will learn more about us as authors as you continue to read. We, sadly, may never know more about you as the reader (unless you decide to make direct contact) though we imagine that you are drawn to the idea of online identity by the fact you are reading our work.

This activity in some way mirrors the realities of working online. Physical distance separates us. We have to think of new and innovative ways to communicate our 'selves' across this barrier. The realities of technology can be both a support and a hindrance to this process and we hope that this chapter will provide a means of reaping the benefits of collaborative reflection, and negotiating the challenges that the platform poses.

Personal Beginnings

This piece of action research started with a very personal enquiry: Our roles in the higher education sector mean that we both teach in face to face, online and blended contexts and have done so for a number of years. As well as being an Associate Lecturer for the Open University Psychology and Counselling Modules, Michelle is also a psychotherapist, facilitator and researcher with an interest in personal and professional identity. Madeleine is a chartered psychologist and Staff Tutor with the Open University. Her interests lie in personal identity and development.

The main online teaching channels used by the authors and tutor-participants in this study are:

- A non-synchronous forum – allowing posting of messages and delayed response. These involve students from one or more groups and are facilitated/moderated by one or more tutors
- Other non-synchronous means such as E Mail
- Synchronous or live teaching via online rooms enabling presentations and activities to be uploaded. Communication is possible via audio and or video as well as chat facility.

Having some experience of teaching in these contexts I (MO) was preparing for an interview to teach on a new OU psychology module, which was to be taught mainly online. One of the set tasks for the interview involved composing responses (and order of responding) to ficti-tious postings on a non-synchronous forum (Knightley 2015) in Withers (2015). Engaging in virtual conversations with imagined students I found myself in lengthy deliberations about the inter-relationship between my own values and needs of the students represented, how I would commu-nicate the self-reflective aims of the new module philosophy, as well as student centred imperatives inherent in the Open University and wider Open movement. (You can see an example response in Appendix 11.A). I wondered how my words on the screen reflected my stance and impacted on the students involved.

I was struck by the considerable reflection this provoked, causing me to think about the importance of genuine and supportive communication in the online context. I pondered how this linked to my values and identity as a person-centred psychotherapist and facilitator, including my belief in promoting a sense of personal value, agency and empowerment in students, in both the face to face and virtual environment. What followed was an investigation into whether other tutors working in online environments felt the same. What is the experience of working genuinely with teaching values and identity in an online environment, what are the highlights and challenges of working in this way and how does the research evidence support or challenge this experience? McNaughton and Billot (2016) ponder this question suggesting, 'Pedagogy, values, and professional and personal narratives of self are all affected, particularly by technological change' (p. 644). These questions are of particular importance given the proliferation of online delivery in the Higher Education sector and the need for tutors, 'to be able to work comfortably and confidently in the online environment.' (Baxter 2012).

The Disembodied Nature of the Online Environment

Early on in the final writing of this chapter I received a thank you card from a student I taught in a face to face context. They commented on my "good humour … smiling eyes and intense commitment to helping me value what I might be able to do, and what I was doing." In that moment I felt heard and understood in my approach, my identity and teaching values. I was connected with the hugely embodied act of teaching – how I was able to successfully communicate my commitment to developing human potential and value through my physical presence. This added an extra dimension to my enquiry. It justified and made sense of the time and effort I gave to the interview task described previously. In the context of a non-synchronous forum there is a literal disembodiment and separateness both from my colleagues and students. I rely on an abstract representation of my embodiment (Ogden and Wakeman

2013) in words and images to convey my hopes, aspirations and passions. Baxter (2011, p. 9) noted feedback from her students suggesting their experience of her was different according to whether they were encountering her in a face to face or online environment. I have noticed my own desire to present a consistent identity in both face to face and online environments and rely on feedback in its various forms, in the immediacy of the interaction, or after the event to determine whether this has been successful.

Professional Identity and Philosophical Congruence: Effectiveness and Satisfaction

As a person-centred therapist, my understanding of my professional identity and its expression in various contexts comes from the idea of 'philosophical congruence'. Tudor and Worrall (2006, p. 17) suggest that we will be at our most effective when our values and the expression of these in the context of our work are closely matched. Baxter (2012) suggests that it is important in terms of our professional development to examine the crossover between our sense of effectiveness and our teaching identity. Since the online context is unique in nature, it seems important to examine whether the reality of online teaching in all its forms allows tutors to be their real selves. This leads to the key question addressed in this chapter:

How Can Online Environments Allow Tutors to Express their Identity and Values in Ways which Contribute to Successful Teaching Relationships?

The chapter continues by describing the method and design of the study. It then goes on to present the findings from the action research and discuss these in the light of the literature reviewed before going on to offer conclusions and practical solutions for those tutors working in online environments.

The Research Study: Data Collection and Analysis

This piece of action research interweaves my own experiences with the perspective of other tutors teaching online in the social sciences. Data was gathered via an online questionnaire asking the following questions:

- How do you see your identity as a tutor, and how does this link to your values and aspirations?
- How is expression of your teaching identity supported or hindered by the online teaching environment? What is satisfying and frustrating about this process?
- What do you experience as the key similarities and differences in expression of your tutor identity in online as opposed to face-to-face teaching environments?
- How does the expression of your identity in online environments support student learning?
- How does the expression of your identity in both online and face-to-face environments support your aspirations as a tutor and link to your teaching values?
- What is the overall impact on your role satisfaction as a tutor when your values and aspirations are reflected in your online interactions?
- How does this role satisfaction benefit you and your students in both the short and long term?

Ethical approval was gained from the Open University Human Research Ethics Committee. Participants were recruited from the online tutor communities for two social sciences courses delivered by the Open University. The sample came from across the United Kingdom and participants self-selected. Seven tutors responded.

Tutor responses to the survey were summarised and synthesised, using a thematic analysis. Themes were combined into short quotations retaining wherever possible tutors' original words. Themes are combined as if to represent the voice of one tutor.

The literature review was the final phase of the study and used participant key words as search terms. The rationale for this was to allow themes to arise from the experience of participants' in this study themselves and to discuss this in the light of the work of previous authors and researchers. This approach draws on elements of Grounded Theory Method (Charmaz 2014, p. 20).

Findings and Discussion

Defining Identity and Its Online Expression

Lasky (2005) cited in Xiao (2016) frames professional teaching identity as the way in which tutors, "define themselves to themselves and to others". Tutors surveyed care deeply about being facilitators in a learner-centred environment. As these comments illustrate:

> I see my identity as a facilitator of learning. My identity is an important part of being a tutor and important in establishing a link with my students.
> I see myself as a learning mentor leading and accompanying adult students on a learning journey. This involves acknowledging and building on their existing and often substantial previous experience and learning.

At the heart of the philosophy of the Open Movement is a pedagogy of abundance (Weller 2014, p. 10), where open content, shared in online relationships benefits a wide and diverse community of learners. This philosophy makes much of the resourcefulness of the community and the value of pre-existing knowledge. It does not site expertise solely with the tutor and for our participants who aligned with this philosophy, online environments seem an ideal platform to engage in student-centred relationships and to share passion for their subject matter whilst drawing on the inherent resources of the learning community. However, some tutors find the online environment draws them away from this aspiration into a top down model of didactic teaching. They feel that most of the interaction in an online tutorial occurs through the tutor who occupies the central position at the wheel of communication making this more lecturer style than genuinely interactive for students. Online teaching can often feel 'top down' rather than facilitative.

This is reflected by Rehn et al. (2016) participants who selected tutor-led styles in synchronous sessions purely because it seemed easier. Xiao (2016) found that distance tutors express a difference in their actual as opposed to their aspirational identity in the workplace. Returning to the idea that satisfaction is fostered when our aspirational values match those which are expressed (Tudor and Worrall 2006) we can see here the potential for dissatisfaction in the shift away from collaborative and student-centred learning.

Relationship: Physicality and 'Visibility'

Tutors in this study miss the physicality of the face to face environment which they see as central to communicating their values and identity, and thus building relationship. They aspire to visibility – a way to be seen and to monitor students' responses and assess their learning when interactions are conducted online with participants stating they, "aspire to having a relationship with the students but this very rarely happens unless they come to a face to face tutorial.".

Rehn et al.'s (2016) suggest that the transition from face to face to online learning requires specific attention and that, "Building relationships and rapport between the teacher and the students is critical to a positive learning environment (Munroe 1998), and the real and perceived distance in a videoconferencing classroom makes it more difficult to create this atmosphere." (p. 303). Participants in the current study agreed saying, "We need to work a little harder to build a relationship with students, as you can't rely on your physical presence." and "How can I even tell whether students are there or not?"

Rehn et al. stress the importance of 'presence' in synchronous online communication defining this as the extent to which a physically dispersed group have a sense of being together. They also draw on Gunawardena and Zittle's (1997) explanation, "the degree to which a person on the other side of a screen (or computer) is perceived as being 'real' (p. 9)."

(p. 303). These researchers stress the need for a 'social presence' in order for cognitive presence or learning to be achieved. This certainly seems to resonate with the aspiration of tutors surveyed to be seen in who they are and in their subject passions.

Although participants in the current study aspired to, "share love of my subject with my students. I aim to motivate and inspire them…" they saw technology as depersonalising and mainly as a barrier.

> "I need to spend time on technical skills as well as building relationships, and course materials. I need to choose topics/activities that will work specifically in an online environment."
>
> "There is no 'Plan B' when things go wrong (e.g. lost connections) as is the case in a face to face session." – this suggests that technological breakdown represents a rupture in relationship that could be worked around in a face to face context, and, "The technology is constraining and dictates how an activity can be presented – or indeed what activities can be covered."

The loss of both visual and auditory cues when chat boxes are employed solely was seen to contribute to distance.

> In online rooms only a tiny minority will use the microphone, and it is not possible to have 'intimate' interactions via the chat box.

Slagter van Tryon and Bishop (2009) ideas of social connectedness are relevant here. Their research actually suggests that where the cues of face to face interaction are not available, learners will disclose relevant information to build and maintain cohesive groups online. They stress, however, that increased and persistent opportunity to share is needed alongside technical support if this is to be successful. I would suggest that a couple of things are relevant here. Firstly that a tutor's own disclosure of identity (for example as a student centred facilitator, their passions) will help students to familiarise themselves with social cues in what may be, for them, a novel (and perhaps intimidating) learning 'event' (Slagter van Tryon and Bishop (2009)). This orientation to the role of the tutor might be followed with opportunities to build relationship with each other. In simple, practical terms giving each participant in a synchronous interaction time to familiarise themselves with the microphone/chat box to say their name and what they hope to get from the session may build some technological confidence as well as allowing some initial bonding.

Turning to my personal experience, I have found it is possible to have depth conversations via a chat box but only when I am a co-facilitator and this is my sole task for that particular section of the session. This means I can focus on giving detailed responses to students who choose or require (for purposes of accessibility) to use typed chat as their method of communication with the group. This kind of more intimate communication is impossible when simultaneously facilitating voice/video and chat interactions. I would suggest that this is a strong case for co-facilitation in synchronous online environments wherever resources allow.

When things go wrong, for example a lost internet connection, this fractures and disrupts online teaching – particularly in live sessions. There is little that can be done about this, though participants saw opportunities for further technological education and training to support both tutors and students with engagement in online contexts. Rehn et al. (2016) citing Koehler and Mishra (2009) highlight that a blend of subject specific, technological and pedagogical knowledge is required for successful teaching in online contexts. I wonder if this alone allows communication of identity and refers to the earlier discussion of communication of presence as equally important. This is supported by Rehn et al.'s findings which showed firstly that technological and pedagogical knowledge do not specifically translate into presence online. Secondly, that presence had a direct correlation with outcomes and student satisfaction. However, it should be noted that there was some loss of the value of presence when technological proficiency was low, showing a multi-directional relationship between these factors.

Fields et al.'s (2016) study describes an online relationship between a cohort of learners which endures beyond the end of a course. It is clear from this example that time was given to a period of face to face interaction in advance of the set up of the online community. It could be argued that this kind of blended learning might allow a deepening of relationship perhaps not possible in a purely online context. Fields et al. specifically looked at online relationships over time which leads me to reflect on whether there is an optimum timescale for establishing a relationship during which a tutor and student can gain a sense of each- others' identity.

The Importance of Disclosure

Participants in our study saw disclosure as a way to get past the lack of physicality in online environments.

Students not 'seeing' me as a person hinders – letting them know a little more about me helps them see me as more than just a distant voice. (Tutor)

As I reflect on the idea of disclosure I am reminded of its multi layered nature by Song (2016). Song cites Benesch (2012) who discusses the importance of emotional disclosure in teacher identity. They stress what we are able to express of our emotional identity depends on the context including institution and culture. This leads me to wonder how far tutors in our action research responded emotionally to the demands of the online environment and felt more or less able to disclose these responses to colleagues and indeed students as appropriate. They might, for example feel nervous at using the online channel, or frustrated at a technological glitch. I personally see disclosure of this nature, where it is appropriate as a key part of my identity. I acknowledge the normalising role of emotional disclosure where my own nervousness or frustration allows others to express their own, perhaps 'clearing the air' for ongoing learning to take place. I would suggest this helps students to see me as a person and enhances the social connection that previous authors and our participants have cited as important.

Physicality is seen as a disclosure in itself. Tutors seek to build on the ways in which their presence can be communicated in online contexts whether through typed or voice communication suggesting emoticons and humour as ways to do this.

Participants suggested, "You can do small things to help such as attaching a picture to your profile but we lack an online persona/image/object that represents each of us that can be moved around. Emoticons can also be useful to create a more relaxed atmosphere." (Tutor).

The seeming lack of use of the range of technology available in the wider industry and its potential to enhance tutor and student experience was commented on, "It seems that there is so much that gets people involved in video games that isn't used."

(Interestingly video was not mentioned specifically by current participants although this is an option in online rooms used by authors and participants.) This resonates with Rehn et al. (2016) who suggest verbal and physical means to communicate genuine presence in synchronous communication. They propose use of participant names and inclusive pronouns, as well as gesture and body language wherever this is possible.

An Accessible Environment

Participants valued the potential for accessibility offered by the online environment stating that, "My approach values education being open to all." There are numerous reasons why students may be unable to attend face to face teaching sessions and participants acknowledged that, "Distance learners can feel isolated and it is good that students who would not normally be able to attend face to face can make it."

Overall, the literature gives support to participants' experiences in this small piece of action research. Table 11.1 gives a summary of findings, questions for ongoing personal and professional reflection and ideas gathered from our own practice as well as best practice observed/offered by colleagues.

Conclusions

I conclude this chapter by highlighting what I have personally learned and how I intend to go forward in my online teaching practice. To do this I utilise ideas from Appreciative Enquiry (AI) (See Appreciative Inquiry Commons n.d., online) to undertake a further level of analysis. AI seeks the 'positive core' present in each situation, using this to promote growth and change (Schiller in Cockell and McArthur-Blair (2012). I have therefore attempted to ask 'appreciative questions' about tutors assertions about what they aspire to deliver and to explore what might allow tutors to achieve their aims.

I reflected on participant experience and the literature using the acronym SOAR (Stavros and Hinrichs (2009, pp. 16–17) in Cockell and

Table 11.1 Summary findings, questions for ongoing reflection and practical suggestions

Findings	Reflective questions	Suggestions for best practice – consider:
Participants described their online identity as **student centred facilitators of learning.** They found the online environment lent itself to teacher centred model and this was a frustration. Participants found that the lack of **physicality and visibility** in the online environment detracted from a sense of presence. There is a sense of **distance and disconnection** and **technology is a barrier to relationship.** For example **few students use the microphone in synchronous settings** and it **is difficult to have depth conversations via the chat box.**	What is your experience of communicating your own values and identity in online environments? How have you maintained a collaborative stance alongside learners? What is your own sense of physicality and presence as you engage in online interactions? How can you enhance a sense of connection between you, learners and co-facilitators?	Disclosing your own aims for the session/ communicating aspirations for collaboration at the beginning of an online session. Creating opportunities for disclosure of personal connection to current topics through direct prompts (e.g. within presentation slides) Including a holding slide/message at the outset of a synchronous session with instructions on how to undertake a microphone/sound test. Creating space for tutor and student 'check in' in with use of specific physical prompts e.g. 'I am sitting in my study and I can see the spring daffodils outside', 'You may hear my dog barking in the background' Use of physical objects such as books to create a sense of connection e.g. 'Bring along a book on x topic and tell us why you would recommend it'. Use of collaborative teaching wherever possible for efficient management of verbal and chat box responses.
Being seen as a person is important and this means that some level of **disclosure** beyond that which is afforded by the physicality of face to face interactions is necessary.	How do you use disclosure in online interactions to convey a sense of yourself and how this relates to the topic you are teaching?	Create opportunities for disclosure of how tutor interests link to the topic at hand, for example use of 'check in' time and use of appropriate examples within sessions.

McArthur-Blair (2012, p. 127)). Adapted from the earlier analysis tool SWOT (Strengths, Weaknesses, Opportunities, and Threats), SOAR invites consideration of:

- "Strengths: What can we build on?"
  In this study participants saw key strengths in their passion for their topic and in their student centred identity.
- Opportunities: What are our stakeholders asking for?
  Current participants and previous studies suggests that student stakeholders appreciate genuine communication from tutors. This supports relationship and learning in both face to face and online contexts.
- Aspirations: What do we care deeply about?
  We care deeply about being genuine and communicating passion. We aspire to utilising the knowledge which resides in the entire community, not just the knowledge of the tutor.
- Results: How do we know we are succeeding?"

And so, I come full circle to reflect again on my own values and identity, including my own passions for my subject matter (psychology and counselling). As I do this an image of a diagram for planning of online interactions comes to mind; this is represented in Fig. 11.1 which is influenced by the participants in the current study (represented in Table 11.1) as well as the reflections of previous researchers cited.

Each circle of the Venn diagram represents an area I can consider in the online interaction. Course content and aims are in focus in the top circle. What I propose in this model is giving equal weight to tutor and student values and identity as well as to the passion and experience they bring to the table. This has a dual focus. Firstly, it brings what might be an implicit hope for genuine reflection of identity into explicit focus in the planning stages for online work. My hope is that this would result in communication of presence as suggested by Rehn et al. (2016), group building as suggested by Slagter van Tyron and Bishop (2009) and thus more 'philosophically congruent', effective and satisfying online interactions. The sections of the Venn Diagram represent how course content, tutor and

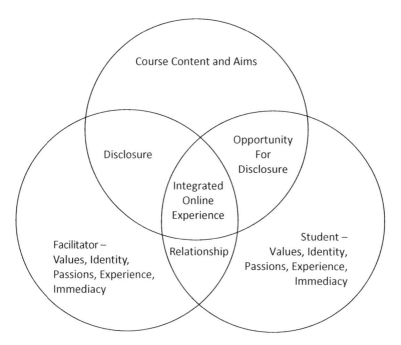

Fig. 11.1 Planning online interactions

student values overlap with each other and translate into practical action. I have suggested that as a tutor I can actively use disclosure (of key aspects of identity, passions and values) which serve to illustrate points about course content and aims. This is supported by Rehn et al.'s student participants who expressed satisfaction and appreciation at their facilitator's disclosure of stories and though use of humour. The students stated that, "We got to know her a lot better because she added a bit of a personal aspect to the classes and this made us feel connected.' (p. 311) This compensates for a loss of physicality in online contexts. In a face to face context for example, it can be seen that I am a Fat Woman. In face to face contexts I have often used this component of my identity to make teaching points in relation to challenging societal expectations and objectification (see Calogero in Mahendran (2015, p. 192)). Undertaking this activity in an online environment requires an added, explicit level of disclosure, perhaps a picture of myself, or a verbal prompt linking this to my passions as a size acceptance activist and researcher. Embedding opportunities for disclosure (for example into slides or activities) allows me to enquire into students' experience and passion. This allows them in turn to communicate their identity and bolsters the relationship between us, as well as enhancing our learning experience. If specific opportunities are created for sharing and relationship building at the outset of a course this could create a solid basis for the ongoing productive learning environment. In an ideal world I might like to create a dedicated period of time for relationship building (as in Fields et al.'s 2016 study), though restraints of timetable pacing and volume of course content may prevent this.

Blended face to face and online interaction allows an element of the physical components and prompts of identity to be held in memory and enhance online interactions. Indeed the tutors surveyed used a blend of face to face and online teaching so this may be the case, though it may not be possible in all settings and for all students.

Results: How Do We Know We Are Succeeding?

This section of the SOAR acronym is not specifically addressed previously. However, it has key importance and I would suggest that success can be assessed on a session by session or course by course basis by creating specific opportunity for reflection on success of the online interaction/relationship alongside key learnings (e.g. what was successful/helped you engage?). I would also advocate for individual tutor and peer to peer reflection (where collaborative working has been undertaken), based on aspects of SOAR and the model presented in Fig. 11.1.

Reflections on the Action Research

This chapter has (as any research is) been influenced by my own values. There may be readers who place more or less emphasis on the importance of expressing values and identity online, and this is a position I respect. I am sure that the participants who consented to take part did so from motivations reflecting a stance similar to mine and therefore the sample is selective. Whilst this might be seen as a criticism of the study, from an appreciative stance it is perhaps an opportunity to undertake further research to reflect a broader range of perspectives. For my part, if I could do this piece of research again I would undergo a collaborative process of asking appreciative questions from the outset, with my initial question-naire participants, following this up with interviews or a focus group. Whilst this particular appreciative analysis was based on my reflections alone, it perhaps represents an opportunity for a later, refined study with a more integrated AI design.

Tips and Discussion Points

- Participants described their online identity as student centred facilita-tors of learning. They found the online environment lent itself to a teacher centred model and this was a frustration.
  - Explicitly disclose hopes for collaboration at the beginning of an online session
  - Create opportunities throughout for discussion of connection with topics being discussed (for example by including prompts in slides/materials)
  - Utilise prior knowledge about students and co-facilitators to pro-mote discussion – for example, 'x … do you mind if I share the example you used at our face to face tutorial?'
- Participants found that the lack of physicality and visibility in the online environment detracted from a sense of presence. There is a sense of distance and disconnection and technology is a barrier to relation-ship. For example few students use the microphone in synchronous settings and it is difficult to have depth conversations via the chat box.
  - Include a holding slide/message at the outset of a synchronous session with instructions on how to undertake a microphone/sound test.
  - Create space for tutor and student 'check in' in with use of specific physical prompts e.g. 'I am sitting in my study and I can see the spring daffodils outside', 'You may hear my dog barking in the background'
  - Consider including a picture of yourself in online profiles or within presentation slides.
  - Use physical objects such as books to create a sense of connection e.g. 'Bring along a book on x topic and tell us why you would rec-ommend it'.

Appendix 11.A Example forum posting (Interview Task: Knightley 2015)

Forum posting	Tutor response	Rationale
Jasmine: 'I'm replying to the post at 14.10, about an approach in psychology. That person is clearly very confused!! The explanation is set out VERY OBVIOUSLY in the module book, you only have to read it closely! Phenomenology is just discussing the things that happen to people. Simple, no?'	Quarantine message and send individual response below via e mail: Dear Jasmine, Thank you for identifying on the forum that one of your colleagues may be experiencing some difficulties in understanding module materials in relation to Phenomenology. Supporting each other with our understanding is certainly one of the aims of the forum so thank you for getting involved. It is interesting isn't it that we are talking about phenomenology (our own subjective experience). When we are not face to face in a room with another person, or in a real time conversation online, we only have our own subjective experience to fall back on when we a reading intention into a communication because we are unable to ask what was meant or get an immediate response. I wonder if, reflecting on your original posting, you might notice aspects of it which might have been interpreted by the reader as less supportive than you intended. I'm really keen for you to offer your own ideas around understanding of this term so would like to offer an opportunity to reword your post to remain more in line with the group agreement we all made at the outset of the module, as well as the OU study skills guidelines on discussion in online forums. You will notice that your post has been removed so that we can give you an opportunity to respond personally (on the same thread) and more specifically to x who posted at 14.10. You could do this by giving further detail on your own understanding of phenomenology with links to the module materials you are using to support this understanding. This will give further opportunity for x and other students to benefit from your experience and bring their own understandings based in the module materials. I have attached a link to some information on 'effective discussion' which might be useful in reconstructing your response. I hope this is helpful, and I would be really happy for you to talk this through with me prior to reposting to ensure that the online learning experience is as useful as it can be for all of us. Looking forward to reading your further ideas on phenomenology and responding to any questions you might have. Warm Wishes Michelle	• Response <u>seems</u> out of line with group learning agreement and study skills guidelines. • Responding directly in the thread may be shaming for the student and miss learning opportunities for this and other students based in knowledge and understanding and key skills learning outcomes and I therefore: 1. Thank the student for their posting, assuming positive intent, and that this is an issue of communication 2. Make links to phenomenology and subjective experience (the topic of the post to enhance knowledge and understanding) 3. Make an invitation to respond more specifically with a summarised understanding of phenomenology (key skills) and specific links to the chapter 4. Make direct reference to study skills and the group agreement to support the student with a reconstructed response 5. Invite further conversation and clarification, thus modelling an open approach to communication

- Use co-teaching wherever resources allow for efficient management of verbal and chat box responses.
- Being seen as a person is important and this means that some level of disclosure beyond that which is afforded by the physicality of face to face interactions is necessary.
  - Create opportunities for disclosure of how your values, identity and interests link to the topic at hand, for example in 'check in' time and throughout. Incorporate reflection on this into planning time.
  - Create opportunities for students to be seen as a person, ask for personal/professional responses to material where appropriate.
  - Both of the above might include linking to examples outside of direct course materials, for example current stories in the media.
  - Communicate personal impact wherever appropriate. For example, in relation to content, 'I am quite moved to think how x issue might affect…'. In relation to the environment, 'I'm a little frustrated with the technical issues we are having this evening but…'
- Participants valued the potential for accessibility in online environments.
  - Wherever possible check for accessibility needs in advance of session and ensure technology is supportive of these.
  - Send accessible materials in advance if required.

Personal and Professional Reflections

- I have made an assumption that the group would have formulated, or been offered a group learning agreement and been signposted to the netiquette guidelines at the outset of the module.
- My rationale overall was based around potential impact on individuals and the group learning environment.
- I am mindful that I completed the activity in isolation – In reality I would have the advantage of reflection and support from colleagues, which I have found invaluable in previous similar situations.

Chapter Acknowledgements We would like to thank the participants of our action research who generously shared their experience of online teaching. We would also like to thank the organisers and participants of the Faculty of Arts and Social Sciences 'Creativity and Critique in Online Learning' seminar where initial research findings on 'Being Human Online' were presented, and inspiration for the final draft was gained.

References

Appreciative Inquiry Commons. (n.d.). *What is appreciative inquiry?* [Online]. Available at https://appreciativeinquiry.case.edu/intro/whatisai.cfm. Accessed 21 Nov 2016.

Baxter, J. (2011). *An investigation into the role of professional learning on the online teaching identities of higher education lecturers.* EdD thesis, The Open University.

Baxter, J. (2012). The impact of professional learning on the teaching identities of higher education lecturers. *European Journal of Open, Distance and E Learrning* 2012: II [Online]. http://www.eurodl.org/index.php?p=archives&year=2012&halfyear=2&article=527. Accessed 23 Mar 2017.

Charmaz, K. (2014). *Constructing grounded theory* (2nd ed.). London: Sage.

Cockell, J., & McArthur-Blair, J. (2012). *Appreciative inquiry in higher education: A transformative force.* San Fransisco: Jossey-Bass.

Fields, A., Lai, K.-W., Gibbs, J., Kirk, A., & Vermunt, J. (2016). The transformation of an online learning community from an organised facility to an organic fraternity. *Distance Education, 37*(1), 60–72.

Mahendran, K. (2015). Self Esteem. In J. Turner, C. Hewson, K. Mahendran, & P. Stevens (Eds.), *Living psychology: From the everyday to the extraordinary book 1.* Milton Keynes: Open University Press.

McNaughton, S. M., & Billot, J. (2016). Negotiating academic teacher identity shifts during higher education contextual change. *Teaching in Higher Education, 21*(6), 644–658.

Ogden, C. A., & Wakeman, S. (2013). *The body and society.* Chester: University of Chester Press.

Rehn, N., Maor, D., & McConney, A. (2016). Investigating teacher presence in courses using synchronous videoconferencing. *Distance Education, 37*(3), 302–316.

Richardson, J. C., & Alsup, J. (2015). From the classroom to the keyboard: How seven teachers created their online teaching identities. *International Review of Research in Open and Distributed Learning, 16*(1), 142–167.

Slagter van Tryon, S. J., & Bishop, M. J. (2009). Theoretical foundations for enhancing social connectedness in online learning environments. *Distance Education, 30*(3), 291–315.

Song, J. (2016). Emotions and language teacher identity: Conflicts, vulnerability, and transformation. *In TESOL Q, 50*, 631–654.

Tudor, K., & Worrall, M. (2006). *Person-centred therapy: A clinical philosophy.* London: Routledge.

Weller, M. (2014). *The battle for open: How openness won and why it doesn't feel like a victory.* London: Ubiquity Press.

Withers, P. (2015, July 21). Email to Michelle Oldale.

Xiao, J. (2016). Who am I as a distance tutor? An investigation of distance tutors' professional identity in China. *Distance Education, 37*(1), 4–21.

12

The Move to Online Teaching: A Head of Department's Perspective

Introduction

Amidst the massive changes within higher education, the integration of online teaching strategies within universities is now well established Gregory and salmon (2013). The impact of the transition to online teaching adds another challenge in terms of both identity and role for the individual academic. Despite some acknowledgement at university level that academics will need training and changes to work load management systems, there is very little literature about what it is like to move as a university teacher from a traditional face to face environment to an almost entirely online one. Support for the individual in making this transition is key and this chapter offers a Head of Department's point of view. One strand of literature in this area suggests that university senior management teams often start from a position that academic staff are not motivated to participate and will generally resist change. This case study offers a challenge to that view by focusing

D. Preston (✉)
Department of People and Organisation, Open University Business School,
Faculty of Business and Law, Open University, Milton Keynes, UK
e-mail: diane.preston@open.ac.uk

© The Author(s) 2018   **241**
J. Baxter et al. (eds.), *Creativity and Critique in Online Learning*,
https://doi.org/10.1007/978-3-319-78298-0_12

on a group of academics who had chosen consciously to move to the Open University in the UK, an online and distance learning provider. Teaching online requires different skills and presents a fundamental challenge to teacher identity; there is a need to not only understand the academics' perspective but also to acknowledge that there is motivation within the academic community. What is critical is the support provided for academics making this transition at all institutional levels.

The Changing World of the University

For some years now the higher education sector has been experiencing a period of extensive change. Factors such as increasing competition, marketisation and higher student expectations have meant the rethinking of university strategies at all levels including that of online learning (Barber et al. 2013; Salmon 2005, 2014). New ways of teaching and learning using digital and web based technologies is now an established trend in higher education across the world. As Tynan et al. emphasise, it is no longer possible to work in ways that belong to a transmission era of university teaching. Instead, they argue that 'as access and connectivity penetrate deeply into our personal, transactional, work and learning lives, interactivity and constructivist pedagogies must be considered routine, not 'add-ons' in teaching' (2015: 15).

The term online is used here to denote the move from traditional, face to face teaching to one that is wholly or largely online and at a distance. Introducing online learning into a university has many implications; not least a massive financial investment and fundamental changes in both infrastructure and professional roles. However, one area that is less often considered is the impact on academics despite them being 'an instrumental constituent whose advocacy is critical to the adoption of online education' (Mitchell et al. 2015: 351) and often the 'first to experience the practical implications of change' (McNaughton and Billot 2016: 644). Throughout the discourse about the transformative effect of online strategies in higher education, very little attention has been paid to those primarily responsible for their implementation (Gregory and Lodge 2015). Teaching online requires different types of work processes and professional skills

(Schnneckenberg 2010) and presents a significant challenge to teacher identity (Sappey and Relf 2010). The challenge for those supporting academics through this transition process is to recognise the learning curve, assuage hesitation and build on academics' motivation and expertise as teachers. Consequently, academics' motivations for, and understandings of, the requirement of online teaching need to be explored explicitly.

The aim of this chapter is to better understand the experiences of a group of academics moving to online teaching and to make some suggestions about the support they might receive based on my personal experience as a Head of Department. University level systems around areas such as development and reward are important but so too are those at the more localised level of the department or team. Hanson (2009) acknowledges the role of teaching programme leaders in terms of both the encouragement of, and negotiation toward, online learning for academics but this is an exception. The Head of Department plays a key part in the implementation of university or faculty strategy at the operational level (Sarros et al. 1997; Floyd 2013; Currie 2014) but also the more immediate tasks of mentoring and inducting those who might be new to the online teaching environment and way of working. She is also often an academic as well as a manager and may well face similar challenges. There is a need to both understand more about academics' experiences but also how universities might provide better support. Given their experience and position in the university strata, the Head of Department is the point at which university senior managers can understand the touch points of both resistance and motivation.

Challenges for the Academic/Teacher

Building on Henkel's (2000, 2005) seminal work, over the last two decades many studies have reviewed the tensions involved for academics in the midst of the changes in higher education (see, for example, Symes 1999; Becher and Trowler 2001; Barry et al. 2006; Deem et al. 2007; Sparkes 2013; Clarke and Knights 2015). One of the biggest changes is the introduction of a management cadre and discourse and its effect on academics' morale (Pritchard and Wilmott 1997; Exworthy and Halford

1999; Fredman and Doughney 2012). In addition, there is also an area of literature based upon a managerialist discourse of academics being the main barrier to change and that university senior management teams can be hampered by academics in terms of their reluctance to embrace change in the higher education sector (Boxall 2015; Mitchell et al. 2015). Schneckenberg argues that the underlying problem for the adoption of online learning is the 'structural peculiarities of universities and cultural barriers which are deeply rooted in the academic community' (2009: 411). Or, more specifically, that academics are reluctant to get involved in training and development related to online teaching (Kukulska-Hulme 2012). In short then, some previous literature in this area has tended to lament academics' lack of participation in the move to online teaching rather than acknowledging that there may be real concerns for the academics involved. An underexplored area of literature looks at the increasing levels of enthusiasm for online teaching from academics; one recent survey in the United States found that nearly half of the four and a half thousand academics questioned said the rise of online education excited them more than it frightened them (Allen and Seaman 2012). Given both sets of literature – the assumed resistance and signs of a counter argument to this – it is argued here that it is important that we know more about why this transition to online teaching is challenging for the individual academic and what we can do to support it.

The Basis of Hesitation

As outlined above, the move to online learning presents a major challenge to academics in that it has 'profoundly changed the way academics teach and research, and the speed at which they are expected to work' (Fanghanel 2012: 5). In their study of academic work, Clarke et al. (2012), for example, found high levels of anxiety from individuals feeling that their authenticity as experts in the academic field were challenged by their current, ever-shifting working lives and contexts. Coping with change as an academic (Kosaker 2008) and taking risks as a teacher (Turkle 1993) are both necessary parts of all types of effective teaching but the shift to online presents a major challenge for the academic and some level of apprehension is inevitable (Ross et al. 2014).

These fears regarding a change in teaching role sit within a much wider literature about professional and personal identity which proposes that identities are complex and fluid rather than fixed, and that anything that has the potential to threaten our identity requires us to undertake significant amounts of 'identity work' (see, for example, Grey 1994; Barry et al. 2006). This is the effort that goes into the dynamic process of forming, maintaining and often revising the sense and practice of who one is (Alvesson and Wilmott 2002). Our work lives, like any other activity, are infused with emotion (Fineman 1993, 2000) and our identities are insecure (Clarke et al.2012) and uncertain because identity depends so much others' evaluations and validations of the self (Luckmann and Berger 1964). Knights and Clarke's work (2014) on 'fragile' academics is about the challenges to individuals in the midst of massive general change in the higher education sector. It is argued here that the move to very different modes of teaching should be included in this because of the challenges it represents. So much of our understanding of ourselves is bound up in our activities and practices, and our sense of ourselves as teachers is very much related to our practice as teachers. One example of a change of practice regarding online is that while teaching always involves others, usually these are other academics on the same module or programme teaching team; whereas the move to sophisticated online teaching is likely to involve many others around the university such as administrators, digital media editors, audio-visual experts and librarians. This not only puts the individual's teaching endeavours in the spotlight but also imposes different sorts of demands and deadlines. If Clarke et al. (2012) are correct, and identity work often takes place in a context of a fear of failure, then radically changing the way one teaches presents an entirely under-estimated complexity. Here it may be helpful to draw on what Barnett (2007) calls an 'ontological turn' in the sense that it involves not only the individual academic becoming a learner themselves and challenging what they know but also developing the skills to cope with the uncertainty which that process brings. Indeed, Barnett suggests that such a 'turn' entails an identity transformation that can impact upon every aspect of our lives, not just in terms of our roles as academics or teachers.

Finally, other literatures outline further reasons why academics may be hesitant about the shift to online teaching, including, for example, a lack of understanding of the differences between this and traditional face to face teaching, inappropriate or much advanced technology, or unsupportive university systems (Conole et al. 2007; Goodyear 2010; Gunn 2010). Other factors related to the challenge to teacher identity might include fear of the unknown, fear of the disruption of interpersonal relationships with both students and colleagues and concerns about the effects of change on status and jobs (Mitchell et al. 2015). In the light of this enormous challenge for academics it would seem sensible to both acknowledge their hesitation and provide support for the move at all levels.

What the Head of Department Can Do

Head of Departments can offer support to academics in a number of ways for those who, like the group under study here, are either brand new to an online distance teaching university or who are existing academics but are making the shift to online teaching. Building systems of peer support amongst all departmental members and early and regular interventions by the Head of Department and other experienced academics are key. At the interview stage, the nature of online work needs clarifying and the differences between this and face to face modes of teaching outlined. As indicated earlier, this could include, for example, differences between working alone and with others, and in different ways and the challenges this presents for an academic role and identity. At the Open University, for example, a large part of the teaching process is the production of online materials. This involves in part the potentially very lonely business of writing units of online learning but also then collaborating with many other, often non-academic colleagues to draw in audio visual elements, links to related journal articles, graphics and imagery and online tutor group forums and tutorials to create online learning activities that would work within a VLE platform. Some part of the recruitment selection process should be based on the applicant designing a multi-media online teaching exercise with some critical reflection on how and why it is different to traditional modes of teaching. Questions at interview could probe the level of knowledge about, and motivation toward, this mode of teaching and the training and support that is likely to be required. Most applicants will have some experience of a VLE but do they understand the pedagogy behind online and blended learning and could this be developed? If newcomers can work in a team together, with regular inputs from more experienced staff, then so much the better. Inputs that allow academics to see the benefits of the move to online teaching for themselves and their students are also important; for example, having greater autonomy over how the curriculum is developed and potentially more control over when work takes place rather than in regular lecture and tutorial slots. As Peach and Bieber propose, for example, online teaching creates opportunities for academics to 'circumvent traditional mechanisms of control and thus gain greater control of their professional lives' (2015: 38).

To address any issues regarding a reluctance for academics to get involved in professional development opportunities associated with online teaching suggest that a significant contributor to this problem is if support is not there at all levels within the university. Depersonalised, off the shelf and sometimes entirely online training provision needs to be replaced or at least accompanied by, for example, group based training about the complex production processes and the roles of others in the process. Optimal support for staff concerned about engaging with online learning may be *aided* by exposure to online learning, but overcoming reluctance effectively may be better supported by employing a range of approaches. Brooks (2010), for example, suggests the need for 'hybridised' faculty development which uses a number of media and methods.

Methodology

This chapter presents the results of a case study investigating the experiences of a small group of academics involved in the redesign of a group of MBA electives within a UK Business School. The case study is located in the Open University (OU) in the UK, a distance learning university which differs from others in that students work online and at a distance and are supported by Associate Lecturers in geographically organised groups of about 20 students. The online teacher at the OU falls into one of two categories, the 'central' academic who creates the online learning and pedagogic design and content and the 'associate' academic who acts as tutor and facilitator in the running of the online module. Baxter (2012) provides a comprehensive account of the experience of moving online for OU tutors, and Salmon (2000) provides an outline of the tutor role in terms of e-moderation. In contrast, this case study is about a small group of 'central' academics. There were 8 interviewees in all, 5 of the academics had been at the university for between 5 and 15 years but were still relatively new to entirely online teaching design and 3 had joined the OU in the previous two years, all from universities with virtually no online provision at that time.

The aim here is a focus on the often under-reported lived experiences (Middlehurst 2008; Kolsaker 2008) of working academics, and specifically how it felt to redesign modules to an almost entirely online platform and how this differed from previous experiences of teaching in a face to face environment. Even though some aspects of the modules' design were predetermined, such as the number of online tutorials and assessments, the academics involved were free to use a range of pedagogical approaches and e-learning tools in both the design and delivery of the module. The group of academics concerned were given the general remit of taking a suite of existing, partially online, 30 credit MBA modules and effectively cutting them in half (making a 30 credit module into a 15 credit module) and putting them online. From this new range of 15 credit MBA elective modules students would then be able to choose three, to make up 45 credits of the overall 180 credits required for the MBA qualification. At the OU 'putting online' equates to the teacher creating a series of online learning activities based in the students' own work practice, leading to consideration of related academic ideas and theories. So, for example, the online teacher would design an activity that asked students to consider the culture of their own organisation and what struck them as being different from other organisations and then reflect on this and how related ideas might help them to understand it better. The module author's main task is to weave an online narrative through the activities, reflections and theories and use a range of media to relay these activities and ideas. Unlike some other online provision, the OU does not rely on filmed lectures but may use this as one of many elements in designing online activities, either for the individual or in collaboration with others through online forums. It is this working alone as narrator and creator yet working with others who, for example, support multi-media, which could be argued to be one of the key differences academics meet when joining the OU. In short, teaching involves bringing together a variety of online teaching sessions into one whole (module) whilst retaining the voice and purpose of all these different elements. So, there is autonomy in terms of the teacher but not as we typically know it in other institutions.

Semi-structured interviews were held with the eight academics who were the designers and producers of the new online module. Each participant was interviewed for approximately one hour and interviews were recorded and transcribed. Interview questions were about what they saw as the differences between old and new modes of teaching, either in the case study university or elsewhere, and about their early experiences of moving to online teaching. A thematic analysis (Braun and Clarke 2006) of the data was undertaken that involved conducting a deductive or 'top-down' analysis of the interview data and coding data against themes identified in the associated literature. A semantic approach to the interview data was used to search for common areas of discussion across participants. The study was framed within a realist framework which is based on the assumption that 'language reflects and enables us to articulate meaning and experience' (Braun and Clarke 2006: 85).

In terms of this study being an academic researching other academics, a lead was taken from Clarke and Knights (2015) who describe how academics conducting research in their own occupation enjoy the advantages of both relatively easy access and a personal understanding of the job. An acknowledged limitation of the study is that online teaching and learning can mean very different things in different universities and disciplines (Kirkwood and Price 2014) across a spectrum of course-delivery modalities in higher education (Porter et al. 2016). So what is described here may not be readily generalisable but it is intended to instigate further consideration of the introduction of an online strategy from the individual academic's point of view.

Findings

In the introduction to this chapter several emerging themes were identified within the current literature. One was that academics were generally reluctant to embrace change and to get involved in the move to online teaching. In this study, however, academics were generally positive about their move from face to face to online teaching. One concluded that:

> I actually loved writing this module; sitting at home and having the time to ponder and to think.

Any sense of resistance to be willing to experiment with online teaching approaches and content was not evident in the study. For example, one interviewee said that he felt that:

> Online gives you greater flexibility, you can use different sorts of media, different technological tools, you have more scope than just a piece of text.

Another interviewee said he'd recognised that the design of online teaching had highlighted for him how:

> In a way you can give the student more information. In a traditional lecture, they sit and listen and then leave the classroom and they don't have anything tangible apart from a set of slides and a few notes.

A further interviewee described here enjoyment:

> Stepping from the position of 'I am now going to present my own and others' learning' and instead 'let the resources do the talking.'

Academics appeared to be positive about embracing change; they recognised that times – and student expectations – were changing and *that:*

> Students are now forking out a lot of cash to go to university and giving them the same old experience is problematic.

Of the differences between this and face to face teaching and the challenges for the teacher involved, one interviewee explained how at his previous university going online had meant 'filming lectures' and that designing for online teaching was something rather different. Another talked of the challenges of teaching and writing online and summed up her worry in the following way:

> How do we know if what I have written will work? You're kind of writing to nobody because you don't know what the reaction is. It's a bit like a radio Deejay where you have to imagine a person and talk to them. It's like you're talking to everybody and nobody at the same time.

This is an important challenge for the individual and for those supporting them. As a head of department it is about creating a balance between allowing individuals autonomy in their teaching but providing enough support from, for instance, other academics going through the same progress on a similar module and/or having established online mentors in place to guide academics through the complex and often lonely process.

Another theme in the interviews was how academics were beginning to see how the new model of teaching would start to impact on them individually, not least that fewer academics will be needed in the future. One commented that it might be:

> Tempting to get younger, less experienced people and throw them in at the deep end which would be very detrimental to quality.

Two of the interviewees did mention the importance of training and development but, in this instance, felt that some support had happened too late to be useful. Early interventions and providing an understanding of the entire process and all its elements is both important and difficult. One way is to get the range of individuals involved in the production of the online teaching to talk about how they perceive their own role and that of others and what stakeholders expect from one another. The importance of capturing the learning from the whole exercise of moving online was mentioned by most of the interviewees in this study.

In terms of the challenges to teacher role and identity, interviewees could see clear differences. One described how, in a lecture, for example:

> You see a person's face change and you realise you have affected the way that they are thinking; you don't get that with online teaching.

Here support interventions are about making sure that the online teacher does get a sense of the effects of their teaching. This could be by encouraging the central academic to work closely with the Associate Lecturers who are supporting students directly, or even by encouraging them to take on an AL role as part of their induction process. At the OU many systems are in place to allow central academics to see how materials and assessment are being experienced by students, such as through participation in online tutor forums, and regular feedback data and results.

Although the benefits of autonomy in creating online learning were recognised, there was also a sense of being in a team, albeit in a slightly different way. One interviewee explained how:

> My previous universities were really different, you didn't work in a team, you designed and did everything yourself and, in that sense, you were largely not constrained by other people. I think that's liberating in one way, but constraining in another.

Another theme that emerged from the interviewees was the permanent nature of online teaching; that included the pleasure taken in being able to work up teaching materials in the way the author wanted without the pressure of an immediate face to face audience. This was not presented as a desire for working in splendid isolation from academic colleagues or indeed students, but speaks to the legitimate space needed to prepare materials and the enjoyment of the autonomy in that process. One comment sums this up well:

> With online learning it's like you're producing something permanent that they can revisit, rather than them thinking 'I wonder what she said about that three weeks ago'.

It was acknowledged by most of the interviewees that online mode challenged the teacher with a new set of issues; one, for example, had recognised how the teacher becomes:

> More of a 'critical friend who still knows more than you do but is putting together an interesting experience. This is rather than saying 'I am the expert and I am going to tell you what to think'

In the same vein, another interviewee talked about how moving online had made him think:

> much more carefully about what to do with our contacts with students.

To summarise, the majority of interviewees acknowledged the challenges they had encountered but tended to see this is a positive way; as one interviewee said, they felt their role as the teacher had "not been usurped but changed".

Conclusions

In this chapter, the intention has been to start a discussion about some individuals' actual experiences of getting involved in online teaching. The case study involved academics who had chosen consciously to join the Open University because of its expertise in online learning but, as this mode of teaching becomes increasingly common through all kinds of universities in the higher education sector, it is worth considering how universities in general, and Heads of Department in particular, recognise and support academics more readily and more systematically. This support may be particularly important at the more localised, departmental level where academics and their peers can be supported and provided with appropriate practical training and development. In addition, the further argument here is that built into this support needs to be some clear acknowledgement of the challenges that moving to online teaching brings to academic role and identity on the basis that the academic persona as teacher is a key part of what academics do and who they are. Changing the practices of teaching has considerable potential to impact the teacher's sense of self.

A broad range of new skills is required for online teaching from academics who almost certainly already have heavy teaching commitments and stretching research objectives. We have seen in this study how academics were aware of the challenges involved but still seem to be open to learning more about online teaching. Academics here were struck by the differences in the teaching experience, for example, in working in different sorts of teams and producing something permanent in a different mode for students. This needs space and support and acknowledgement that this is a very different type of work.

Universities and their senior management teams may need, for instance, to change workload planning systems in the university (Gregory and Lodge 2015; Tynan et al. 2015) in recognition that academics will find it difficult to allocate sufficient time to acquiring or enhancing the skills necessary without this provision. In addition, systems of peer support, mutual encouragement and the setting of clear expectations are important at all tiers within the university but perhaps particularly so at the localised level of the department. Induction and training has to be of the type where the challenges to the identity of the academic are acknowledged and where academics are recognised as individuals whose personal values inform their professional practice (Angerkind 2011). Any initial and ongoing interventions by Heads of Departments and others should acknowledge that, where values are threatened, it is extremely important that opportunities are offered to discuss new meanings and discourses.

In the introduction to this chapter the vast changes both in the higher education sector and the professionalization of teaching were outlined. Appropriate support and training for lecturers moving into online learning has been slower to develop. In the UK context, perhaps a compulsory part of Higher Education Academy Fellowship submissions should be in the area of online teaching; and the different skills and challenges of online teaching be acknowledged in university preparations for the 'Teaching Excellence Framework'.[1]

Lastly, rather than university senior management teams assuming resistance from academics, the opportunities and benefits of the move to online – and ways of facilitating these – should be the focus of management intervention. Academics should be supported to enable the transition and to begin to see the advantages of online teaching in order to be committed enough to deal with the changes it brings for themselves and the student. Understanding more about individuals' experiences of moving online can only enhance this process. We must think in terms of academics, as knowledgeable practitioners, being sensibly cautious about, rather than resistant to, the radically different business of teaching on line compared to more traditional forms. Academics are expert practitioners, therefore their caution is understandable – they recognise the radically different task. Management, then, has the responsibility for making available the resources for academics to take on this radically different task.

Tips and Discussion Points

- Recognise that the move to online is a challenge to teacher identity/persona, not just a change in job role.
- Build systems of peer support for newcomers with early and regular interventions and sharing of experience using a variety of methods.
- Clarify the differences regarding expectations of online working and type of work at recruitment, selection and interview stages, incorporating a design exercise for teaching through multi media technologies.
- Challenge the notion of resistance from academics and build on the enthusiasm and positivity of online teaching.

Work at the departmental/team level and don't rely on university wide, top down training and policies.

Note

1. The Teaching Excellence Framework (TEF) is a scheme introduced by the government in England in 2016–17 to measure the quality of teaching at Higher Education Institutions (HEIs). Universities are given a rating to indicate the level of teaching quality that they provide, their demonstration of a strategic and effective approach to intellectual challenge and student engagement, and student satisfaction ratings.

References

Allen, I.E., & Seaman, J. (2012) *Conflicted: Faculty and online education,* Insider Higher Ed. Babson Survey Group.

Alvesson, M., & Willmott, H. (2002). Identity regulation as organizational control: Producing the appropriate individual. *Journal of Management Studies, 39,* 619–644.

Angerkind, G. S. (2011). Separating the 'teaching' from the 'academic': Possible unintended consequences. *Teaching in Higher Education, 16*(2), 183–195.

Barber, M., Donnelly, K., & Rizvi, S. (2013). *An avalanche is coming: Higher education and the revolution ahead.* London/England: Institute for Public Policy Research.

Barnett, R. (2007). *A will to learn: Being a student in an age of uncertainty: Being a student in an age of uncertainty.* Maidenhead: SHRE and Open University Press, McGraw Hill.

Barry, J., Berg, E., & Chandler, J. (2006). Academic shape shifting: Gender, management, and identities in Sweden and England. *Organization, 13*(2), 275–298.

Baxter, J-A. (2012). The impact of professional learning on the teaching identities of higher education lecturers. In European Journal of Open, Distance and E-Learning, 2012(2). Available online at http://www.eurodl.org/index.php?p=archives&year=2012&halfyear=2&article=527

Becher, T., & Trowler, P. R. (2001). *Academic tribes and territories: Intellectual enquiry and the culture of disciplines* (2nd ed.). Buckingham: The Society for Research into Higher Education and Open University Press.

Boxall, M. The UK's outmoded universities must modernise or risk falling behind29/06/15 The Guardian newspaper, HE Network at http://www.theguardian.com/higher-education-network/2015/jun/29/the-uksoutmoded-universities-must-modernise-or-risk-falling-far-behind

Braun, V., & Clarke, V. (2006). Using thematic analysis in psychology. *Qualitative Research in Psychology, 3*(2), 77–101.

Brooks, C. F. (2010). Toward 'hybridised' faculty development for the twenty-first century: Blending online communities of practice and face-to-face meetings in instructional and professional support programmes. *Innovations in Education and Teaching International, 47*(3), 261–270.

Clarke, C. A., & Knights, D. (2015). Careering through academia: Securing identities or engaging ethical subjectivities? *Human Relations, 68*(2), 1865–1888.

Clarke, C. A., Knights, D., & Jarvis, C. (2012). A labour of love? Academics in UK business schools. *Scandinavian Journal of Management, 28*(1), 5–15.

Conole, G., Oliver, M., Falconer, I., Littlejohn, A., & Harvey, J. (2007). Designing for learning. In G. Conole & M. Oliver (Eds.), *Contemporary perspectives in e-learning research: Themes, methods and impact on practice*. Oxford: Routledge Falmer.

Currie, G. (2014) Hybrid managers in business schools, in Building the leadership capacity of UK Business Schools, Association of Business Schools, Winter 2014, p.12-14 ISBN 978-0-9567461-9-1

Deem, R., Hillyard, S., & Reed, M. (2007). *Knowledge, higher education, and the new managerialism : The changing management of UK universities*. Oxford: Oxford University Press.

Exworthy, M., & Halford, S. (1999). Professionals and managers in a changing public sector: Conflict, compromise and collaboration? In M. Exworthy & S. Halford (Eds.), *Professionals and the new managerialism in the public sector*. Buckingham: Open University Press.

Fanghanel, J. (2012). *Being an academic*. New York/London: Routledge.

Fineman, S. (1993). Organizations as emotional arenas. In S. Fineman (Ed.), Emotion in organizations (pp. 9-35). Thousand Oaks, CA, US: Sage Publications, Inc

Fineman, S. (2000). *Emotion in organizations* (2nd ed.). London: Sage.

Floyd, A. (2013). Narrative of academics who become department heads in a UK university. In L. Gornall, C. Cook, L. Daunton, J. Salisbury, & B. Thomas (Eds.), *Academic working lives: Experience, practice and change* (pp. 86–93). London: Bloomsbury.

Fredman, N., & Doughney, J. (2012). Academic dissatisfaction, managerial change and neo-liberalism. *Higher Education, 64*, 41–58.

Goodyear, P. (2010). *Teaching, technology and educational design: The architecture of productive learning environments*. Strawberry Hills: Australian Learning and Teaching Council.

Gregory, M. S., & Lodge, J. M. (2015). Academic workload: The silent barrier to the implementation of technology-enhanced learning strategies in higher education. *Distance Education, 36*(2), 210–230.

Gregory, J., & Salmon, G. (2013). Professional development for online university teaching. *Distance Education, 34*(3), 256–270.

Grey, C. (1994). Career as a project of the self and labour process discipline. *Sociology, 28*, 479.

Gunn, C. (2010). Sustainability factors for e-learning initiatives. *ALT-JResearch in Learning Technology, 18*(2), 89–103.

Hanson, J. (2009). Displaced but not replaced: The impact of e-learning on academic identities in higher education. *Teaching in Higher Education., 14*(1), 553–564.

Henkel, M. (2000). *Academic identities and policy change in higher education.* London: Jessica Kingsley.

Henkel, M. (2005). Academic identity and autonomy in a changing policy environment. *Higher Education, 49,* 155–176.

Kirkwood, A., & Price, L. (2014). Technology-enhanced learning and teaching in higher education: What is 'enhanced' and how do we know? A critical literature review. *Learning, Media and Technology, 39*(1), 6–36.

Knights, D., & Clarke, C. A. (2014). It's a bittersweet symphony, this life: Fragile academic selves and insecure identities at work. *Organization Studies, 35*(3), 335–357.

Kolsaker, A. (2008). Academic professionalism in the managerialist era: A study of English universities. *Studies in Higher Education, 33*(5), 513–525.

Kukulsa-Hulme, A. (2012). How should the higher education workforce adapt to advancements in technology for teaching and learning? *Internet and Higher Education, 15,* 247–254.

Luckman, T., & Berger, P. (1964). Social mobility and personal identity. *Archives of the European Journal of Sociology, V,* 331–348.

McNaughton, S. M., & Billot, J. (2016). Negotiating academic teacher identity shifts during higher education contextual change. *Teaching in Higher Education, 21*(6), 644–658.

Middlehurst, R. (2008). Not enough science or not enough learning? Exploring the gaps between leadership theory and practice. *Higher Education Quarterly, 62*(3), 19–321.

Mitchell, L. D., Parlamis, J. D., & Claiborne, S. A. (2015). Overcoming faculty avoidance of online education: From resistance to support to active participation. *Journal of Management Education, 39*(3), 350–371.

Peach, H. G., & Bieber, J. P. (2015). Faculty and online education as a mechanism of power. *Distance Education, 36*(1), 26–40.

Porter et al. (2016). A qualitative analysis of institutional drivers and barriers to blended learning adoption in higher education. *Internet and Higher Education, 28,* 17–27.

Pritchard, C. and Wilmott, H. 1997. Just how managed is the McUniversity?, Organization Studies, 18 no 2:287-316

Ross, J., Sinclair, C., Knox, J., Bayne, S., & Macleod, H. (2014). Teacher experiences and academic identity: The missing components of MOOC pedagogy. *Journal of Online Learning and Teaching, 10*(1), 57–69.

Salmon, G. (2000). *E-moderating: The key to teaching and learning online.* London: Kogan Page.

Salmon, G. (2005). Flying not flapping: A strategic framework for e-learning and pedagogical innovation in higher education institutions. *Research in Learning Technology, 13*(3), 201–218.

Salmon, G. (2014). Learning innovation: A framework for transformation. *European Journal of Open Distance and E-Learning, 17*(2), 220–236.

Sappey, J., & Relf, S. (2010). Digital technology education and its impact on traditional academic roles and practice. *Journal of university teaching and learning practice, 7*(1), 3.

Sarros, J. C., Gmelch, W. H., & Tanewski, G. A. (1997). The role of department head in Australian universities: Tasks and stresses. *Higher Education Research and Development, 16*(3), 283–292.

Schneckenberg, D. (2009). Understanding the real barriers to technology-enhanced innovation in higher education. *Educational Research, 54*(4), 411–424.

Schneckenberg, D. (2010). Overcoming barriers for eLearning in universities—Portfolio models for eCompetence development of faculty. *British Journal of Educational Technology, 41*(6), 979–991.

Sparkes, A. C. (2013). Qualitative research in sport, exercise and health in the era of neoliberalism, audit and new public management: Understanding the conditions for the (im)possibilities of a new paradigm dialogue. *Qualitative Research in Sport, Exercise and Health, 5*, 440–459.

Symes, C. (1999). 'Working for your future': The rise of the vocationalised university. *Australian Journal of Education, 43*(3), 241–256.

Turkle, S. (1993). *Life on the screen: Identity in the age of the internet.* New York: Touchstone.

Tynan, B., Ryan, Y., & Lamont-Mills, A. (2015). Examining workload models in online and blended teaching. *British Journal of Educational Technology, 16*(1), 5–15.

13

The Future of Online Teaching and Learning and an Invitation to Debate

George Callaghan, Jacqueline Baxter,
and Jean McAvoy

Students as Customers?

The 1979 election of Thatcher in the UK and the 1980 election of Reagan in the US heralded a radical turn in terms of the marketisation of the public sphere across much of the western world. In the realm of economic policy, the UK underwent severe de-industrialisation, a loss of worker influence in the labour market and a liberalised financial sector

G. Callaghan (✉)
Department of Economics, Open University, Milton Keynes, UK
e-mail: George.callaghan@open.ac.uk

J. Baxter
Department of Public Leadership and Social Enterprise, Open University,
Milton Keynes, UK
e-mail: Jacqueline.baxter@open.ac.uk

J. McAvoy
School of Psychology, Open University, Milton Keynes, UK
e-mail: jean.mcavoy@open.ac.uk

© The Author(s) 2018
J. Baxter et al. (eds.), *Creativity and Critique in Online Learning*,
https://doi.org/10.1007/978-3-319-78298-0_13

261

(Hutton 1995, 2015). The ideological core of this outlook: a desire to shift rights and responsibilities from the collective to the individual; an ideal premised on the responsibilisation of the individual as imagined within rational choice theory. Within the context of economics this implies, for instance, shifting the risk associated with providing financial security in old age from employers to employees. An example of this process is the declining number of defined benefit occupational pension schemes, in which the employer possesses responsibility for guaranteeing a pension, and a concomitant increase in defined contribution schemes, in which the employee bears the investment risk (Callaghan, Fribbance and Higginson 2012). The shift towards marketisation has reached into many other aspects of UK economic life, with the NHS in England introducing competition reforms (Brerton and Vesoodaven 2010) and numerous areas of the public sector being out-sourced and privatised.

University education has not escaped the process of atomisation and individualisation associated with the neo-liberal and marketised mind-set. This is perhaps most apparent with the introduction of student fees in England. These were initially set at £1000 in 1998, rising to £9000 by 2017 (UK Government 2017). The logic is premised on the idea that the individual student financially benefits from a degree and therefore they should bear the cost. Fiscal alternatives, such as recognising the collective benefits of having doctors, lawyers and a more educated citizenry and sharing the costs through higher progressive taxation, have less traction in this ideological outlook. Individualism, price and profit take primacy (Scott 2000).

The introduction of fees does not only create a market in Higher Education with the student as a customer, it also places competitive pressures on Universities to increase market share and build a unique brand: in short, to behave in a similar fashion to traditional businesses (Chaplea 2006). As we argued in the introduction, this means Vice Chancellors look to increase customer value – and simultaneously cut costs.

It is possible that some in HE see digital technology as an opportunity to provide education while at the same time making vital cost savings; thus increasing competitive advantage. Certain senior managers might even be wondering what kind of teaching tasks can be completely automated. The tacit knowledge inherent within the teaching experience may be side-lined in the universal pursuit of what some might see as efficiency, with the teaching task being relegated purely to a number of tick box competencies. As Frey and Osborne comment "occupations consisting of tasks following well-defined procedures that can easily be performed by sophisticated algorithms" (Frey and Osborne 2013: 2) might see significant shifts in employment. Within academia this could mean that elements of marking or assessment which lends themselves to quantification, such as plagiarism checking or correcting grammar, could be automated, with the ultimate aim of stripping out 'expensive' academic labour. Indeed as Martin Hamilton argued at the 2017 Digifest conference: academics "might be surprised at just how much can be automated" (Hamilton 2017).

It is of course possible to turn this dystopian future around, to imagine a more progressive educational environment where academics utilise all available means with which to create, enhance, enable and energise a critical citizenry. Within this optimistic scenario, automating routine tasks could increase the amount of academic time spent encouraging deep learning and thinking. The HE sector is involved in this debate, with University leaders and academics working through the complexities (and potential contradictions) associated with digital education. The case studies and discussion presented in this edited volume make a vital and valuable contribution to this debate, illustrating (as we go on to argue in this chapter) that e-learning contains both creative potential and potential pitfalls for both students and teachers.

Revisiting Theory

We have argued in this book that technology is (and always has been) in constant interaction with, and intrinsically linked to education. From the development of the printing press, through to photocopying, video, TV and now the web, teachers use technology in their work. This book has allowed us to both record and reflect upon how new technology impacts on different aspects of education at a large distance learning University. In this concluding chapter, we will firstly reflect upon relevant educational theory and then move on to examine emergent themes. We then highlight fruitful areas for future research and revisit the aims of the book in provoking ongoing discussions within higher education.

As an editorial team we have been careful to balance the creative, looking at the creative and innovative approaches in using new technology in teaching, with the critical, that is being aware of problems associated with such technology. The glittering novelty of new technology can easily lead to an unqualified acceptance that it must in some ways be superior to what teachers have done in the past and therefore must be introduced immediately and without question. It is a small step from this to institutional techno-determinism, where University leaders develop strategies and workshops for the uncritical implementation of digital teaching; just as the plenary speakers in the Digifest warned (see Chap. 2 this volume).

While we argue against such technological determinism we acknowledge, in common with Veletsianos (2016), that new technology in general and social media in particular, are core elements of the dominant culture. Universities, perhaps especially the Open University (Weller 2011, 2013), must use this technology to augment their social role as repositories of knowledge and generators of critical thinking. It could even be argued that the civic mission of a large scale provider of supported distance learning such as the Open University, implies it should be a pioneer in this area. That is should ensure its students graduate not just with formal academic knowledge, but also with the skills and confidence necessary to function in a digital world.

In terms of educational theory, the chapters in this edited volume draw on a multiplicity of theoretical perspectives. For example, virtual learning environments which rely on multiple choice tests as part of self-assessment, relate to behaviourism (Skinner 1968; Illeris 2009). Also students clearly use their own cognitive processes when they engage in e-learning (Riding and Sadler-Smith 1997). However, the theoretical approach which emerges from the action research case studies contained in this book is most strongly associated with constructivist and social /experiential theories of learning (Wenger and Lave 1991; Wenger 2010; Bates 2014). Emerging themes include the links between formal and informal learning associated with social media, the potential for online forums to develop a sense of trust between students and teachers and the link between teacher and student identities in the physical and virtual worlds.

There are also clear pointers in many of the chapters to the related (and developing) theory of connectivism, which argues that increasingly knowledge resides in electronic networks (Schreurs et al. 2014; Boitshwarelo 2011). Support for this perspective comes from virtual libraries, the use of "google" and "YouTube" in searches for information and the capacity of social media to transfer information. As we argued in an earlier chapter, there are links here to Wenger's discussion of learning networks (2008), in particular their potential for connectivity. Wenger puts forward the argument that while learning communities and learning networks are different, in the sense that one emphasises identity and one connectivity, they can combine to produce powerful communities of learning practice. An example from within a University setting might be an institution creating such communities by utilising both informal and formal learning. The latter is especially useful at teaching technical skills, knowledge and specialised expertise (the shape of a demand curve in Economics, the geomorphology of a landscape in Geology) and also to drill home important study skills (critical reflection, building an argument and then backing it up with data and supportive references). Informal learning, such as that associated with social media and electronic forums, assist in building the connections and networks which creates a community of critical learning practice.

Emerging Themes from the Action Research

An important characteristic of the chapters in this edited volume is that they are written by practitioners describing and analysing their own contemporary teaching practice. This means that the observations and reflections are grounded in the everyday reality of organising and delivering teaching. The practical aspects of this approach are demonstrated by the fact that each chapter contains a tips box with advice for teachers seeking to introduce similar innovative learning techniques. Three key themes emerged from the chapters. One relates to using electronic forums to facilitate collaboration between students, the second links to using digital technology to build academic communities while the third relates to the impact of technology on the identities of academics.

In terms of electronic forums, three of the chapters deal in some way with using such technology in teaching. In Chap. 3 Rachel Manning and Donna Smith look at the structure and function of forums as part of blended learning (Irvine et al. 2013); in Chap. 4 Helen Kaye and Jane Barrett focus on forums as facilitators of collaborative learning and in Chap. 10 Paige Cuffe and Jean McAvoy examine how academic managers organise a large number of tutors to deliver team teaching through forums. In different ways each of these forum chapters points to both the creative potential but also the critical practical challenges in using such digital spaces in teaching.

According to these chapters, the attraction of forums from a pedagogical perspective is their flexibility: the geographical location of students and tutors is not important; they can be synchronous, meaning tutors can teach in real time or asynchronous, offering the ability to create and sustain a pedagogical dialogue. They also permit students to learn from each other as well as from a subject expert. However, in practice there are significant issues. These range from the practical, in that there are resource implications in terms of staff development and training, to the pedagogic: in that it can be difficult to encourage students to participate in forums and also difficult to encourage tutors to enthusiastically embrace these new teaching spaces.

In advice to academics seeking to introduce electronic forums into their teaching, the authors emphasise the importance of having clear structure and learning outcomes that both the students and tutors understand. Some also highlight the importance of giving students an incentive to participate, for example by formally assessing forum participation. Another interesting pedagogic observation is that students report a learning gain even if all they do is passively participate in forums by reading the postings of others. This is an interesting finding which offers a different dimension to the learning process and which is supported by other research in this field (see for example Baxter and Haycock 2013). It also supports Henri's taxonomy of interaction which identifies particular stages of participation in online forums (1992). This model takes a constructivist view of identity formation with learning and community integration as central to online student identity formation and illustrates the ways in which the student moves from a relatively peripheral role in the community through to full integration. The increasing levels of learner confidence gained through this form of forum integration links positively to motivation, retention, and learner resilience (Burke and Reitzes 1981; Duemer et al. 2002 in Baxter and Haycock 2013: 1).

Another important observation, which particularly relates to collaborative work, is the need to develop techniques and practices which encourage sociability (or friendliness) on forums. This helps to create a sense of trust between students which encourages participation. All three chapters also emphasise that successful forums require substantial investment of time and effort: students take time to learn new skills and to develop trusted relationships with fellow learners. Tutors also require time to train and learn new skills and time for moderation and active teaching on forums. From a management perspective such teaching time is quite difficult to measure compared to gauging how much time is needed for a face-to-face lecture or tutorial. It is a flow process, requiring tutors to regularly check on forums, initiate and nudge discussions along. The resource intensive nature of such innovative practices has important consequences for those in higher education to see digital education as a way to cut costs: successfully operating electronic forums requires significant teaching time.

The second theme relates to the potential of digital technology to assist in the building of connections between those involved in teaching and learning. This emerged during George Callaghan and Ian Fribbance's Chap. 5 on using Facebook to facilitate informal learning and Karen Foley and Ian Fribbance's Chap. 9 on synchronous and asynchronous digital conferences.

From a theoretical perspective these authors draw on the conceptual framing of social constructivist and social learning theory, in particular the work of Wenger (2008, 2010) to argue that informal channels of learning have the potential to add value by encouraging students separated by time and space to be self-reflective, critical and to develop and deploy agency. For example, the digital *Student Connections* conference discussed in Chap. 9, illustrates that it is possible to bring together a large number of geographically dispersed students to view and engage with teaching material. Taken together these chapters demonstrate that social media and digital technology can be useful building blocks in creating an academic community. While such capacity is particularly relevant to a distance learning organisations such as the Open University, it is likely that in the future, as the nature of teaching and learning becomes increasingly digital, more traditional universities will also benefit from these technologies and techniques (Weller 2011).

These chapters on using technology to help build community again provide technical tips. These include starting out with a clear pedagogic purpose. This might sound obvious, but it is possible to imagine a situation where an especially keen senior university manager is so beguiled by new technology – and empowered by the marketisation of HE – that they strongly suggest (instruct) teaching staff change their learning design to include twitter or another form of social media. It is a far better approach that academics retain ownership of the learning design and develop a learning plan which mixes social media content, so including, for example, academic material, visual material and more conversational and possibly even humorous content. Academic staff should also consider how they might make multiple uses of any digital assets. For example a blog or short video might be used in Facebook with a click through to a more substantial teaching piece which is on a module website. The authors also conclude that it is worth building in an evaluation strategy at the beginning of a digital learning project.

In terms of challenges, the question of resources is again an issue. If the faculty or academic school is to successfully use Facebook or similar social media to contribute to the creation of an academic community they must invest in staffing and training. To keep a Facebook page alive and engaging is like tending a delicate plant or looking after a complex piece of machinery, it requires constant vigilance, tinkering and maintenance. As the chapter on use of Facebook to stimulate academic debate illustrates, continual effort must be put into writing interesting posts and academic contributions need to be regularly scheduled. In addition, some form of moderation should be put in place.

The need for staff development is also apparent. As we expand upon in the next emerging theme of identity, this training includes not just the mechanics of using a new technology, but also in appreciating and managing the changing the nature of the relationship between teacher and student. As opposed to giving a lecture or running a tutorial and leaving, an academic (or academic team) needs to build a more constant and more public series of interrelationships with their students. Many academics, particularly those who are research intensive, will find this approach distinctly challenging. Callaghan and Fribbance also emphasise that teaching teams must be aware of overloading students with too many channels of informal learning and that such innovative pedagogical tools must not impinge upon the deep learning required at University level – a finding which also emerged during earlier studies into Facebook (Ellison et al. 2007). Finally, in relation to using large social media companies in education, there are ethical issues to consider – Universities must balance gains to student learning against the fact that they are encouraging students to use commercial companies who make money through targeted adverts.

A third theme to emerge from the chapters relates to identity. This is discussed in Michelle Oldale and Madeleine Knightley's Chap. 11 on values and identity in online teaching and also in Diane Preston's Chap. 12 which explores the challenges a Head of Department faces managing staff working in an increasingly online teaching environment. Many academics learn their trade and spend much of their professional lives engaged in face-to-face teaching. Even in a supported distance learning institution such as the Open University the shift to teaching digitally is relatively new – in 2018 most tutors provide a blend of face-to-face and online tutorials. This means that the move to an online environment represents a significant change to ways of working and consequently can represent a challenge to academic identities (Baxter 2012; Sappey and Relf 2010). As one of Preston's interviewees commented when discussing traditional teaching "You see a person's face change and you realise you have affected the way that they are thinking; you don't get that with online teaching." This creates a potential for disconnect and distance and represents a significant change in the nature of the relationship the teacher builds with a group of students. As Preston reports, these changes can lead to insecurity, anxiety and feelings of uncertainty around professional status.

Oldale and Knightley recommend a number of practical tips to help overcome some of these issues. These include building connections between the tutors and students. One way to do this is by disclosing aspects of their teaching environment and perhaps some aspects of the personal life. As one tutor comments "Students not 'seeing' me as a person hinders – letting them know a little more about me helps them see me as more than just a distant voice." The suggestion is that tutors tell the students about themselves and the physical environment they are teaching in (their room or study at home) and ask students to also share elements of their lives. For both students and academics this represents quite a change to the teaching environment and teaching relationship: in a face to face situation the cognitive, affective and situative elements of learning are inherent within the learning environment. Lecturers are able to see when students 'get it' and to judge if what they are teaching is being absorbed by looking at students. They are able to immediately "feel" the effects of the learning environment – be it in the classroom or the workplace. This influences the how and why of teaching. The online environment does not offer such tangible feedback and so compensatory measures must be developed.

Managing the transition of academic staff to teaching online also emerges as a challenge. In order to help initiate change within a teaching team, Preston recommends setting up a system of peer support at departmental level, with enthusiastic colleagues initiating meetings where observations, problems and breakthroughs are discussed. She also emphasises, echoing the findings in many chapters, that time and money has to be spent on training and staff development.

While the themes of using electronic forums to facilitate teaching, using social media to build community and thinking through issues of online identities brought together most chapters in the book, there are three chapters which offer interesting insights into additional elements of on-line teaching. One of these is Stefanie Sinclair's Chap. 6 which examines online opportunities for students to use multisensory learning and assessment to learn through being creative (Stefani 2017). In her use of case studies from Open University Religious Studies and Philosophy modules she explores how digital audio and photo imagery can be used in teaching and learning and introduces readers to a number of ways in which the online environment can be exploited to offer new and creative assessment solutions. Sinclair describes a sound bank activity where students listen, comment and upload sounds associated with lived religion and religious traditions. In another task students take a photograph of an object or place which they see as representing an aspect of 'religion' in their locality and then post this image together with a description on an online platform. Such innovations have an important element of widening participation as they open up opportunities to a range of different senses and skills which can help students with particular study issues (such as those with dyslexia). However, Sinclair reports familiar challenges. These include staff time in setting up and managing the process, overcoming anxieties around the use of new technology and the problem of persuading reluctant students (and sometimes tutors) to engage with an innovative approach. Again, she emphasises the importance of having clear learning plans, thinking about evaluation at the beginning of the process and collaborating with colleagues working on different modules.

David Pell's work in Chap. 7 on online plagiarism strikes a sobering note within the book. The potential for plagiarism, essay mills and impersonation are greatly enhanced by new technology and Pell argues that this type of student behaviour represents a serious threat to the credibility of higher education awards. Potential explanatory variables for such behaviour include study skills issues (e.g., students not knowing that 'cut and paste' is poor academic practice) and time or outcome pressures which can push students to prioritise scores over learning. As Universities come to rely more on online learning and assessment the range of online opportunities for plagiarism increases, a process Pell describes as an 'arms race', with universities combating online plagiarism with ever more sophisticated detection software.

In Chap. 8 Graham Pike and Hannah Gore discuss MOOCs through the lens of a forensic psychology course case study. When these massive online courses first took off in 2012, the high student numbers and international reach were seen as a breakthrough in widening access and providing educational resources at scale. But problems immediately emerged, particularly around poor engagement and completion rates (Kizilcec et al. 2013). In the OU MOOC examined here, Pike and Gore hypothesise that by using innovations such as creating a narrative through serialising materials, it is possible to increase retention rates (in their example up to around 30%). Again though, it is clear that to successfully lead students through digital innovations such as massive open and online courses, additional resources are required. As Martin Weller (2015) comments *"It has been mildly entertaining to see many of the **MOOC** companies making 'discoveries' of things that we have known for ages (e.g. that students* *require support). "* As this approach to learning at scale develops, with for example some institutions offering (occasionally professional) accreditation, senior managers within the educational sector need to be aware of the resource implications both in the production and the presentation of these modules.

An Ongoing Conversation

Whilst at the start of this chapter we stated that technology has always been in constant interaction with education, digital technology represents both a broadening and an intensification of this interaction. The pace and range of change associated with digital technology is rapid, constant and complex. The challenge for Universities is to harness this technology in the pursuit of providing teaching and learning which creates a more informed, engaged and critical citizenry. As Howard Rheingold, the writer and thinker on social media notes in his book about how to thrive online: "those who understand the fundamentals of the digital participation, online collaboration, information credibility testing and network awareness will be able to exert more control over their own fates than those who lack this lore" (Rheingold 2012: 2).

Of course the social and economic context within which academics are working both shapes and constrains the opportunities for them to pursue this objective. For example, in a highly marketised educational system there is (as we have already highlighted) pressure on and from university leaders to cut costs and improve the student or (as some might put it) customer experience. There is also evidence that students are behaving in an increasingly instrumental consumer orientated manner (see Azevdo 2017). As Michael Tomlinson writes in his 2014 study for the Higher Education Academy "A goal-driven approach was evident among many of the students in terms of wanting to enhance their future outcomes and employability, reinforcing the perceived post-experiential value of their studies" (2014: 6). Within this constrained and marketised environment academics need to use all of the resources at their disposal both to teach their subject and to help students learn reflective and critical study skills which will be useful throughout their lives. The contribution of this book is to offer an honest description and analysis of case study examples of academics in a large distance learning University doing exactly this using digital technologies.

The authors not only describe a range of innovatory practices; they also show that providing quality supported distance learning online is a challenging process. Similar to many learning journeys, learning to teach online involves hard work, making mistakes, following blind alleys for a time, experiencing occasional breakthroughs, building relationships with colleagues and slowly taking the pedagogical project one step further.

One substantial change that permeates the chapters within this volume is to be found in the nature of the relationship between academics and students. Rather than teaching being provided through two lectures a week and a face-to-face tutorial, it becomes much more of an ongoing and more nebulous process, with fewer boundaries between 'contact and non-contact' time. In forums, this means teaching staff regularly responding to student queries and in the case of social media it means relatively constant posting. It also involves considerable pressure to rapidly respond to emails generated by, for example, University systems which feed through information on plagiarism to academics – information which requires a response within a very tight timeframe. Furthermore, the lack of physical presence on the part of students and colleagues impacts upon identity and presents challenges to forming relationships of trust and reciprocity. It also, as previous studies suggest, impacts on tutors' ability to model their teaching on that of more experienced tutors- a key element within learning to teach in a face to face environment (see Baxter 2012; Baxter and Haycock 2013). If acute work intensification for academics, which will invariably see them spread too thinly and thus negatively impact on the learning experience, is to be avoided, university leaders must become far more proactive in seeking to address these issues with staff. If not, there will be a detrimental impact on the recruitment and retention of talented academics.

Despite these issues, which are real and which must be engaged with and worked through by management and staff, the need for Universities to use digital methods to reach and teach students, in our view, remains paramount. The ubiquity and everyday nature of such technology offers myriad ways for Higher Education teachers to connect with students and as such forms part of their mission to educate and actively develop critical thinking and other skills. This should not be limited to formal teaching environments but should in essence take advantage of students' willingness to extend this outside of the university. Setting up successful groups and networks that extend beyond the period of study and in which students encourage one another in their pursuit of lifelong learning was one of the founding principles of the Open University (Weinbren 2014). Digital learning offers new mediums through which to pursue this principle.

There is great potential to use digital technologies in order to impart subject related knowledge, improve learning skills and encourage the analysis and critical reflection necessary for independent thinking. As Bayne and her colleagues in digital education at the University of Edinburgh argue in their manifesto for online learning: "Online can be the privileged mode. Distance is a positive principle, not a deficit. Place is differently, not less, important online. Text has been troubled: many modes matter in representing academic knowledge" (Bayne et al. 2014).

We see the contributions in this book as part of an ongoing conversation amongst the academic community around the technical practicalities and developing pedagogy associated with digital education. As Weller (2011) argues in *The Digital Scholar*, new technology offers the potential for open, real-time communication within academic networks. As such we would welcome responses from readers to the issues examined in each chapter. Which institutions or individuals has tried similar initiatives? What opportunities did they exploit and what challenges did they meet? Did they explicitly consider particular pedagogies and to what extent are they being led by cost reduction measures?

Research and Development

There are a number of areas which would benefit from more research. From a theoretical perspective, the interplay between social constructionism and the developing field of connectivism is likely to be a lively area of debate (Bates 2014; Anderson and Dron 2011). In particular further data gathering and analysis to explore how the knowledge and skills associated with digital teaching fits within either of these explanatory frameworks would benefit the teaching community. From a more practical perspective, it would be interesting to compare how students and academic staff in traditional universities are using digital learning compared to a supported distance learning university such as the OU. It would also be interesting to compare how Higher Education institutions in other countries are engaging with digital learning. Such future studies and contributions need to be mindful of the social and economic context, as the constant interplay between the forces of globalisation and neoliberalism necessarily pressurise and constrain academics. The challenge for those working in Universities is to recognise and make explicit these constraints while attempting to move beyond them to provide quality education. As the cultural theorist Raymond Williams argued, part of a society's common culture should be the creation of an educated citizenry and a participating democracy "… It must be the case that the whole tradition of what has been thought and valued, a tradition which has been abstracted as a minority possession, is in fact common human inheritance without which any man's [persons] participation would be crippled and disadvantaged" (1989: 37). Universities have a responsibility to use all means at their disposal, including online learning, to create and sustain such an educated citizenry and participating democracy.

References

Anderson, T., & Dron, J. (2011). Three generations of distance education pedagogy. *The International Review of Research in Open and Distance Learning*, Special Issue, *12*(3), 80–97.

Azevdo, C. (2017) *Through the looking-glass: An exploration of students' discourse within the managerialised university* (Unpublished MRes dissertation). The Open University Business School.

Bates, T. (2014). *Teaching in a digital age*. https://opentextbc.ca/teachingina-digitalage/chapter/section-3-4-constructivism/

Baxter, J. (2012). The impact of professional learning on the teaching identities of higher education lecturers. *European Journal of Open, Distance and E Learrning 2012:II [Online]*. http://www.eurodl.org/index.php?p=archives&year=2012&halfyear=2&article=527. Accessed 23 Mar 2017.

Baxter, J., & Haycock, J. (2013). Roles and student identities in online large course forums: Implications for practice. *International Review of Open and Distance Learning, 15*(1), 20–40.

Bayne, S. et al. (2014). *Manifesto for teaching online*, digital education at the University of Edinburgh. https://onlineteachingmanifesto.wordpress.com/. Accessed 6 Nov 2017.

Boitshwarelo, B. (2011). Proposing an integrated research framework for connectivism: Utilising theoretical synergies. *The International Review of Research in Open and Distributed Learning, 12*(3), 161–179.

Brerton, L., & Vesoodaven, V. (2010). The impact of the NHS market. *Civitas*, http://www.civitas.org.uk/content/files/Civitas_LiteratureReview_NHS_market_Feb10.pdf. Accessed 2 Nov 2017.

Burke, P. J., & Reitzes, D. C. (1981). The link between identity and role performance. *Social Psychology Quarterly, 44*, 83–92.

Callaghan, G., Fribbance, I., & Higginson, M. (Eds.). (2012). *Personal finance*. Basingstoke: Palgrave Macmillan/ The Open University.

Chaplea, C. (2006). Barriers to brand building in UK universities. *International Journal of non-profit and voluntary sector marketing, 12*(1), 23–32.

Duemer, L., Fontenot, D., Gumfory, K., Kallus, M., Larsen, J. A., Schafer, S., & Shaw, B. (2002). The use of online synchronous discussion groups to enhance community formation and professional identity development. *The Journal of Interactive Online Learning, 1*(2), 1–12.

Ellison, N. B., Steinfield, C., & Lampe, C. (2007). The benefits of Facebook "friends:" social capital and college students' use of online social network sites. *Journal of Computer-Mediated Communication, 12*(4), 1143–1168.

Frey, C.B., & Osborne, M.A. (2013). *The future of employment: How susceptible are jobs to computerization* (Working paper). University of Oxford. http://www.oxfordmartin.ox.ac.uk/downloads/academic/future-of-employment.pdf. Accessed 2 Nov 2017.

Hamilton, M. (2017). Loving the alien: Robots and AI in education In *Digifest conference*. https://www.jisc.ac.uk/events/digifest-14-mar-2017/programme. Accessed 2 Nov 2017.

Henri, F. (1992). Computer conferencing and content analysis. In A. R. Kaye (Ed.), *Collaborative learning through computer conferencing* (pp. 117–136). Berlin: Springer.

Hutton, W. (1995). *The state we're in*. London: Jonathan Cape.

Hutton, W. (2015). *How good we can be: Ending the mercenary society and building a great country*. London, US: Little Brown.

Illeris, K. (Ed.). (2009). *Contemporary theories of learning : Learning theorists in their own words*. London: Routledge.

Irvine, V., Code, J., & Richards, L. (2013). Realigning higher education for the 21st century learner through multi-access learning. *Journal of Online Learning and Teaching, 9*(2), 172.

Kizilcec, R. F., Piech, C., & Schneider, E. (2013). Deconstructing disengagement: Analyzing learner subpopulations in massive open online courses. In *Proceedings of the third international conference on learning analytics and knowledge* (pp. 170–179). New York: ACM.

Rheingold, H. (2012). *Net smart: How to thrive online*. London: MIT Press.

Riding, R. J., & Sadler-Smith, E. (1997). Cognitive style and learning strategies: Some implications for training design. *International Journal of Training and Development, 1*(3), 199–208.

Sappey, J., & Relf, S. (2010). Digital technology education and its impact on traditional academic roles and practice. *Journal of university teaching and learning practice, 7*(1), 3.

Schreurs, B., et al. (2014). An investigation into social learning activities by practitioners in open educational practices. *The International Review of Research in Open and Distributed Learning, 15*(4), 1–20.

Scott, J. (2000). Rational choice theory. *Understanding contemporary society: Theories of the present* 129.

Skinner, B. (1968). *The technology of teaching*. New York: Appleton-Century-Crofts.

Stefani, L. (2017). Realizing the potential for creativity. In L. S. Watts & P. Blessinger (Eds.), *Creative learning in higher education: International perspectives and approaches* (pp. 196–209). New York and London: Routledge.

Tomlinson, M. (2014). *Exploring the impact of policy changes on the student approaches and attitudes to learning in contemporary higher education: Implications for student learning engagement, Higher Education Academy*. https://www.heacademy.ac.uk/system/files/resources/exploring_the_impact_of_policy_changes_student_experience.pdf

UK Government. (2017). *Student finance*. https://www.gov.uk/student-finance. Accessed 2 Nov 2017.

Veletsianos, G. (2016). *Social media in academia: networked scholars*. New York: Routledge.

Weinbren, D. (2014). *The Open University: A history*. Manchester: Manchester University Press.

Weller, M. (2011). *The Digital Scholar: How Technology is transforming academic practice*, Bloomsbury Open Access. https://www.bloomsburycollections.

com/book/the-digital-scholar-how-technology-is-transforming-scholarly-practice/. Accessed 7 July 2016.

Weller, M. (2013). The battle for open – a perspective. *Journal of Interactive Media in Education*, (3). http://jime.open.ac.uk/articles/10.5334/2013-15/. Accessed 24 June 2016.

Weller, M. (2015). *Open education Europe*, Summary. https://www.openeducationeuropa.eu/en/news/martin-weller-mooc-hype-definitely-over. Accessed 4 Nov 2017.

Wenger, E. C. (2008). *Communities of practice: Learning, meaning, and identity* (18th Printing, first published 1998). Cambridge: Cambridge University Press.

Wenger, E. (2010). *Communities of practice and social learning systems: The career of a concept.* http://wenger-trayner.com/wp-content/uploads/2012/01/09-10-27-CoPs-and-systems-v2.01.pdf. Accessed 9 Sept 2016.

Wenger, E. C., & Lave, J. (1991). *Situated learning: Legitimate peripheral participation.* Cambridge: Cambridge University Press.

Williams, R. (1989). *Resources of hope.* London: Verso.

Printed by Printforce, the Netherlands